Loving Him
without
Losing You

8 STEPS TO
ACHIEVING INTIMACY
AND INDEPENDENCE

CAROLYN BUSHONG

BERKLEY BOOKS, NEW YORK

LOVING HIM WITHOUT LOSING YOU

A Berkley Book / published by arrangement with
The Crossroad Publishing Company

PRINTING HISTORY
Continuum Publishing Company edition published 1991
Berkley edition / May 1993

ISBN: 0-425-13667-1

A BERKLEY BOOK® TM 757,375
Berkley Books are published by The Berkley Publishing Group,
200 Madison Avenue, New York, New York 10016.
The name "BERKLEY" and the "B" logo
are trademarks belonging to Berkley Publishing Corporation.

PRINTED IN THE UNITED STATES OF AMERICA

10 9 8 7 6 5 4 3

LOVING HIM WITHOUT LOSING YOU IS . . .

With useful, step-by-step advice on working through guilt, communicating anger, redeveloping a sense of identity, and more, *Loving Him Without Losing You* is the essential handbook for any woman who wants a stronger self *and* a stronger relationship.

To my family, especially my sister,
whose sharing of her pain and hurt
through her bout with cancer
caused me to soften and really say,
"I'm sorry," and mean it for the first time in my life.

And to Alan, the man of my dreams—
who helped me learn how
to love without losing myself.

Acknowledgments

I want to thank my parents for making me feel intelligent and special enough that I believed there was nothing I couldn't do. Though for years I resented their leaning on me to fix their volatile relationship, after working through my own program of confrontation and rebuilding, I can now see benefits from this experience. They gave me confidence and early training that made me the kind of therapist I am today—one who is caring and compassionate, but not afraid of confrontation.

Because our relationship has changed, I now thank my father for teaching me that when a man really does love you, and you let him know he's hurting you, he *will* listen and stop. And thanks, Dad, for finally letting me get to know you. And thanks to my mother for showing me that no matter how dysfunctional a woman's family was, she *can* still change. I appreciate her desire to grow and become stronger right alongside of me.

And thanks to my nephew, Brett, for providing me with the experience of loving and guiding him as if he were my own son. And similar thanks to Alecia, Alan's only child, who I now love like a daughter.

Thanks to my many professors, but especially to Dr. Virginia Moore, who forced me to deal with my own issues, taught me how to confront, and became a second mother to me. Thanks also to my professor, Dr. Chuck Combs, who gave me the basics in humanistic psychology, and who personally enlightened me about love, sex, and men. Both of their personalities and philosophies helped me create the foundation of my program.

And thanks to Dr. Ida Truscott for pushing me back into the field of psychotherapy when I was a floundering hippie in Aspen, for her friendship and her respectful non-stifling style of supervision of my practice since then.

Many thanks to all those teachers and friends who believed in me and made me believe I had something to offer the world—particularly Todd Oliver, my sophomore English teacher, who inspired me to write my first short story, and to Leslie Lewis, who helped me get into newspaper syndication and then became my best friend.

Thanks to Kyle Miller, my editor, who believed in the book after I had given up, and who gave me great feedback without interference that kept me improving the book without becoming discouraged.

Thanks to all the editor/teachers I've had along the way who taught me what they knew—Ed Bryant, Woody Page, Mary Ann Fitzharris, Karen Trinidad, Leonard Paris, Kathy Kanda, Kris Robbins, and Sandi Gelles-Cole. And thanks to Julie Beardmore for her editorial assistance that kept me smoothing the manuscript out just one more time. And thanks to Sarah Smith, whose persistence and dedication allowed me to consistently meet my deadlines.

And thanks to my Aspen girlfriends and the many men in my past who played with me as I went through my adult adolescence, leaving me with some of the most unforgettable experiences of my life.

And thanks to the various and sundry other people who influenced my decisions in life. A few of them are Tammy Nordin, Mrs. Gilbert, Mary Ellen Border, Russell Stewart, Joanne and Bill Wilson, Jean Yancey, Lu Krueger, Jay Kenis . . .

A special thanks to my numerous clients, without whom this book wouldn't be possible.

And thanks to my two kitties who sat by my side the entire time.

And last but not least, thanks again to Alan—first, for enduring the last few months with me while I worked day and night, but also for getting past my wall of anger and showing me that all men are not alike. Without our relationship, this book would be about becoming a self-reliant woman alone in the world. Instead, with him, I was able to go one step further and learn to love again—this time without losing myself.

Author's Note

The identities of the people written about in this book have been carefully disguised in accordance with professional standards of confidentiality and in keeping with their rights to privileged communication with the author.

Contents

Part IV: The Self-Reliant Woman 233

Loving Him
Without
Losing You

Introduction

I was camped in the woods at Dead Man Lake on Independence Pass, just outside of Aspen. I believed that I was the most self-reliant, independent woman I knew. I had hiked eight miles into the backwoods by myself. I had backpacked alone in a hailstorm. That took courage and guts. What dependent woman would do that?

Lying in my tent, I read *The Cinderella Complex*, by Colette Dowling, with a flashlight. I had brought the book to skim, as many of my clients were talking about it. I felt I needed to read the book for professional purposes, but that I would not have much personal interest in it, since I didn't see myself as dependent on men in any way.

I knew women who were dependent. They were patients of mine in counseling. They felt they couldn't live without a man. They didn't know how to handle their own lives. They often couldn't or wouldn't financially support themselves. They never made decisions on their own. They were afraid of being alone.

I had been like that in my early twenties. Though I had always supported myself, back when I was twenty-one and married, I had leaned on my husband. I was afraid to stay in the house alone. At that time I felt I couldn't live without a man. When my marriage began to fall apart, I had an affair with my psychology professor and leaned on him. I had gone from man to man. But now I had been living alone for seven years and seldom had a steady boyfriend. I had completely supported myself financially during that time, traveled all over the country alone, and even packed up—leaving friends and financial security behind—and moved to Aspen.

However, as I read *The Cinderella Complex,* I knew I was reading about myself. I particularly related to the section about women who cover up their dependency needs with a counterphobic facade of fake strength and independence. These women are the rebellious type, but deep down inside they're insecure and needy. However, they deny it vehemently, hoping their dependencies will never be found out.

I read the entire book that weekend and cried my heart out. It was as if I'd been found out. The book cracked my macho shell—which no man had been able to do. However, when I came to the last chapter, "Springing Free," I was very let down. The activities listed that would supposedly help me break my dependency were activities that I was already quite comfortable with, such as hiking alone. I sat there wondering what my next step should be. That day, I decided that I would seek new answers and write a book that would help women become emotionally self-reliant, that would help break their *emotional* dependencies on men.

As I began to search for the answers, I came to realize that breaking financial dependence on men had little to do with breaking *emotional* dependence. When I used to ask my mother why she didn't leave my father if she was so unhappy, she always said that she had no way to support herself and two children. I had believed her up until the time my sister and I both left home and married. Mom was working then and no longer had two children to support, but she continued in the destructive relationship with my father for another eighteen years, complaining about it the entire time.

When women ask their mothers why they stay in bad relationships, most of them respond as my mother did. So most of us went away believing that the key to independence was financial security. We certainly knew that our mothers, without their own income, had little power in their relationships. But what we didn't understand is that financial independence is only one step closer to, but is not synonymous with, emotional independence.

Though it was hard for me to admit, I had been fooling myself about my dependency needs—my feeling that I no longer needed a man was simply covering up my fear of becoming dependent. But the clues to my emotional dependence were there. I had my own private practice in psychology, but I was barely making a living at it. I was not afraid to be alone, but when I was around a man, I felt incredibly needy. I was financially supporting myself but secretly wishing I didn't have to.

I was dating a man, Kevin, who was supposed to inherit several million dollars when he turned forty. He was thirty-six and I was thirty-three at the time we were dating. When we fought, he often accused me of wanting him for his money. I totally denied it.

After reading *The Cinderella Complex* that night in the woods, I realized that Kevin was right. I decided to break that part of my dependency immediately, so I went to him and ended our relationship by telling him, "You're right, I must be 'hanging in there' for the money, since you certainly aren't giving me anything emotionally." I realized that I hadn't been planning my future. Though I talked about it a lot, I hadn't taken the necessary risks to become as successful as I said I wanted to be. I was hoping that my private practice was something I would only have to fall back on from time to time while creating a glamorous lifestyle with Kevin.

I also pretended that it didn't hurt that he would never make a commitment to me. He said that since his divorce, he had trouble loving anyone. I thought I could save him emotionally by helping him learn how to love, and in return, he'd save me financially. I didn't stop to realize that he didn't want to change, or that all my "hanging in there" did was enable him to stay the way he was. He had closed off all his feelings and opted for a glitzy, one-dimensional existence. He was a hopeless case, yet I continued to try to win his love and approval for three years. Though it was difficult and painful, I was finally able to walk away from my addiction to trying to win his love and my secret fantasy of being rescued by his money.

I had come to Aspen to find myself and had lost myself to another man. Nothing I had done had worked so far. I had tried marriage, living with a man, and waiting to be rescued by the million-dollar cardboard man. It was time to quit. I vowed to give up the search for Mr. Right and to never get that deeply involved with a man again.

At this point, I still believed that financial independence would help me break my dependency on men, so I decided to focus on money and career, so I would never be tempted to give my power away to any man again—even if he was rich.

I became obsessed with making money. I moved to Denver and began to write and give seminars. I was so driven that people used to ask me why I tried so hard, where I got my energy, and if I was on drugs. When they asked why I didn't have a special man in my life, I told them, "because I choose not to."

I decided to give up on men and work on myself. My goal was to make myself as happy as possible as a single person. My motto, "I'm single, secure, and satisfied,"[1] became the first article I published in a national woman's magazine. In my psychology practice and speaking engagements, I became the specialist in teaching women how to be strong and not need a man.

I continued to date, but always several men at a time. I got on with my life as if I would never fall in love again—and I believed I never would. Secretly, I thought I had become too strong for any man to handle. But that was fine with me—that was "their" problem.

I bought a house and settled in. I set long-term career goals and spent most of my time alone—writing, reading self-help books, and working on *me*. I ultimately created a program that finally broke my emotional dependence on men. Then the void went away. And as soon as I made myself happy without a man, I met the man of my dreams.

Over the past eight years, I have gradually developed and successfully used this program with my clients—a program that helps women develop emotional self-reliance, which then allows them to love others without giving themselves away.

Most of my clients are normal, functioning women. Most are financially independent and no longer consider themselves victims of society or men. They simply desire to be happier in their lives and don't understand why they aren't. Though this is a book for women, I have many male clients for whom the program works just as well.

Many self-help programs today, particularly the popular Twelve Step program, is intended for women who have come from severely dysfunctional backgrounds. Though my program also works for alcoholics, drug addicts, adult children of alcoholics, and victims of sexual and/or physical abuse it was designed for women who do not see themselves as coming from abusive backgrounds—average women who had so-called "normal" childhoods.

Depending on how eager, determined, and motivated you are, you can complete this program in anywhere from three months to two years, with the average time being about eight months if you are consistently working on a regular basis.

This program will take you through the process I discovered in developing the emotional self-reliance that first made me feel "single, secure, and satisfied," and the steps that helped me create a wonderful, loving relationship with a man without losing any of the strength or identity I had worked so hard to develop.

This book will guide you through the program, but it will require motivation and commitment from you for it to work. Change is possible *only* if you are determined.

This program is not simple or easy; you may want to quit many times. It requires that you: accept the fact that you really are alone in this world, go against many of society's standards and teachings, look into, and deal with, your past, and give up the fantasy that *anyone else* has the power to make your life happy. Neither I, nor this book, can do it for you. I am only a teacher, and I can show you the way. The book can give you direction, but *you* must take the action to change.

My intention is not to make you my follower, but to expand your thinking and help you create your own direction. I want to "unbrainwash" you from previous training you've received that is no longer working for you. I hope to lead you to challenge any and all beliefs and values that you presently have—so you can learn who you are, what you truly believe, and become the leader of your own life. If you work through the program, you'll become strong enough to realize that you don't have to choose between a man or a career, independence or love. You'll know you can have it all, as long as you have the courage to stand up for who you really are and take—and remain in—control of your life.

You will discover the "real" you—the one you had "trained" out of you as a child. You will go through the adolescence that you missed. You will learn to rely on and give nourishment to yourself, instead of trying to pull it from those you love. You will learn how to be in control of your own destiny and, more importantly, you will be able to love others without losing yourself.

Part I
Why Can't I Find Happiness in My Relationships?

Most of the women who come into my office for therapy appear self-reliant. They are usually attractive, well-dressed women who seem to have it all: style, charm, intelligence, sophistication, a great career, many female friends, and enough money to buy most of the things they want. Many of these women have admittedly been addicted to love in the past but consider themselves strong. They run their own lives, pay their own bills, and aren't afraid to be alone.

But whether single or married, these women aren't happy. Even though most of them have what their mothers would consider "everything," they are dissatisfied with their lives. They still long for a *good* relationship with a man, but not at the expense of giving up their identities.

Men don't have to choose between having themselves or having a relationship, and it's time women get out of this bind too. To be happy, we must stop giving ourselves away when we love.

1

I'm Not Happy
With a Man
or Without One

My clients can't seem to find happiness in or out of a relationship. They say they want a healthy relationship with a man, yet many of the single women have stopped looking for one because of their past history with men. They've usually been burned or taken advantage of—or both—and now wear a sign that says, "I don't need you." Even women who are married *and* have a career aren't satisfied. They still feel that they give more than they get and that they have two jobs instead of one—a career *and* housework. Financial independence has brought them no closer to having equal relationships with their husbands.

We Can't Win

Many women today feel like they can't win. They feel as if *they've* grown and men haven't. They see men as either womanizers or wimps. They believe that most men still want a weak, dependent woman who will take care of their every need. When these women do get into relationships, the men they're involved with usually become more controlling, and the women end up catering to them in some way. Sometimes, they willingly give up their own interests and spend less time with their girlfriends to spend *more* time with the man they love. They may even lose interest in their careers. In general, they feel that they are putting more energy into the relationship than their men are.

Once married, the situation sometimes gets worse. More often than not, "wives" feel taken for granted. They say men pull away from them, spending more time on their male friends or special interests like hunting and fishing. Women say that, especially after marriage, a man often expects his wife to carry the relationship both romantically and emotionally—whether or not she contributes financially. It seems like if a woman wants a relationship, she still has to do most of the work and the sacrificing to have it.

Single women are also disappointed and disillusioned. They aren't where they expected to be at the age of forty, or thirty-five, or thirty. Though they don't want a relationship like the one their parents had, they hadn't fathomed the thought that they'd be living their lives alone. They've learned to handle their loneliness through close friends and/or throwing themselves into their careers. Some now fear that since they've learned not to need men, they've become too strong and independent to ever attract one again. Most women believe that men and personal success are mutually exclusive—that it's an "either/or" proposition. They think that to have a relationship with a man, they have to give up their own desires and goals because they'd have to give so much to the relationship. They think they must choose between a relationship and being independent and successful. They continually waver back and forth between the two choices, because they really want both.

Most of my female clients have read all the self-help books, trying to figure out why they've been unable to have healthy relationships with men. Many have realized that they're in co-dependent relationships, that they are choosing men "who are bad for them," or that they are involved with men who are commitment-phobic. They've analyzed their problems, but they still don't know what to do about them.

All they *do* know is that they aren't happy when they're with a man or when they're without one. They never give up the chase, but they never succeed at it either. They're never able to get the love and intimacy they crave or to be content without it.

Beyond Feminism

The women's movement led us to believe that financial independence would make us happier and make our relationships with

WHY CAN'T I FIND HAPPINESS? 11

men more successful. That was the promise. Though the feminist movement did help us in many ways, it didn't deliver its promise.

When we were young and didn't know better, we followed what our mothers taught us. We sacrificed for the men in our lives ("always take care of his needs, and he'll end up taking good care of you . . . get married, have children, and live happily ever after"). We believed our mothers. We tried their way. It didn't work. We soon found out that in traditional relationships in which we had no financial independence, our self-esteem suffered. We felt deceived by our mothers. So we quickly moved into the world of work, ready for financial independence and a new equality with men—thinking that would finally bring us the joy we were searching for.

It felt good to no longer accept the trade-offs we had faced with dependency—no begging for money, no trading sex for dinner, no longer allowing men to criticize and talk down to us so we could get money for clothes. In fact, some of us even enjoyed having the power so much that we switched roles. My client Lana enjoyed wining and dining younger men. She told me about taking a man home, coming on to him sexually, and him saying, "I hope that just because you bought dinner, you don't *expect* me to have sex with you!" She replied, "You're damn right, I do!" She thought that was the way the game worked, and now it was her turn.

But money didn't bring Lana or the rest of us the equality and happiness we were searching for. In some ways, it just gave us more responsibility. Lana soon found out that some men enjoyed having her pay for everything. She began attracting wimpy men who wanted her to not only take care of the relationship's financial responsibilities, but also teach them about business *and* cook for them.

Those men who weren't wimpy often felt scorn for us as we competed with them in the business world. Few men became our partners as we had hoped. We hadn't counted on the abandonment we began to feel from men. Many of us felt tricked by the women's movement.

Even women who are involved in relationships often feel abandoned. Take Kay, for instance. She lives with a man and is still *very* independent. She and Bob have lived together for four years, but he certainly doesn't expect her to come home and fix dinner for him. After work, Kay goes to her exercise class, comes home, and takes the dogs for a run. Then she fixes dinner for only herself, because Bob has usually eaten by then, either at home or with friends after work. Neither worries about what time the other one comes home or where they've been. She goes to bed at 10 P.M., and he stays up until midnight or so. No one gets jealous or worries about what the other is doing.

In fact, their relationship is so nonpossessive and nontraditional that when Bob started having an affair, Kay didn't notice anything unusual. That is, until he spent several weekends away on business, never called, then came in late Sunday night without waking her up.

Kay thought she had independence in her relationship with Bob, when what she really had was no relationship at all. She and Bob were living like roommates. After his affair, she realized that she'd never really felt close to him. She never felt a sense of commitment from him; they never had any joint goals; there was never any real communication. She had never told him that she wanted more from him emotionally for fear that he wouldn't give it to her. She might have had independence, but she was not self-reliant. Instead of taking care of her needs, she was denying her feelings and desires.

Many women fear that relationships not built on dependency all turn out like Kay's. It scares some of them so much that they abandon their feminist teachings and run back to traditional relationships, in the hopes that it's not too late. They think that relationships not built on *need* can't be built on anything. But it's not true, as you will learn in Part III of this book. Many of us, like Kay, are behaving with men the way we think we *should*. We're acting more independent than we feel. We're telling men we don't want to marry them when we do. We're looking for life-long careers when we don't really want them. We're saying we're happy without a man when we're not. It's in vogue these days to be independent and career-oriented. So we pretend we are happy in this life-style—even when we don't really feel it. We must be honest with ourselves before we can fix the problem.

Four Women's Stories

Take thirty-eight-year-old Alicia, for instance. She appears to be independent. She lives alone, has a great job as a computer engineer, and is paid well. She acts like she's in charge of her life, especially around her friends. She listens to their problems, helps them find better jobs, and loans them money.

However, she came into my office quite depressed. She's been involved with a married coworker for two years, and her obsession with him caused her to lose her last job. Though she can be strong for her friends, she is putty in her married boyfriend's hands. Ever since she's been involved with him, she has let her life fall apart. On the weekends that she doesn't see him, she sleeps constantly, eats herself into oblivion, and spends money to feel better. She hasn't paid her bills in three months and has gained forty pounds.

Alicia has been through many therapists, looking for a quick fix for her problems. Sometimes if the therapist got too close to the problem, she switched to another one. She's tried almost every weight-loss program and sees a psychic regularly. Instead of hanging out at the bars chasing men, as some love-addicted women do, she fills her time with health-care professionals and down-and-out friends, whom she calls when she feels depressed. They tell her about their problems, and in return they listen to her complain incessantly about how her married lover treats her. When their problems involve money, she bails them out. She bought one friend a computer, another an operation for her cat, and one friend relies on her to put food on the table. Taking care of them makes her feel good and helps her believe she's stronger than they are. At the same time, it also makes her feel needier and encourages her to hold onto the fantasy that someday she'll find someone (a man) she can really lean on, that someday her married lover will leave his wife—even though he says he won't. When she hangs up the phone, she feels incredibly lonely. Thank God that tonight she's got her cats, and *thirtysomething* on TV.

Alicia would envy Valerie's life-style. Valerie is an attractive thirty-nine-year-old trainer for a large communications company and married to Ken, a real-estate developer who makes five times her salary. Each morning she strides confidently into her office, with a leather etui on her arm and a wool-and-silk suit on her back. Her hair glows and her makeup is subtly perfect—in sum, she appears to be a healthy, beautiful success story.

She's worked hard at becoming successful. She takes night classes, carries projects home on weekends, and works longer hours than most of the men in her office. She's been moving up in her career for five years now, and it's really beginning to pay off.

When she married Ken nine years ago, she didn't have a career. She worked part-time in a dance studio, did the housework, and nagged Ken because he never helped her with anything. But that was before she was affected by the women's movement. She feels she's changed a lot. She's made it in the world of business and is making good money. She certainly didn't get where she is by being easily intimidated, and her confidence at work shows that. Yet, at home, it doesn't. She knows that her marriage is far from perfect. She wishes she could handle Ken as well as she handles her employees. Her mother tells her that she's expecting too much from him, and she thinks maybe her mother is right. After all, she doesn't really know many men who treat women well ("that's just the way men are"). Valerie believed that by creating her own financial power base, she would feel less intimidated by Ken. But her newfound strength in the outside world hasn't done all it was supposed to do. She's proud that she doesn't have to ask Ken if she can buy a new dress or get her hair done. But the pressure of her career and keeping up the home is getting to her. Besides, Ken is always on her case because she spends so much time at the office. Lately, the more he pressures her, the more she withdraws. He's even started accusing her of having an affair with her boss, and she thinks he's hired a private detective.

Sometimes she wonders if she did the right thing by joining Ken in the world of work. Her mother thinks she should be back home having babies, especially since her biological time clock has almost ticked away. Even though Ken has two children from a previous marriage, he agrees with her mother and wishes she would stay home and be more available to him. However, they already fight about the fact that when his children visit the responsibility for taking care of them gets dumped on her. She doesn't see how she could raise a child, along with everything else she's doing. As much as she enjoys her work and her independence, she's constantly in conflict between her career goals and her fear that her mom and Ken could be right.

Like Alicia and Valerie, thirty-four-year-old Lana certainly looks like she's independent. An ex-cheerleader and prom queen, Lana has always attracted men wherever she goes. She drives a

Mercedes convertible and owns her own stationery business, with offices in both Denver and Los Angeles. She constantly has some man begging her to marry him, yet she chooses to remain single—though she says she wants to marry someday. She looks as if she's really together.

Lana's energy never stops. Her employees marvel at her aggressive pursuit of difficult business deals. Her friends watch in awe as she juggles her work schedule with exercise classes, weekend business trips, dinner parties, and volunteer work for black-tie events.

But, when Lana leaves the office at night, she goes home and her facade crumbles. Though she has friends, they usually end up wanting her to help them with a problem. Besides, most of her free time is spent with her brother and her mom. Her friends think it's wonderful that she has such a close relationship with her family. But Lana often feels drained by them. They lean on her emotionally and financially. All of her time is filled with business engagements and calls from her family and friends, but tonight no one needs her to be anywhere or do anything. It's times like this when Lana wonders, Why am I doing all this? What's the point?

She looks at her apartment filled with designer furniture, her closets full of expensive clothes, and her Mercedes parked in the garage. She wonders, Wasn't all this supposed to make me happy?

Sometimes she thinks she should have married good old George, the forty-five-year-old restaurateur who promised to take her away from all this. Her mother certainly thinks she should have; she worries about Lana living alone. Lana tells her mom that her life is great and not to worry. She says she's happy being single. And sometimes she believes it. But, at other times, she wishes she had someone to share her life with. Right now she doesn't know how she'd have time for a man, anyway.

She's discarded the dependent, whiny side of herself that can't live without a man. She's proud that she's stopped worrying about whether she has a date on a Saturday night. Besides, she can't remember the last time she met a man she really liked. They all seem to be such wimps. She spends her time working on projects that keep her on her road to success, whereas her friends are devastated when a man doesn't call.

What brought Lana into my office, besides the stress of her present life-style, was her surprising diagnosis of breast cancer. Her illness has made her take a new look at her life, and she's decided to make some changes.

Unlike Lana, Valerie, and Alicia, Peggy doesn't pretend to be independent, but she's just as confused as they are. She's a lady of leisure with a husband, two small children, and a nanny that helps her. She's active in several volunteer organizations and paints in her spare time. Before she married, she was on her way as an artist and had shown several of her paintings in a local art gallery. Now she spends most of her time playing tennis and working out at the local health club. She may be forty-three, but she sure doesn't look it.

She and Tom have a traditional relationship, though they married late in life, in their thirties. Tom owns a beautiful house from a previous marriage, and she moved in and redecorated it. He earns the money and she takes care of his personal needs. For a while, the marriage seemed all it was supposed to be.

In many ways it's just like her parents' relationship. The only difference is that her father gave her mother complete access to their bank account. Tom hasn't been so free with his $250,000-a-year income. But instead of fighting with him over money, she overdraws the family account, hides her purchases, and asks him for more money, claiming it's for household expenses. He knows what she's doing and gets upset about it, yet he would rather put more money in the account than fight with her. Tom learned from his mother that he couldn't win battles with women, so he shuts down—emotionally *and* sexually.

Peggy isn't as happy as she believes her parents were. This isn't how it was supposed to be, after all. Every night Tom comes home and plops down in front of the TV with a drink and the remote control and pays no attention to her. As he unwinds with the TV and the newspaper, she's constantly trying to get his attention. She's always reminding him of something he promised to do for her or for the children: "You forgot to . . . ," "How come you never . . . ," and "You always . . . ".

She's always craving more from him, whereas he seems to want less from her. Sometimes she gets the courage to ask, "Why do you always ignore me? Why don't you want to make love to me anymore?" He responds with, "I work hard all day, why can't

I just have a little peace around here? Don't I deserve to be left alone to read the paper and relax once in a while? Why are you always on my case?" The scenes at her house are like reruns of *The Honeymooners*.

Peggy wonders if her husband is having an affair with a young coworker, since he never sleeps with her anymore. When she confronts him, he says he's tired and stressed out from the job. She's beginning to question her decision to stay home and raise the kids. Though she loves her children, Tom doesn't seem to appreciate the time she devotes to them. And they're both in school now.

She doesn't know what to do. Her friends say, "Leave the bastard." But they forget that she and Tom have two children to consider. Besides, she doesn't want to leave him. She was single for years and has no desire to get back in that rat race. In fact, she wants to win Tom back. But the harder she tries, the more hopeless it seems. She's tried every trick to put the spark back in their marriage. Maybe he's bored with her. She wonders if getting a job outside the home would make a difference. He says it would help, because then she would understand how hard he works. She certainly wouldn't mind having her own money to spend. Then maybe Tom wouldn't be so irritated with her.

Emotional Dependence

Though these four women seem very different, their problems are much the same. None of them are happy with their lives. None are emotionally independent or in control. Each one thinks if only she had what the other has, she would be happier. All of these women still want someone or something outside themselves to make them happy.

All four blame different things for their unhappiness—having no man, having a married man, having the wrong man; being married and not having children, having children; working too hard, not working at all; having too much money or not having enough money. None of them want to admit to their emotional dependencies and thereby take the responsibility for making themselves happy.

Peggy's dependencies on her husband are obvious, because they are both financial and emotional. But the other women described try to hide their dependencies—even from themselves. Valerie doesn't need Ken for financial support, but she's still regularly affected by his lack of approval, or she wouldn't be so intimidated by him. In addition, she has transferred some of her dependency to her boss and is deeply affected by his approval or disapproval. Lana is still dependent on her family but has switched some of her dependency needs onto her career and a variety of social activities. Alicia spends money on her friends and married lover and does extra projects at work for her boss to win approval. These four women are emotionally dependent on the approval of others to feel good about themselves.

Desire for approval is normal, but it's unhealthy when it makes you do things that are not in your own best interest—like waiting for someone's phone call, over-scheduling your life, staying in a bad relationship, or not standing up to someone.

Why are our self-concepts so low that we will make fools of ourselves trying to win a man's love and approval like Alicia does? Why does rejection affect us so intensely that, instead of walking away with our self-respect intact, we try harder with those who reject us, like Peggy does with Tom? Why are we so afraid to be alone, yet at the same time afraid to be close, like Lana? Why do we let others hurt us, yet we fear hurting them so much that we won't express our true feelings? Why are we willing to sell our souls for the love of a man?

For years, I was just like the women I've described. No matter how strong and competent I tried to become—or pretend I was—I still craved approval from men, approval in my career . . . approval in most areas of my life.

No matter how many men were attracted to me, no matter how much money I made, no matter how many career advances I gained, it never felt like enough. One small rejection in the midst of numerous accomplishments knocked me down, depressed me, reminded me that I was imperfect.

At those times, I felt an emptiness in my life that I couldn't put my finger on. The only time the feeling seemed to go away was when I was excited about a new man, or when I published another article, or when I was planning for an upcoming event where I might meet someone new. The relief was only temporary. It was like a fix. When I was in love, I felt okay about myself. When I was alone, there was always a sense of something missing.

I knew my life wasn't the way I wanted it to be. I longed for a sense of peacefulness that I sometimes thought I saw in others. I believed that they were happy and I wasn't.

Down deep inside, I felt like I wasn't good enough.

2

Why We Lose Ourselves in Love Relationships

Is It Love or Addiction?

When we crave being with someone to the point of ignoring our own needs or jeopardizing ourselves, that is addiction—not love. Low self-esteem and love addiction go hand in hand. Most of the time when we think we're in love, we're really feeling a void, which we think this person can fill. We feel empty because we feel inadequate. This man seems better than we are in some area—he's smarter, richer, has more friends, or has more power. There's something about him that we admire that's missing in ourselves. Somehow, we believe that by winning him, our own insecurity will go away in that area. Maybe we believe that if he chooses us, we can't be as bad as we think, or that his strength will make up for our weakness.

Deep inside, most of us still believe, and *want to believe,* that men are stronger than we are. Most women will deny it, but our behavior proves it. One of my female clients brought her husband in so that I could help teach him to open up. When I did and he shared his fears and insecurities with her, she was appalled. She turned to him and said, "And you expect me to attach my wagon to you?" She immediately began having an affair with a man she believed to be stronger than her husband.

We tell men to be emotional with us, but we really don't want to give up the idea that there really is someone out there stronger than we are—someone for us to fall back on when the going gets tough. This belief allows us to *feel* secure. But it also keeps us dependent.

Secretly, most of us have a fantasy that we will find that perfect man who will love and appreciate us enough to make our bad feelings about ourselves go away—and then we will be truly happy. But it isn't possible. And even if it were, we would have to give total control of our lives over to him as the trade-off. He would have to be perfect, have no insecurities of his own, and *always* be able to put our needs before his.

Men don't take away our identities. We do it to ourselves. We give them the power to control us. Alicia admits that she chased her married lover. Why would she chase someone that was unattainable? Maybe it was easier for her to fail in a relationship that she knew couldn't work anyway.

We give men power over our lives, and then get angry because they take it. But why do we feel so intensely that we need a man to prop up our self-esteem? Why do we try so much harder in personal relationships than men do? Why will we so gladly sacrifice our identities to try to hold onto a man?

Society Promotes Love Addiction

We're taught that self-sacrifice is the key to a loving relationship. We hear stories about the man who is so persistent that he continues to send a woman flowers and to pursue her even when she tells him to get lost—and we say, "How romantic." We hear stories about a woman working two jobs to put her husband through medical school and we say, "She must really love him." Giving too much to others while disregarding our own needs is what "good" people do, according to society's teachings. Missionaries and saints are glorified, but no one asks if they are happy. Loving so much that we can't stop giving is considered a positive attribute by our society, although other addictions, like alcohol and drugs, are severely criticized.

Society Teaches Us Denial

The Bible teaches us to do unto others as we would have them do unto us, and that if we follow this teaching, justice will prevail.

So we are good and kind and give to others, never asking for anything in return, hoping that we will get our reward in the end. Asking for something back seems selfish. We want to believe that when we "give" to someone, we're doing it out of the goodness of our hearts. We often, in fact, *deny* that we expect something back, but we do. We expect love and approval in return. At the very least, we expect those people to whom we give to to be appreciative, considerate, and treat us with respect. And when they don't, when justice doesn't prevail, when people don't treat us the way we thought they would, we feel angry. But we think that it's wrong and selfish to feel angry, so we *deny* our feelings. Then we build up resentment from never having our needs met, and we deny *that*. We continue to give more and more, still waiting for justice to prevail. When it never comes, we either build up a wall of bitterness or feel sorry for ourselves, believing that we just aren't "good enough" for others to love us and give to us. Our self-esteem drops even further and we find ourselves on the *downward spiral of unhappiness*.

Pleasing, Resenting, and Feeling Guilty

The progression of dependency works like this: We try to please a man by giving too much to him—as we were taught to do. Then we feel hurt and victimized by him because he doesn't give back. Because we fear losing him, we don't stand up for ourselves by telling him we're hurt, expressing our anger, and asking him to stop hurting us. Because we don't stop him, he hurts us again and again until we become resentful. Because we're resentful, we criticize, punish, and abuse him—or someone else we're less afraid of (like our children). Then we feel terribly guilty and bad about ourselves for being so mean, so we go back to pleasing and giving too much, starting the entire cycle over again.

Often we stay stuck in one role or another. We may become a *martyr/victim*, whereby we remain stuck in the hurt and bad feelings about ourselves, always whining about how terrible our lives are. Or we may become a *controller/abuser*, whereby we stay stuck in our anger, determined to get others before they get us. In this role we blame others by judging, criticizing, and reminding them of how imperfect they are, while hiding our own imperfections behind thick walls of coldness.

We repeat these patterns again and again in our relationships. We either hurt others or feel hurt by them. Although in the past men have more often been the controller/abusers, many women today have followed in their footsteps. That's certainly what both Lana and Valerie have done—put up cold walls so no man can reach them. Peggy, on the other hand, plays the martyr/victim role most of the time, but her anger comes out as nagging. Alicia lets her married lover abuse her, then she takes a controlling/abusing role with her girlfriends.

Most of us don't realize that we're behaving this way. And if someone accuses us of being a martyr or controller, we usually deny it. We hold onto the idea that we wouldn't be having these problems if the person we love loved us enough to treat us better. This idea keeps us feeling that we are unloved, so we feel needy and continue the pattern of pleasing. We end up losing ourselves in the relationship because we have denied our angry feelings.

That's what Peggy and Tom do. Tom denies his anger at Peggy for spending so much money. Peggy denies that she spends it. She also denies that she knows it upsets Tom. Tom builds a wall of resentment against her, which he denies, but which eventually has killed the sexual spark he once had for her. Peggy denies the reason for his sexual disinterest and accuses him of having an affair. She nags him to spend more time with her, which pushes him further away. She has lost her identity and becomes the woman of his worst nightmares. Because of their denial, Peggy and Tom have never dealt with their real problems but have switched their focus to everything else, allowing negative feelings to kill their relationship.

Our Parents Taught Us to Chase Love

Our parents were the first love-givers in our lives. When we were born, we were dependent on them and their love. As children, we learned to trust them more than we trusted ourselves. And now we often transfer that trust to others we believe we love.

We were taught to obey our parents. When we didn't, we were punished and made to feel that we were bad. We were never able to feel that we pleased them. No matter what we did, it was never good enough. When we made Cs, we heard that we "should have made As." If we made As, "why weren't we more social?"

When our imperfections showed through, instead of their consoling us, our parents usually made us feel stupid and incompetent.

Though our parents probably loved us, we seldom felt their love. We wanted more from them—more time and more nurturing. We wanted them to talk to us—*really* talk to us—about how we were feeling and what was happening in our lives and theirs. Because they didn't, we went away feeling unlovable. We thought the problem was us, when it was them.

Their criticisms still haunt us. We fear that the reason they were never really there for us—and why no one else is either—is because we aren't smart enough, pretty enough, strong enough, or lovable enough, just like they told us.

Dysfunctional Families

We hear a lot today about dysfunctional families. A dysfunctional family is one that did not function as a healthy family should have—loving, caring, sharing, and working together. In the childhoods of adults from dysfunctional families, everyone pretended that everything was fine, children's problems were ignored, there were too many rules or too few; parents were either so bonded to each other that they ignored their children, or they weren't bonded at all; children were to be seen and not heard. Most of us grew up in families like this. "Normal" families of the past were dysfunctional families. Dysfunctional families create emotionally dependent women who have no identities, women whose only role is to please others in hopes of finally finding the love they desire so desperately—or women who have shut down and isolated themselves, trying to hide their craving for love.

Why We Chase Men Who Are Bad for Us

Because we feel we never got the unconditional love we craved from our parents, we became addicted to trying to win their love. The more we felt rejected, the harder we tried. Now when someone rejects us—blatantly, or they just don't allow us to get close to them—we think something is wrong with us, as we did with our parents. We often idolize the rejecting or abusing persons, assuming that they are better than we are since they rejected us. Our goal then becomes to prove that they are wrong about us.

This is why we often desperately want the men who don't want us, and we aren't interested in those who do.

If he thinks I'm wonderful but *I* don't think I'm wonderful, then something must be wrong with him—he's either desperate or stupid. Like Groucho Marx once said, "I wouldn't want to belong to any club that would accept me as a member."

Men who treat us badly become a challenge to us and to our self-worth. The more they reject us, the more we chase them. Just as with our parents, we forget to stop and think that it could be *their* problem.

They say that opposites attract. They often do, but usually for the wrong reasons. Often, a person who is overly warm and nice is attracted to someone who is cold and inconsiderate or vice versa, so they can play out the "rejection game."

Codependency

The definition for codependency given by Robert Subby in the chapter, "Inside the Chemically Dependent Marriage: Denial and Manipulation," in his book *CoDependency, An Emerging Issue,* is:

> An emotional, psychological, and behavioral condition that develops as a result of an individual's prolonged exposure to, and practice of, a set of oppressive rules—rules which prevent the open expression of feelings as well as the direct discussion of personal and interpersonal problems.[1]

The term codependency is popularly used to describe those who put up with and cover for alcoholics, drug addicts, and/or abusive men. But only recently has it been acknowledged that codependency also refers to people who put up with and cover for their psychologically abusive partners. Most women have experienced some sort of psychological abuse in their relationships with men. It is psychologically abusive when a man criticizes, judges, has affairs, controls, uses you financially or sexually, withholds emotions, and/or withdraws love from you because you don't do things his way.

Anytime we accept psychologically abusive behavior from someone, we are behaving in an emotionally dependent way. We are accepting someone else's opinion about us without challenging it for fear of losing their approval. This in turn keeps our self-esteem low, helps the abuser continue in his or her behavior, and keeps us addicted to their love.

For instance, the fact that Alicia will continue to see a married man who does not intend to leave his wife promotes his noncommunicative, dishonest behavior with his wife, besides promoting his insensitivity to Alicia's needs. This makes her codependent. Alicia can't understand why he doesn't change, but she's the one "enabling" him to stay the way he is. In fact, his affair with her may keep his needs met well enough to prolong his marriage for years, whereas without her, he might get miserable enough to leave. She continues to hope he will leave his marriage, yet she enables him to stay.

Valerie is codependent too. As long as she continues to withdraw from Ken when he becomes controlling, he will become more and more controlling, and she will have to withdraw more and more. She plays into his problem rather than confronting it. Although Peggy is dependent on Tom, Tom plays a codependent role with her. And Lana is codependent with her friends as well as with her mother and brother. The codependent partner helps the dependent partner stay that way. We lose ourselves when we play either role.

Our parents taught us that we should try to please them. They taught us to deny our feelings and therefore our problems. They taught us to be codependent and sacrifice our needs for theirs as they supposedly did for us. They discouraged us from being our own persons and developing identities that didn't depend on the approval of others. They taught us to chase love.

Switching Love Addictions to Other Addictions

You may say that you're not dependent on men. Many women today don't have a man in their lives to be dependent on. But the low self-esteem that comes with love addiction leaks out into other areas too. As I've mentioned, Lana and Valerie have transferred much of their dependency on approval to work. The reason Valerie's husband thought she was having an affair with her boss was because once Valerie became a workaholic, she did become dependent on her boss's approval instead of Ken's. Like Valerie,

I stopped worrying about who asked me out on Saturday night and, like men often do, began to measure my self-worth by the amount of money I made.

I believe that it's the desperate craving for love that is at the core of all addiction, it's the denial of the need to be loved and approved of that causes such incredible pain that we want to drink or use drugs to hide from life. Popular theories on alcoholism claim it's a disease with genetic origins, and is not curable. Stanton Peele in his book *Diseasing of America*[2] disagrees. He believes that the theory that alcoholism is a disease that's never cured is a seriously flawed and unproven premise, developed by Alcoholics Anonymous (AA) and embraced by mainstream medicine and psychotherapy. "Convincing people that they are passive victims of uncontrollable 'disease' undermines their feelings of efficacy. It also excuses lawlessness by wildly mixing up moral responsibility with disease diagnosis." I agree with Peele that assuming that alcoholism is incurable lets the addict off the hook from taking charge of his or her own life. Alcoholics Anonymous support groups are extremely helpful in aiding alcoholics to "separate" from their chemical addictions. However, in my experience in treating clients with alcohol and drug dependency who were involved in AA, the dependency on love and approval still remains and is simply transferred to the AA groups and to a "higher power," instead of the person becoming completely self-reliant. Possibly the desire to use alcohol in order to play out denial instead of choosing other addictions has a genetic link. But I believe that the addictive personality comes from denying the need for approval instead of choosing to face the problem and work it through. If my premise is true, the alcoholic simply needs to go one step further and break the love addiction so he/she can break the dependency on AA and stop considering him or herself a recovering alcoholic for the rest of his or her life.

From Leaning on a Man to Leaning on Christ

When some women become disillusioned with their lives and/or love relationships, they decide to turn control over to Christ. In fact, the Twelve Step Program developed by AA recommends this. Organized religion not only provides dependent women with an acceptable crutch but also can take over as another male authority figure to guide them, much as a father or husband would.

Churches are perfect for women who don't want to take charge of their lives and are searching for someone to lean on. Ministers tell them that there is something greater than they are—a Christ—another male they can't talk to or hold accountable, but who has given them permission to run their lives. Clergy often use fear and guilt to control them, just as their parents did. They're told to trust *Him* instead of themselves, to decide what's right and wrong. After all, they *are* sinners—and their only chance for happiness and salvation is to ask *Him* for forgiveness for their inadequacies.

That's what happened to Diane. She felt lost after her divorce from an overly controlling husband. She was looking for someone to lead and guide her. She reached out to a church singles group for help. She was needy and vulnerable, and her minister took advantage of it. He encouraged her to have a relationship with Jesus through him. Diane's married minister not only manipulated her into an ongoing sexual relationship but also into setting up business deals and doing his secretarial work for free—all in the name of the Lord. She put up with it for years, never questioning him and always keeping their secret from the congregation and his wife. In group therapy, we begged her to end the relationship and turn him in. She said she couldn't and dropped out of therapy. Now, three years later, I received a note from her telling me that she has filed charges against him. I called and asked her what made her finally do it; she said it came down to choosing between that and suicide.

Some could argue that Diane *did* have a choice in the matter, so some of the blame could be put on her. But what about those women brought up with strict religious upbringings and taught to look up to authorities. How can it be their fault? Patti's father was a minister. For years, her religious training kept her depressed and needy for some man to love her. She had kept a family secret about her brother, believing, as abused women do, that it arose because of *her* fault. Her story is told here, through excerpts from a letter to her father:

> Growing up in a minister's family didn't seem to have many advantages, now that I look back over my life. I left the church because I was angry that I felt I had to do whatever I was told. I've always felt I have to hide from you those things I know you

won't approve of, and I'm tired of it.

I feel you've always avoided issues by saying everything was God's will. In our family, we were never allowed to disclose our feelings—especially anger—so obviously incest wasn't something I could talk to you about.

I can no longer keep the family secret. When I was growing up—I don't remember exactly when—Ed had sex with me. I felt so alone and abandoned because I thought I was supposed to be able to trust my brother not to hurt me, and I couldn't understand how my father could let this happen. There was no way I could hurt you by telling you about this. I was so afraid of you punishing me for this mortal sin, and that I would be told I had to leave the church and family. I feel betrayed by both you and Ed.

You've always wondered why I've been depressed and in therapy for years. This secret has kept me feeling alone and alienated, both from the church and the family. I want you to talk to me about it instead of pretending it didn't happen. I want you to tell me I'm okay and it's not my fault. I want you to tell Ed that what he did was wrong.

Patti worked the problem out with her father, and she was able to successfully deal with the issues of her brother's betrayal and the church and finally complete her therapy. Most women are not as drastically abused by religion as Diane and Patti were, but most of us were taught religious beliefs like sacrificing for those we love that affirmed our second-class status, and taught us passivity. The Bible says that we should turn the other cheek, never feel malice, never covet—never feel or do anything that isn't perfectly "nice." These expectations are inhuman and make us continually feel bad about ourselves. We're taught that if we feel anger, envy, resentment, greed, lust, depression, or loneliness that we're bad—as if these weren't a natural part of being human. Religion continually reminds us of our imperfections, keeping our self-esteem low and pushing us to look to others for happiness.

Other Experts We Lean on

Even many of my successful female clients who are experts in their fields become dependent on other experts. Female doctors, lawyers, corporate women, and even other psychologists tell me that they feel like imposters and feel more comfortable leaning on authorities, rather than having to be the authorities themselves—even over their own lives.

As savvy as Lana seems, she totally trusted her accountant and never looked at her tax returns after he prepared them. Last year when she was audited and owed ten thousand dollars in back taxes, she couldn't believe what he had done to her. Although she considered suing him, the IRS said that her taxes were her responsibility, not her accountant's.

We've had this problem with doctors for years. We give them too much power over our lives and then expect them to handle it by being superhuman. Then we file malpractice suits against them when they don't deliver.

We let our lawyers, doctors, stockbrokers, teachers, priests, and bosses run our lives. We give them too much of our trust because we are looking for someone to relieve us of the burden of responsibility for our own happiness. These experts often send us the message that "I know what's best for you. Trust me. I care about you and I'm only trying to help." And we naively believe them because we want it to be true.

I'm not denying that authorities in special fields do have information that can be very valuable to us. However, we need to see them as our employees instead of gods. We should sort through their information and combine it with our own feelings and needs in order to make decisions about our lives and never give them complete control.

Letting Therapists Run Our Lives

Women who are looking for someone to switch their dependencies onto are prime candidates for abuse by their therapists. Because clients often want to believe that a therapist knows all, they lean too heavily, and the therapist ends up becoming codependent with the client. The client feels better after her sessions because of the attention and empathy lavished on her by her therapist, but the therapist is often *enabling* the client to stay locked in her situation by giving her positive attention and a release for her frustrations. The client then switches her dependency onto the therapist instead of moving forward and learning to trust herself. (It's normal, however, for a therapist to sometimes encourage a client's dependency early in the relationship and then gradually wean the client from this dependency.)

Therapy groups, self-help books, and therapists can easily play on a woman's insecurities, claiming they will teach her more about herself so that she can ultimately take control of her life when in reality, they often make her look outside herself for answers. However, sometimes when a therapist tries to push a dependent woman toward becoming more self-reliant, she simply switches to a therapist who will allow her to become dependent. Many women will go from expert to expert trying hypnosis, meditation, psychics, medication, or any psychological fad before they will try to take charge of their own lives.

Andrea became addicted not only to therapy but also to her therapist. She came to see me, trying to break her addiction to her male therapist of ten years. At times she felt sure she was in love with him. "I can't give him up," she said. "I don't feel I can let go until I win his respect and friendship, and he won't give it to me."

Andrea began seeing this therapist right after her husband walked out on her and their two sons, owing thousands of dollars that Andrea ended up taking responsibility for. Andrea was devastated and needed help getting back on her feet. Her therapist took advantage of the situation. For a long time, Andrea didn't realize that she was chasing her therapist's approval and letting him run her life, just as she had done with her husband and her father.

A critical question for women who are considering therapy is, "Through therapy, am I gaining more control over my life and mental well-being, or am I giving away control to yet one more authority figure?"

Where We Go From Here

To break emotional dependencies and become self-reliant, we must learn to stop caring whether others are pleased by our behavior, and learn to enjoy being alone. We must forgive ourselves for not being as perfect as our parents and society—and we—wish we were. We must know who we are, understand why we're this way, and learn to appreciate our differences. To relate to others in a healthy way, we have to get in touch with our feelings and communicate those feelings and desires to others. To keep others from abusing us, we must learn not to fear our anger but to express it constructively through confrontation. To rid ourselves of our defensive patterns from the past and gain strength as adults, we must confront our parents and tell them how they have affected our lives. To fulfill our fantasies of the future, we have to take risks in those areas in which we've been fearful. To take control over our lives, we must stop muddling in and analyzing our problems, and instead take the action necessary to make our lives the way we want them to be. Then—and only then—will we truly have an identity that no man, parent, or authority can ever take away from us.

The following chapters concentrate on these issues, teaching you self-empowerment, and guiding you down the road of self-reliance through my program—the Eight Steps to Emotional Intimacy Without Addiction.

Part II

**The Program:
Eight Steps to Emotional
Intimacy Without Addiction**

The Program Process

EIGHT STEPS TO EMOTIONAL INTIMACY
WITHOUT ADDICTION

Step One: Recognize, understand, and admit your emotional dependency and commit to change.

Step Two: Withdraw, separate, and develop your own identity.

Step Three: Forgive yourself for not being perfect.

Step Four: Understand why you are the way you are.

Step Five: Get in touch with your feelings and communicate them.

Step Six: Confront your parents.

Step Seven: Complete your adolescence through risk-taking and experimenting.

Step Eight: Take responsibility and control in every area of your life.

These eight steps will guide you through the process of defining your own identity, becoming your own person, and taking charge of your life. If you are dedicated and work through these steps, you will break your love addictions and become a stronger person in the process.

The goal of this program is to help you take charge of your life by overcoming your love addictions and emotional dependencies. The program contains quizzes, questions, and exercises developed to make you think and feel and explore yourself. Because our minds often play tricks on us and try to make us forget things, you may want to start a journal or workbook to help you stay on track. If you're doing the program on your own without the help of a therapist, write down every important thought, feeling, insight, and significant childhood incident you might remember, so that you can act as your own therapist. If you have any doubts about being able to do the program on your own or are deeply depressed, read "Seeking Therapy" in the next chapter before you begin the program.

It is important to follow all the steps of the program though you may want to choose a different order. Although it's possible to gain valuable information and insights from each step, to become truly emotionally self-reliant, it is important that you complete the entire program. This will not be an easy journey, but it is one that I know you will never be sorry you took.

Are you ready? Let's start the most exciting trip of your life— your journey toward self-reliance!

3

Step One: Recognize, Understand, and Admit Your Emotional Dependency and Commit to Change

Like with other addicts, a love addict's first step in breaking emotional dependency and becoming self-reliant is to recognize your dependent behaviors, stop denying the problem, and admit that your life is not as you want it to be. Then you must make a commitment to do whatever is necessary to change it.

Along with the new sense of strength that we gained through the women's movement, we also gained a sense of embarrassment about admitting our dependencies—especially on men—and our deep desire to be taken care of. Housewives who choose to stay home and raise their children aren't respected. Women without careers are considered boring. It's difficult to admit to other women today that you have a hidden desire to be taken care of because most pretend they don't.

We were all taught to find a rich (or at least well-educated with the potential of becoming rich) man to take care of us. It's unlikely that most of us have been able to give up this idea simply because we were told to do so. Intellectually, we understand the trade-offs of powerlessness when we don't have our own security, but, emotionally, we deny how bad we feel when we're powerless. And as long as we deny the conflict we feel, we can't solve the problem.

Even though the women's movement forced many of us into taking charge of our own financial security, most of us still feel a void. We thought that by no longer needing men to take care of us financially, we would no longer care what they thought of us or crave their love. But the need to feel loved and approved of didn't go away with financial success, as our behavior proves.

Single women still act desperate when they're around an "eligible" man. Married women put up with emotional coldness from their husbands. Most of us have increased our checkbook balances, but few of us have stopped trying to win the love of a man.

Society's Messages, Tradition, and Women

Most of us were brought up in traditional families. The man provided and the woman took care of the home. That was the way we thought it was supposed to be. Because our mothers were in denial, most of them wouldn't admit that they weren't happy. My mother used to say, "So who's happy anyway?" She, and many women like her, settled for a life of existing. She and my father wanted me to do the same. They wanted me to accept a life like theirs, a so-called "normal" life consisting of getting married, raising children, spending weekends running errands, fighting about money, and never expecting anything more than that. But I couldn't do it.

My sister did. Now forty and an empty-nester with no career, she wonders if she did the right thing.

Alicia and many of my other single women clients believe that if they could just find the right men and have marriages like my sister's, they would be happy. From the outside, it looks good. In many ways, my sister and her husband are happy; they're best friends, they've been quite successful financially, and they've raised a child who is healthy, graduated from high school, and is not on drugs. Many people would be glad to have a life like theirs. But my sister feels the same void that Alicia does. Though she has a man in her life, he isn't able to share with her emotionally. Though she has a great kid, it hurts her that he's not appreciative of the sacrificing she's done for him. Now, as he prepares to go off on his own, she feels purposeless and lost.

Traditional relationships are usually built around a division of labor in which the man is the provider (in this role he is usually codependent, controlling and avoidant), and the woman is the caretaker (in this role she is usually dependent, a victim and overly emotional). Because they take on such extreme roles, they usually end up either in a power struggle, fighting like my parents did, or emotionally avoiding each other like my sister and her husband do.

Alicia and other single women like her have to give up the fantasy that people in traditional marriages are happier than they are. What they believe to be happy marriages are often relationships built on dependency and codependency—and do not breed happiness. Until women give up the fantasy that these dependent/codependent relationships are good ones, they will continue to seek them and therefore never change.

It's important to remember that most of us were taught to be dependent, whether we were aware of it or not. And though we don't usually behave like whiny wifelets of the past, such as Peggy, we've found new ways to play out our emotional dependencies and lose control of our lives. Valerie, Alicia, and Lana have done what men have been doing for years—thrown themselves into their careers and transferred their emotional dependencies to jobs, friends, coworkers, and bosses. Without admitting that they are emotionally dependent, they can't solve the problem. As an adult, the decision is yours. You *can* change and break these dependency patterns, but you must first *admit* you're dependency—or fear of it.

What Is Your Emotional Style?

We've talked about the two main roles in most relationships: the martyr/victim (who is dependent) and the controller/abuser (who is codependent). The martyr/victim is usually openly dependent, whereas the controller/abuser is most often avoidant. Most people are either emotionally dependent or emotionally avoidant and both men and women can use both styles. Emotional avoidance often appears as strength, but it is simply a cover-up for a fear of emotional dependence. Some people can play both roles and many of us are able to adopt either role, often switching roles with different partners.

Lana is basically emotionally avoidant. She pretends she doesn't care what others think. Men think she's cold and uncaring. They feel abused by her. She acts like no one can get to her, yet she goes home and suffers in silence. Because she's been hurt many times before, she chooses to put up a wall that keeps others at a distance, so she can't be hurt again. Though she may appear to be "strong" and in control, in her most recent love relationship with a controlling doctor, she has reverted to being an emotionally dependent woman who allows herself to be abused. Kay and her live-in boyfriend were both emotionally avoidant, so they stayed together for seven years without discussing any of their problems. Valerie is emotionally avoidant, clearly locking her feelings out, whereas Peggy and Alicia are emotionally dependent. Most of us make a decision in childhood to be one way or the other—we choose to be like either mom or dad. Lana, Valerie, and I looked at our weak, dependent mothers and said, "I won't let anyone take advantage of me like that," so we tried to be more like our emotionally avoidant fathers. Both styles are unhealthy.

Which are you? Are you emotionally avoidant, emotionally dependent, or healthy? Do you wait for others to make you happy? Do you try to hide your lonely feelings—even from yourself? Or do you take charge of your life by recognizing and working through your emotions? Find out.

Take the time to carefully consider your responses to the following questions. Be honest with yourself. If you think you may be in denial about your behavior, ask a good friend to help you answer the questions below.

DETERMINING YOUR EMOTIONAL STYLE

1. When someone makes you angry, you most often
   a) cry.
   b) avoid that person.
   c) tell them how you feel and why.

2. You most often feel
   a) lonely.
   b) stressed.
   c) happy and comfortable with yourself.

3. When someone criticizes you, you
   a) think he's probably right and get down on yourself.

b) criticize him back or withdraw.

c) tell him you don't want to hear his judgmental insults, but you would like to know what he's really upset about.

4. When you're upset, you usually
   a) think you're probably overreacting and wait, hoping the feelings will go away.
   b) let it build and then explode.
   c) speak up and say something.

5. You often think
   a) that something must really be wrong with you since you can't seem to get your life under control.
   b) that others are usually holding you back from success and happiness.
   c) that as soon as you figure out what the problem is, you'll handle it.

6. Do you
   a) feel constantly pressured by others' expectations of you?
   b) not care what others think of you?
   c) care what others think, but don't let it run your life?

7. You often feel
   a) unappreciated.
   b) that you're better than others.
   c) loved and loving.

8. With friends, family, and lovers, you
   a) usually expose more about yourself than they do.
   b) let them talk about themselves, but share little about yourself.
   c) talk about yourself, but make sure they open up to you as much.

9. Your life is
   a) disorganized and confusing.
   b) rigidly organized down to what you "usually" eat and when you "always" work out.
   c) organized, but you're not afraid to miss exercise class or change your schedule if it's for a good reason.

10. You are
    a) rather flighty.
    b) mostly serious.
    c) sometimes serious and sometimes silly.

11. You prefer
    a) to have people around you all the time.
    b) to be alone.
    c) a balance of time with others and time alone.

12. Your friends
    a) feel sorry for you.
    b) look up to you.
    c) like you, but know your life isn't perfect.

13. In your relationships with others, you are
    a) a giver.
    b) a taker.
    c) a partner—both giving and taking.

14. Are you
    a) submissive in personal relationships?
    b) aggressive in personal relationships?
    c) submissive or aggressive depending on what's called
       for?

15. When you feel afraid to do something, you
    a) think "I don't know enough to be doing this."
    b) pretend you're not afraid.
    c) remember that everyone feels frightened at times and as-
       sume it will pass.

16. Do you
    a) often overeat, exercise too much, drink too much, and/or
       spend too much money?
    b) always try to stay in control?
    c) usually stay in control, but sometimes indulge yourself?

17. Do you
    a) cry all the time?
    b) rarely cry, and if you do, no one ever sees it?
    c) cry whenever you feel sad—sometimes in public but
       mostly at home when you're alone?

18. Your emotions are
    a) like a roller coaster.
    b) stable—you're hardly ever too up or too down.
    c) consistent, but with a full range from sadness and hurt to anger and joy.

19. You are critical
    a) mostly of yourself.
    b) mostly of others.
    c) seldom.

20. When someone seems sure to hurt you, you
    a) wish he wouldn't, but it usually happens.
    b) get him first.
    c) ask him what's going on and then try to work it out.

21. When you first meet a man you like, you
    a) feel desperate and often do whatever he wants.
    b) usually act cool and disinterested.
    c) are friendly, but not too eager.

22. Once you start to care about someone, you
    a) stop looking at anyone else.
    b) talk about other men and/or push him away in other ways.
    c) let him know you care, but also let him know that you plan to date other men until the two of you make a commitment.

23. When you really enjoy a man and want to sleep with him, you
    a) jump in bed with him as soon as possible.
    b) reject him sexually so he'll keep calling back.
    c) tell him you're attracted to him but want to wait until you know each other better before you sleep together.

24. When the two of you become an item, your social life
    a) revolves around his, with your friends going on a back burner.
    b) continues exactly as it was since you expect him to fit into your schedule.

    c) continues basically as it was but with some adjustments to make sure that you have time for him as well as for others in your life.

25. When you care about a man, you
    a) send him little cards and notes and make special things for him, even if he never does these things for you.
    b) expect him to send you cards and do special things without your reciprocating.
    c) do special things for him, but stop if and when he doesn't reciprocate.

26. When you're involved with a man, he usually
    a) acts cold, condescending, and/or unemotional.
    b) becomes a little boy who "needs" you.
    c) shares his emotions with you but handles his problems himself.

27. When you have problems developing a relationship with a man, you think
    a) my neediness probably scares men away.
    b) most men can't handle a strong woman like me.
    c) I'm probably just going through a dry spell.

28. When a man acts macho with you, you
    a) scream, yell, cry, and/or beg him to stop treating you so badly.
    b) think, Oh well, that's just the way men are.
    c) hold him accountable by saying something like, "I'm not letting you get away with that."

29. When you are in a relationship, and if you have a problem, you
    a) usually ask his advice and follow it.
    b) usually assume he couldn't help you.
    c) ask his opinion and incorporate it into what feels right to you.

30. When it comes to spending money in a relationship, you
    a) expect him to cover all the expenses.
    b) make it a point to pay your own way, and often have to pay for his.

    c) usually cover your own expenses, or take turns, even paying his on special occasions.

Scoring

If you chose mostly As, you behave in an emotionally dependent way. The more As you chose, the more dependent you are. You're "waiting" for someone else to make you happy. You don't want to have to take charge of certain areas of your life.

If you chose mostly Bs, you behave in an emotionally avoidant way. The more Bs you chose, the more avoidant you are. You are faking your strength. You think it is strong to walk away. You hide your dependencies from yourself. You'd rather blame others than work through issues. You probably have very few "real" relationships in your life. You must first let down your facade and admit your emotional dependencies before you can work them through and be close to others.

If you chose close to the same number of As and Bs, you probably switch back and forth between behaving emotionally dependent and emotionally avoidant, depending on the situation and the person. The emotionally dependent/avoidant woman often falls apart over one issue and pretends that the next one doesn't bother her. A woman who does this may believe it's stronger to avoid her emotions, but she can't always pull it off. If you are emotionally dependent/avoidant, you must give up the idea that avoiding is strong and then begin to deal with your real emotions.

If you chose mostly Cs, and didn't lie to yourself, you are basically an emotionally healthy woman. You've probably worked hard to take charge of your life. You've learned to be comfortable alone with yourself. You don't let others' approval run your life. You aren't afraid to be yourself and speak your piece. You'd rather deal with a problem head-on than avoid it.

How Emotionally Dependent Are You?

Whether you *act* dependent or avoidant, most of us are much more dependent than we think, but we don't always realize it. Here is a checklist. Answer Yes or No to each question to find out how dependent you are.

1. Do you feel constantly pressured by others' expectations of you?
2. Do you have difficulty questioning your doctor and other professionals about their diagnoses or advice?
3. Do you often experience conflict between what you think you "should" do and what you feel you want to do?
4. Do you go from one therapist to another or from one self-help program to another, in search of the "right" answer to your problems?
5. Are you intimidated by people who appear to be confident?
6. Do you assume that you don't know as much as others do?
7. Do you behave differently around men than women?
8. Do you follow what others tell you to do and then blame them for giving you "bad" advice?
9. Does your self-esteem depend on what others say and think of you and/or on your possessions or job?
10. Is it hard for you to say no to others?
11. Do you often obligate yourself to too many people and things?
12. Do you often get on your own case for not being perfect?
13. Do you often feel like your life would be much better if you were younger, had more money or more education, or had the right man?
14. Do you hold back sharing your true feelings for fear that you'll hurt someone or they won't like you?
15. Do those you care about seldom seem to appreciate you?
16. Do your relationships turn into power struggles of who's right and who's wrong?
17. Are there major areas of your life in which you feel inadequate?
18. Do you find yourself waiting to make changes—until the kids are older? until you lose weight? until you have more money? until things get better?
19. Do you constantly ask others to help you make your decisions?
20. Does it sometimes feel like your boyfriend or mate is like your father?
21. Are you afraid to be alone, and/or when you are alone, do you stay occupied so you don't have to think about yourself?

22. Do you feel that others never give back to you as much as you give to them?
23. Are you afraid to give ultimatums?
24. Do you talk about and analyze your problems but never resolve them?
25. Are you afraid of people in positions of authority?
26. Do you have severe mood swings and/or fear you'll never be happy?
27. Are your expectations of your abilities too low, whereas your expectations of what you *should* be doing are too high?
28. Did you grow up in a family in which there was little communication, in which expressing feelings was not acceptable, and in which there were either rigid rules or none at all?
29. Do you often feel like crying?
30. Are you a compulsive eater, drinker, smoker, lover, spender, shopper, etc.?
31. Do people say you're too sensitive and emotional, or too in control?
32. Do you feel that "life isn't fair?"
33. Do you think your unhappiness comes from what others seem to do to you?
34. Do you find yourself being abusive or covering for another person's abuse?
35. Do you spend a great deal of time talking about—and worrying about—other people's behavior/problems/future, instead of living your own life?
36. Do you find yourself taking on more responsibility at home, in a job, or in a relationship than you really want or are paid to do?
37. Do you ignore your own needs in deference to meeting someone else's (family, friends, husband, boss, lover)?
38. Are you afraid that if you get angry, the other person will leave or not love you?
39. Do you worry that if you leave a relationship or stop controlling, your partner will fall apart?
40. Do you spend less time on you—alone or with friends—and more time with the man in your life, your children, and other family members, in activities you wouldn't normally choose to engage in?

If you answered yes to sixteen or more questions, you are *very* emotionally dependent on others. If you answered yes to five or fewer questions, your level of dependency is low. If you answered yes six to fifteen times, you are average in your level of emotional dependency. Although average dependency is normal, it is not healthy.

Why Some Women Decide to Change
(and Why Some Don't)

You probably think, ''I don't have any more problems than anyone else does, so why do I need to do all this work? Most of the people I know are a lot worse off than I am.'' You can have a ''normal'' life that is quite similar to that of others that you know, without ever going through this program. To people who are starving, or have no friends, or live with an abusive man, Lana's, Valerie's, Alicia's, and Peggy's lives may sound great. But these women want more than a ''normal'' life. They want happiness.

Few people try to obtain greater happiness in their lives, because most are in codependent relationships in which they are being maintained in a dysfunctional fashion—their insecurities feed off the insecurities of their partners, and it seems ''safer'' to stay in the relationship than to take the risks necessary for emotional growth.

Many people remain in denial for their entire lives. Some people are so *unaware* of their feelings that they don't know there's more to life than merely existing. In fact, many people don't deal with their emotions or their lives until and unless they face a major crisis, such as an illness, a divorce, the death of a child, or a major job loss.

It's difficult to admit that you feel insecure and unloved, and that you wish someone would take care of you. It's difficult to admit that you aren't and haven't been in charge of your life. Finding out that you may have been simply following a script written for you by others, instead of choosing the life you really want, can be devastating. Your basic beliefs about life are challenged.

For some, giving up this fantasy can throw them into a deep depression. Most of my clients feel worse before they feel better.

Hitting bottom and feeling that "I hate my life as it is" seem to be necessary for major change.

Fear of Knowing Yourself

Most people are afraid to look inside themselves for fear of what they might find. Most of us believe that down deep inside, we are "bad" people. We fear that digging into our past will somehow prove this to be true. We've spent years covering up thoughts and feelings about those inadequate parts of ourselves so that others won't see them. The idea of looking at those parts that we consider imperfect, flawed, or deficient—and how they got that way—is much too scary for most people to deal with.

It is this fear—the fear of finding out about and working through the parts of ourselves that we don't like—that keeps many of us from taking this first step of admitting that a problem exists and deciding to fix it. Few people admit their real fears, which is *critical* to growing and changing with or without a therapist.

We don't need to fear what we will discover in ourselves. We are imperfect, but so is everyone else. Within, all of us is good *and* bad—love *and* anger. We've been taught that anger is bad. We need to go back and learn why we believe this and realize now that it's not true, so that we can begin to express our anger. In doing so, we will become healthier and repair our damaged self-esteem. If we don't, we will continue to feel bad about ourselves.

Looking back into our past and understanding who we are and how we got that way is hard work. But it's the only way to start loving yourself and truly learn how to love others in a healthy way.

Seeking Therapy

As you work through this program, you may decide to do it alone, or you may decide to seek therapy. It's very important that you seek outside help if you become deeply depressed. Appendix I on page 249 gives you the signs of major depression as described by the American Psychiatric Association.

Initially it's often very difficult to make major changes without help and feedback from someone else, especially because we have a difficult time seeing the patterns and defenses we're caught up in. When we are hurting, our tendency is to avoid instead of explore our issues. If, and when, we avoid, we end up feeling angry at ourselves, become more depressed, and act out self-destructive behaviors.

If you do seek therapy, be sure not to choose a therapist who is in denial about his or her *own* life. Such a therapist may try to keep you from doing the difficult parts of the program that he or she has been unable to accomplish. If you believe in this program, show it to your therapist and ask for support in working through it. Friends and relatives may try to talk you out of completing the program because they wouldn't have the courage to do it themselves. This may also be true of your therapist. Don't let them hold you back. It may be necessary to switch therapists. Guidelines for selecting a therapist are excerpted from my article, "Choosing the Right Therapist," and are provided in Appendix II, page 251.

My Clients

The women who come into my office are usually there because of their problems with men. Most often a woman comes in to see me because a man has left her, or she can't win a certain man's love and approval, or she is incredibly lonely and wonders what's wrong with her. What brought Bonnie in to see me was her desire to win over the married man she was having an affair with. She even brought him in, hoping I could talk him into leaving his wife. Bonnie was unhappy in her marriage. Her husband was much like her father—the strong, silent type. She never felt his love and approval. When they'd have a fight, he'd go out drinking with his buddies and become so disabled with alcohol that Bonnie had to take care of him. A married male coworker who was attracted to Bonnie began listening to her complaints about her husband. Before they knew it, they were in bed together. Bonnie feared her husband and did not have the strength to confront him or leave him. Instead of dealing with the problem, she switched her dependency onto another man. By the time she came to me for therapy, she was close to losing everything—her lover, her marriage, and her job.

Valerie and Ken came in because Ken believed Valerie was having an affair. Peggy just felt depressed. She didn't want a divorce, but her marriage was getting worse and worse. Alicia came in because she knew deep inside that she needed to end her relationship with her married lover, but she wasn't able to do it on her own.

Sometimes these women realize that they are emotionally dependent, but usually they don't. Take Sheri for instance. She's a twenty-six-year-old airline stewardess who recently came into my office after being involved in three destructive relationships in a row. She went from a bad live-in relationship, to a man who ended up running off with her girlfriend, and finally to a pilot who says he cares for her but won't sleep with her. Sheri saw my article "How to Succeed at Love Without Really Trying"[1] in *New Woman* magazine and called, asking, "What am I doing wrong with men?" She was hoping for a quick, easy solution. After a few sessions, however, it was obvious to me that her problem was deeper than she thought. When I pointed out that her pattern of choosing an unavailable man again and again came from a need for approval stemming from her childhood, Sheri became depressed. I also pointed out that she was choosing men that were unemotional and unavailable, as her father was when she was growing up. She was trying to win their love to prove that she was good enough, because she never really felt her father's love and caring. She knew that what I was saying was true. But she didn't want to deal with it. She had hoped I could just tell her how to win the last guy back and her problem would be solved. I told her I could give her simple behavioral techniques to help her with her relationships with men, but to break her patterns, she would have to deal with the root of the problem. Besides, she'd be back in a few months wanting more techniques for more problems—which would create a dependency on me. It was important for her to deal with her low self-esteem issues, with my help. She, unlike many clients, let go of her fear and eagerly asked, "Okay, where do we begin?"

She responded very differently from Florence, a fifty-seven-year-old woman who was going through her second divorce. After the third or fourth session, she came in, stating, "This will be my last session. I came to you to get help getting through this divorce, and I feel that you've helped me a lot. I feel sure now about ending the relationship. But, last week, when we got into my past and you told me that my relationship with my father probably helped cause my bad marriages and would create bad relationships with men in the future, I got real depressed. I don't want to think that about my father. I left feeling worse last time, not better, and that's not what I came here for. My father is dead, and I refuse to have any bad thoughts about him.''

Florence was braver than many of my clients. When some clients find out that solving problems involves action on their part rather than simply talking over issues with their therapist, they never call back. Some say, ''There must be another way.'' If I call them to find out why they haven't rescheduled, their excuses are, ''I can't afford it,'' ''I'm too busy at work,'' ''I have a health crisis that is more important right now,'' and my favorite—''I just met a new man and I'm in love, so now I don't need therapy.'' Usually what is really getting in their way is their fear— fear of admitting and dealing with their own dependencies.

Upward Spiral of Self-Reliance

When many of my clients begin to see all the ways they are dependent on others' approval, they become overwhelmed. Alicia certainly was. At first, she felt like giving up.

But once you decide to change and take a few of the necessary steps, the process gets easier. Just as there is a downward spiral of dependency, there is an *upward spiral of self-reliance.* One positive step leads to greater confidence and helps you get to the next step.

There will be many times in the next few chapters when you will want to quit. You may become frightened, or the program will seem too hard. Make a commitment *now* not to quit. When something feels ''wrong'' to you, as it may when you change your belief system, ask yourself, ''Does it feel wrong because I've never tried it before and I'm afraid to risk? Does it go against what I think I should believe because of society's teachings, and I'm afraid to go against them?'' Don't let those reasons hold you back, but if an action does go against a belief that you choose to keep as part of your new identity, don't do it. Be true to yourself, but recognize fear and don't give in to it.

Remember—what you've done in the past hasn't really worked

for you, or you wouldn't have picked up this book. It's time to break out of your love addictions and move forward. If you now *know* you are emotionally dependent and have decided to change that, go on to the next step. If not, you may still be in denial and not yet ready for the program.

4

Step Two:
Withdraw, Separate,
and Develop Your Own Identity

Though Alicia and Lana live alone, they spend very little time alone with just themselves. In fact, they will do anything to avoid being really alone: join groups they aren't truly interested in; sit through movies they dislike; hold conversations with people who bore them; listen to friends and relatives complain all night. This doesn't mean that Lana and Alicia never spend time alone; they do. In fact, many emotionally avoidant women claim to feel very comfortable being alone. Overwhelmed by others' problems, they often need to be alone and escape from their friends' needs and emotions, which is good. But they usually don't use their aloneness as an opportunity to focus on themselves. Instead, they escape into trashy novels, or they overeat and/or overdrink, watch TV, or sleep the time away. Their time alone is not used wisely—to develop a relationship with themselves.

But most of us don't want to get really clear about who we are. We've been told by our mothers, "Don't get too set in your ways, honey, or you'll never be able to find a man to marry." So many of us want to wait to get our lives together until we see which man we'll be needing to adjust to.

Fear of Being Alone Forever

We are so driven by the fear that we might end up living alone—without a man—that we don't want to get our lives too much in order. We know it doesn't make sense and that we should try to make ourselves happy, but the fear overrides our intelligent thought.

Married women often tell me, almost secretively, that they felt stronger and happier with themselves when they were unmarried and living alone. Yet, they—and most single women—feel frightened and devastated about the possibility of being without a man. They can't take their focus off finding or being with one long enough to try and make themselves happy. They cannot fathom the idea of happiness without a man. Or if they do, they still think they'll be happier with one.

The truth is that happiness comes from inside, and that you will not be any happier with a man than you are with yourself right now.

But society pressures us. Twenty-eight-year-old Barbara, though basically happy being single, feels constantly pressured by her friends to get married. She feels that they talk behind her back about why she can't find a man. A woman alone has always been looked at by our society as less, purposeless, and "not good enough" in some way. Single women who buy into this ancient belief make remaining single seem negative.

Marrieds Aren't Happier than Singles

Lonely feelings only go away temporarily during the addictive "high" we feel in the early phase of a dependent relationship. Ultimately, that void of loneliness does not get filled with a relationship. Like with other addictions the craving continues and we need more and more to feel satisfied. The addiction to being loved continues because it was created in our childhoods. No man—not even the "right" man—can make it go away.

In reality relationships are often draining. In a relationship, you often must choose between doing what's best for your mate or for you. Because of our training, most of us end up deferring our needs and desires to his. If we do what's best for us, we often fear we're being selfish.

When we're involved in a relationship, we're more often limited in the ways we can deal with our intimacy needs. When we're single, on the other hand, we can call lovers or friends or choose to meet someone new without having to answer to the person who is not meeting our needs. Being single can often be a better choice than being married, as long as we don't keep our lives on hold. The antidote to loneliness comes from knowing ourselves and then from the quality and intimacy of our relationships with others, not from finding the "right" person.

As a single person, you're more likely to follow your career goals. You don't have to worry how a drop in income or move to a new city will affect someone else. And waiting for someone to make you happy doesn't go away when you marry. Contrary to popular belief among singles, marriage is no guarantee against loneliness. I found out when I was married that it's much lonelier lying in bed next to a man who won't talk to you than it is lying in bed alone reading a good book. Married women still wait and hope that their husbands will be more intimate and make the void go away. Marriage gives them someone else to blame for their loneliness and unhappiness, instead of themselves.

But whether you're single or married, the real issue is learning to face the world alone and letting go of the desperate need to lean on someone else, especially a man. Finding the right man is like applying for a loan: To get the best deal, you must be able to prove you don't need it. And as with money, it's difficult not to appear desperate when you really are.

Living alone can be an exhilarating, freeing, constructive experience if a woman does not choose to believe that doing so means something is wrong with her. A woman can use the time alone to do whatever is best for herself without worrying about anyone else's needs.

Not until I surrendered and made a decision to become "single, secure, and satisfied" did it work for me. I put my life in order as if I would never be involved with a man again. I moved to a new city for my career, bought a house, developed a new group of friends with whom I felt a sense of belonging, and completely planned my future *without* a man. I dated around but felt sure I would never be married or even involved in a monogamous relationship. *I let go.* And you must do the same. Until and unless you *let go* of the search for the right man, you'll never be happy—and you can be sure you'll never find him. Or if you do fall for someone, you won't be able to love him without losing your identity.

You don't have to be single to complete this program, but you must become "secure and satisfied" within yourself. And to do this, you must learn to be comfortable alone and happy on your own.

Withdraw and Separate From Love Addiction

Just as alcoholics go cold turkey, you must similarly withdraw from your love addictions. Alicia not only had to pull away from her married boyfriend, but because she was so emotionally attached to her family and friends, she had to disengage from them as well. Even though her family lived two thousand miles away, she relied heavily on their approval. And with her friends a day couldn't go by without several codependent calls to them. The first step I asked Alicia to do was to spend an evening or weekend (four hours minimum) alone, at home or away, without talking to anyone—friends, lover, or family—trying to get in touch with herself. Then she was to schedule at least one evening every week to do this. It can be a very uncomfortable thing to do. At first, you may feel overwhelmed or frightened or lonely. But as you spend more time with yourself, the more comfortable you will become.

As children, we learned to be carbon copies of our parents and others we came in contact with. The development of the individual personality is supposed to be a slow and gradual process beginning in infancy. As we get older, we should be progressively pulling away from our parents, becoming more independent, and deciding who we really are. To separate and individuate, we must spend the time necessary to discover our own distinguishing qualities (our feelings, ideas, needs, philosophies, wants, etc.) that make us unique from our parents and other people.

Boys usually go through a stage where they separate from their parents and form their own identities by experimenting with new ideas and exploring different values. Parents excuse this process by saying, "Boys will be boys!" Women more often remain suspended in a preadolescent, childlike state whereby they transfer their dependency needs onto someone else instead of completing this separation.

Withdrawal and separation—the second step in becoming self-reliant—is what we needed to do during adolescence, instead of suspending our identity development by waiting to attach to someone else. Developmental psychologist Erik Erikson states that successful resolution of this stage of development (separation) leads to a clear adult identity, whereas an unsuccessful resolution "leads to a scattered, fragmentary, diffuse, shifty sense of who you are."[1] And, the problem is that women don't usually complete this "separation-individuation phase." Usually, we only leave our parents when we transfer our dependency onto a man. Often, if it doesn't work out with him, we will transfer this dependency back to mom and dad. Several of my female clients will admit that when a relationship ends, they feel a desire to run back home.

Men consider such an option less often because they learned to fear being close, especially to their mothers. They discovered at an early age that they had to separate from their mothers to grow up—or they would be labeled sissies or maybe even become gay. This is why men are often accused of "compartmentalizing" their feelings—and are able to walk out on relationships, even when they're in love. This is not necessarily "good" for them either, but it gives them power. Love addicted women envy it. Emotionally avoidant women try to copy it.

There is a necessary and happy medium. Though men often quit relationships too soon, women must learn when to give up. *We must know when to quit.* Because we haven't learned to separate, we often can't let go of an unhealthy relationship. We continue to hope it will get better, and in the process, we allow others to destroy us. Learning to separate from others and walk away is an extremely important step and must be completed for you to become a self-reliant woman.

Rebelling Is Not Separating

Women often believe they've separated from their families, because they've moved away or because they have, and still do, rebel against their parents' wishes. Even those who fought back and rebelled as teenagers usually did not reach the point of truly separating and breaking away from their parents' approval. Rebelling is just the flip side of dependency. Instead of blindly following what is expected of us, we blindly reject our parents' teachings. Rebelling is an angry, revengeful, reactionary path instead of a self-directed, self-reliant one.

Rebelling is however a first step and is a necessary and natural part of breaking dependency on and separating our identities from others. We must first feel angry about what we were taught. *But rebelling is only a partial step.* Although we may angrily fight our parents or do something behind their backs, we usually feel guilty afterward for what we've done—until and unless we've taken a stand with them. Guilt makes us feel bad about ourselves, which keeps our self-concept low. With a low self-concept, we revert to pleasing others and thereby never separating from them, keeping the cycle of dependency going.

Statistics have proven that battered children usually grow up to become battering parents, even though most vow they won't. Why? Because they've learned no other way to relate to others or communicate or handle problems. Like their parents, they deny and hold back their feelings until they can't take it anymore. Then they explode and have no control over their actions. Feeling bad afterwards, they vow not to feel angry again, which forces them to hold in their feelings, putting them back into the abusive cycle. On the other hand, some adult children of abusive parents don't abuse their children and instead go to the other extreme—they rebel against the way their parents treated them—and become too permissive with their children. Then their children often rebel against the way *they* were raised, again passing on the abusiveness to *their* children.

We may intellectually say that we refuse to be like our parents. But when we don't separate our identities from our parents, we gradually take on their traits without even knowing it. Until we have consciously evaluated our values, decided on the way we want to be, and psychologically *let go* of our parents, we can't break the cycle.

Learning to Be Happy Alone

When I talk to women about learning to be alone, many of them say, "But I don't want to learn to be alone. I've spent my whole life making sure I wouldn't have to be." Women often believe that being alone means that no one wants to be with them and that they're unloved. The main reason many women fear being alone is because when we are alone, our paranoias and insecurities appear. Being with someone else is like having a fix—we stay so involved with them that we don't have to deal with our own thoughts and fears. As little girls, we learn to try very hard to hide from things we're afraid of. When we're afraid of the dark, we leave the light on; when we're afraid of being yelled at by dad, mommy covers for us. We are never taught how to, or are expected to, face fears and overcome them.

Without spending time alone, you cannot feed the soul, stay in tune with yourself, or learn to face fears. The void that you feel from time to time will be filled by developing a relationship with yourself and learning to handle your fears. A sense of spirituality and a feeling of oneness with the universe will develop as a natural by-product of spending creative time alone focused on yourself.

Without time alone, we become confused as to who we are. We feel empty because we don't have an intimate relationship with ourselves. Then we feel scattered and unclear when dealing with others because we have no solid core; therefore, when we're around others constantly, we become reflections of them. We end up so confused that we don't know who we are or what we want from someone else. Reflecting our identities off of others can also be incredibly draining. People often ask me how I have so much energy and I tell them, "I spend a great deal of time alone re-energizing myself." Once you take the time alone to know yourself, you will find that your time alone will give you energy and help you stay strong and "on track" in your relationships and with yourself.

You must give up the fantasy that anyone can, or ever will, "be there" for you totally, and accept yourself as ultimately alone in this world. Terri Schultz says it best in her book *Bittersweet:* "Until you know that you are the most important person in your life, you cannot let anyone else become important to you without feeling threatened by it."[2]

You must make a promise that your primary relationship will always be the one with yourself. Continual peace with yourself must be your ultimate goal. Staying in touch with your feelings and desires as you change is the process by which you learn about the "real" you—and how to keep the "real" you. As Anne Morrow Lindbergh says in her book *Gift From the Sea,* becoming self-reliant involves learning "how to remain whole in the midst of the distractions of life; how to remain balanced, no matter what centrifugal forces tend to pull one off center; how to remain strong, no matter what shocks come in at the periphery and tend to crack the hub of the wheel."[3]

Aloneness is a requirement for facing fears and issues and

working them through. Only when we're alone can we get in touch with our feelings of insecurity so that we can overcome them. Only when we're in touch with these insecurities can we become clear about a direct course of action needed to take charge of our lives.

Alone time can be one of the most positive and creative times in one's life. It's a time to find and appreciate our own uniqueness, a time to get in touch with our real feelings without fear of how others will perceive us, a time to open our senses to the world and really see, smell, touch, hear, and taste. You will get stronger and stronger, learn to rely on yourself more and more, and finally fall in love with yourself!

Setting Aside Alone Time

Though it may seem difficult, in order to work through this program it will be necessary for you to set aside this time alone by making dates with yourself. You won't be able to do these exercises at the office, at home with family, or in the presence of the TV or ringing phones. You must have as much uninterrupted time as possible. You will need to set limits with yourself and others, such as turning on your answering machine and recording something like, "I'm working on a project this weekend and won't be answering the phone. Please leave a message and I'll return your call if it's urgent. Other calls will be returned next week."

To get to know yourself, you must make this alone time a priority—the way you would make time for a new man in your life. Instead of trying to figure out what he would like or what his favorite foods might be, think about *yours.*

You may have trouble telling a friend, "I can't go skiing this weekend because I need to spend the weekend alone working on myself and becoming self-reliant." He or she might think you've lost your mind, or at least think you're being rude and self-centered. But you will have to have the courage to go against the grain of approval to be able to complete this program.

Spending a short time alone now and then won't do it. This must be a creative, committed endeavor. Limiting the time you have with yourself will keep you from accomplishing the task. You must have enough time to allow your mind to wander, to go on an inward journey on an internal winding staircase of thought.

The answers to your life are in there and only you can find them. No one else!

To some it will seem silly to spend some time alone every week or every day. It may even seem selfish, especially if you have a husband and children and/or a job that demand your time. Your instinct will probably be to feel unjustified in doing this. *But finding and spending time alone is one of the most crucial steps in attaining and maintaining emotional self-reliance.*

Maintaining Alone Time in a Relationship

Though it may be more difficult to create alone time when you're married or involved in a relationship, you don't have to be single to do it. We all need and deserve time alone.

As a single woman, I often declared to my friends, "I'm spending this weekend alone working on my garden." But once I became involved in a long-term relationship, alone time became more difficult to find. At first when I told Alan, my present mate, that I needed a weekend alone, he was hurt and didn't understand why I wouldn't prefer to be with him. When I suggested he might need time alone, he said "No." I told him that made me feel obligated to him, as if he were dependent on me for his happiness. When he said things to me like, "The guys wanted me to play golf this weekend, but I told them I'd rather be with you," I felt guilty for not feeling the same. I continued to take my time alone, but I also talked to him about my guilty feelings. When we got together after my alone weekends, I was always happier, more energetic, eager to talk, and much more loving. He finally began to understand how my alone time feeds me personally, and now he often says, "Do you need some alone time, honey?" He's no longer threatened, and he feels and appreciates the rewards of my spending time alone. In fact, he's learned to use his alone time more creatively, and now admits he needs it.

If you're married, I know it may be hard to take an entire weekend alone, but you can start by taking some time after work a couple of evenings per week, or once a week to begin. Make arrangements to do something special for yourself, like taking a walk or a drive alone.

But, whenever you are able to, take a weekend away from your daily routines as often as you can. Make it clear to your family and friends that you need your rest and recreation. Make arrangements for crucial errands and tasks to be handled by others, or by you in advance, and then do only what you want to do.

You might also encourage your husband or boyfriend to take a regular night out with the boys so you can have time at home alone. Don't think that the two of you have to be Siamese twins and do everything together, or you'll lose your identity and, in the long run, you'll lose him. You'll both be more exciting, interesting people who will enjoy each other more if you can both learn to allow each other to enjoy your time apart.

What to Expect When Spending Time Alone

Many of my clients say, "When I'm alone all I do is feel sorry for myself and wish I was with someone, or I think about what a terrible person I am."

Once you are completely alone for a period of time, just letting yourself be, your paranoias and insecurities *will* appear. This is normal. You have put so much energy into being able to hide "you" from yourself, that all the bad feelings must now pour out. And the longer you've avoided yourself, the worse it will be. My sister avoided her real feelings for forty years, but once she was diagnosed with breast cancer, her emotions flooded out. Although they frightened her, she had no choice but to deal with them.

If you practice self-degradation and/or feel sorry for yourself when you're alone, then you are still hanging on to a hope of being rescued and have not really committed to change. You are not truly experiencing yourself or what is around you. Instead of thinking about what a terrible person you are, you must refocus your attention to why your life isn't as you want it to be and what you need to do to change it, and then concentrate on the strengths you have that can help you accomplish these goals.

You must accept the fact that dealing with your repressed emotions will be very painful at first, and even awkward, in the same way that getting to know someone new can be. But the hurt, pain, and problems you've denied for years must now be worked through. You must go back and look at the old issues and feelings you've kept buried for so long. You must be sure you don't avoid any information or feelings about yourself. You must dig out those pieces of yourself that are the clues to your identity.

The "answer" you've been searching for, the answer to the point to life, will become clear when you rid yourself of everyday clutter and focus on you.

What to Do While Alone—Developing Your Identity

Take away the roles you play and ask yourself, "If I am completely alone on a mountaintop, who am I? What am I about? What adjectives describe me?" We've all heard "You can't love others until you love yourself." It may sound trite, but it's true. Right now is the time to learn to love yourself.

Spending Time With Yourself Creatively

During your time alone, promise yourself that you will *stay* alone and *enjoy* it. If you're afraid, you can desensitize yourself to your fear. Begin at whatever stage you're at right now. Take baby steps. Your first step could be to go to a movie alone, take a walk alone, go to the grocery store alone, or climb a mountain alone, but it must be an activity one step above whatever you are not afraid to do alone now. Maybe it's spending an afternoon or an evening alone, then a day, then an entire weekend.

Don't overanalyze everything you already know about yourself or muddle in your problems. Instead, choose something you enjoy enough to *lose yourself* in for a while. Not something that will cause you to deny your feelings but intensify them. For instance, if you are watching a sunset, you may want to focus on the colors and designs and how you feel when you see them. If you are manicuring your fingernails, you may want to focus on how each nail looks and feels as you finish it. If you are reading, you may want to focus on what feelings the material evokes in you, or how the information stimulates you intellectually. You can use outside sources to experience yourself more fully. In *losing yourself* this way, you really *find yourself,* because feelings you've been avoiding will emerge.

Your Weekend Alone

Make sure that your special weekend will exclude all interruptions from the outer world. If you stay home, unplug the phone, or put a message on your machine that you're taking time out. Stay away from trashy novels, nonstop TV, and other obsessions, as we discussed earlier. Tell your friends not to stop by. Make no obligations to anyone but yourself. Fill your environment with everything you consider nurturing—favorite foods, sunshine, a favorite tape, a few favorite thought-provoking books to skim, cuddly blankets, comfortable clothes, loving pets, and beautiful flowers.

During the weekend, nurture yourself by doing some of the following:

1. Don't structure your time. At every moment, concentrate on, What do I want? What do I feel like doing? Don't be afraid to waste time; you need unstructured time to see what feelings and thoughts surface and to open yourself up to the unconscious reservoir of creativity that exists in you.
2. Daydream and fantasize. Let your thoughts go. Let feelings bubble up, and don't fight them.
3. Create your favorite dish. Enjoy making it and eating it.
4. Take a two-hour bubble bath.
5. Go cross-country skiing or hiking, plan a picnic with wine and cheese and/or your favorite foods.
6. Write about your feelings and desires in a journal.
7. Write a poem or story about your life or something of beauty like a flower or rock.
8. At your leisure glance through, but don't read cover-to-cover, self-help or inspirational books.
9. Set up a new exercise program for yourself, with new music or targeting a certain area of your body.
10. Take a drive alone and enjoy the scenery—but don't set a destination. Be spontaneous and go anywhere you want.
11. Lie in the sun, feel the warmth, and sort out your feelings.
12. Let yourself cry over a sad movie or song—or over everything or nothing.
13. In your head, go over conversations that you need to have with certain people. Write them down, and be ready to confront the necessary parties.
14. Buy tapes of your favorite music and listen and sing along with them, trying to feel the emotions that they convey.
15. Spend a day with memorabilia: your yearbooks, photo albums, scrapbooks. Remember good things about yourself and

about the person you were, the person you see in all these mementos.

16. Make a promotional tape in which you advertise all your good qualities. Play it back anytime you are tempted to put yourself down or feel sorry for yourself.

17. Make a list of everything you enjoy doing, and promise yourself that you'll do at least one thing on the list every day.

18. Make a list of questions to ask your family about yourself when you were little.

19. Make a list of people who may be holding you back from getting what you want in life, and think about how you need to deal with them.

20. Complete the Identity Workbook on the following pages.

Identity Workbook

Because you have avoided the real you for so long, you have to do a lot of work to find that wonderful, emotional, curious, vital person you were before your parents and society trained their "shoulds" into you and forced you to be what they wanted you to be instead of yourself.

How well do you know yourself? In the workbook and/or journal you started earlier, do the following exercises.

I. *Write down the answers to the following questions.*

1. What's your favorite color, song, movie? Why?

2. What are your values and beliefs?

3. What are your feelings right now? your wants? your needs?

4. Is there anything you take a stand on? Anything you would fight for?

5. Where do you stand politically? Why?

6. How do you feel about religion? Why?

7. What kind of music do you prefer? Why?

8. What are your goals in life?

9. Where do you stand on abortion, animal rights, and other issues that the country seems divided on?

10. What's your favorite sport? Why?

11. How did where you grew up have an effect on who you are today?

12. What is your definition of love?

13. Overall, what one thing about you makes you the most different from every other human being you know? Are you proud of it or embarrassed by it? Why?
14. What do you believe is the point to life?
15. Is having possessions important to you? Why or why not?
16. Do you believe anyone is happy? Why or why not?
17. What matters to you the most in life? Friends? Lovers? Family? Feeling committed to something?
18. Do you want children? Why or why not?
19. If you're dating someone, do you think you're with this man for the right reasons?
20. Why do you often do what others want rather than what you want to do? Is their approval more important than enjoying your life? Should it be?
21. What would it take to make you ever feel like you were good enough?
22. Whose approval do you seek the most? Why?
23. What's something that's important to you that you're not doing? Why aren't you?
24. Do you believe you deserve the best? Why or why not?
25. How would your life be if it were perfect?

Think through these issues. For instance, if you believe it's wrong to take care of your own needs first before others', how are you supposed to get them met? If you expect others to meet them, that's dependency. If it's not wrong to take care of your own needs first, why aren't you doing it? Spend as much time as you need, thinking about these and any other questions that come up.

II. *Interview yourself.*
Pretend you know nothing about *you.* What do you need to ask? What do you need to know? Make a list of questions, then answer them. How are you different from most people?

You might ask, "What's important to me? What in my life makes me feel proud? Angry? Embarrassed? What do I want to do that I put off doing? What would I like to change about myself? Do I have a secret I have never shared? What is it and why don't I share it?" Write up the interview and title it.

III. *Discover your various selves.*
Discover who you are in public. What is your "public self?"[4]
Who do you try to present yourself to be? What public do you
try to perform for? Describe yourself as others would describe
you. If your parents, boss, friends, etc., were to have a discussion
about who you are, they would say "She's _____."

Discover your "private self."[5] What do you know about yourself and intentionally keep from others? What are your secrets?
Fantasize yourself as vulnerable and weak, ineffectual, inadequate, and passive. What happens to you when you picture yourself this way? What are your worst fears? What is the worst thing
that could happen?

Now fantasize yourself as strong and aggressive, domineering,
and bossy. What happens to you when you picture yourself this
way? What are your worst fears? What's the worst thing that
could happen?

Now fantasize yourself as the fulfillment of your ideal self—
putting parts of the vulnerable and strong self together. What's
the best you? What's the best thing that could happen to you?
The worst? What did you learn about yourself? Write it down.
Don't lose any valuable information about yourself.

Now try to discover your "unknown self"[6] with the following
exercises.

IV. *Analyze your dreams*
Keep paper and pencil by your bed and write down your dreams
as soon as you wake up. To find out what they mean, you might
want to ask yourself the following questions:[7]

1. What are my emotions during the dream? What am I feeling
   or *not* feeling, and how are these emotions familiar?
2. What is the action of the dream pointing to? What does the
   action say needs to be done?
3. What does the dream say I am avoiding? What is not being
   said or done?
4. Where is the power in the dream? What is controlling it?
5. What is missing from the dream? What would ordinarily be
   there that is not?
6. From where or what is a threat coming?
7. Does the dream stop short of something happening? What con-
   clusion do I fantasize?

8. In what way does the dream say I frustrate myself? What comes in to thwart or change the course of action?
9. What is the mood (setting) of the dream, and how is my life like this mood?

V. *Draw a picture of yourself.*[8]
Don't read further until you stop and draw a picture of yourself on a large sheet of paper. Use colored pencils or crayons if you can.

What does the picture say about you? Did you take up the whole page or just a corner? Whether you drew yourself large or small relates to your self-concept. If you are in the middle of the page, you are probably self-directed.

What does your picture tell you about the way you relate to the world? Do you fill all or part of your space? How realistic or symbolic is your representation of yourself? Is your outline sharp, fuzzy, disconnected, flowing? Is your figure open or closed? What parts of your body are missing? Out of proportion? Hidden? Are you clothed or nude (exposed or covered up)? Is your body designed to be seen? Touched? What colors predominate? Give your drawing a name. What mythical (fairy tale, movie, television, storybook) character does it bring to mind? Why?

VI. *List ten personality characteristics that you positively do not have.*
Do not continue reading until you have done this. Then answer the following questions:

- Which of these traits does your mother have?
- Which of these traits does your father have?
- Which of these traits sometimes creep into your behavior when you are off guard?
- Which of these traits can you not tolerate when you see them in others?

Take a careful look at these traits that you disclaim as your own.

- How intensely do you dislike each of them?
- How strongly do you fight them?

These traits probably represent some of your greatest fears about
who you really are and who you want to be. Now, be your opposite.
Fantasize yourself being everything on your list. Think about yourself that way. What is the worst thing that could happen if you had
those characteristics? Next, act out some of these personality traits
that you say are not yours. Spend one day or one hour or one minute being everything you usually are not. Example: If you say
you're not a bitch, try being one. If you say you're not nice, try being that way. See how it feels and how others respond to you. Did
you find out something new about yourself? Write it down. Don't
lose any information that you learn about yourself.

My greatest strides in my own personal growth used to come
from backpacking alone in the mountains for a weekend. I had
no one but myself to lean on, and no one but nature to be close
to. I worked through exercises like these. I kept a journal and
pieced together my identity. I came out of those trips feeling like
a new person.

To become a vital, self-reliant person, it will take effort to stay
focused and centered on you. The Eastern self-defense/dance of
Tai Chi teaches us that when we are physically centered, others
can't pull us off balance, others can't harm us. This is also true
emotionally.

Most people regress, stop spending time alone, and go back to
avoidance and denial or fall into self-pity and self-deprecation,
stay where they are, gain no new insight, and repeat their old
patterns again and again. This causes depression, immobilization,
and puts them back on the downward spiral of self-destruction of
their self-esteem and self-image.

If necessary, go over these exercises again and again until you
feel like you're starting to know who you are. Come up with your
own exercises if you want. But, take this time to really get to
know who you are. Because you will grow and change and your
needs and goals will change, alone time will continually be necessary to stay in touch with yourself.

One Woman's Journey Alone

A few years ago Elaine successfully worked through this program. When she first came to my office, she was trying to get

the courage to divorce her husband. She was confused and afraid. She didn't know if she was doing the right thing or not. Her husband was critical of her and never followed through with anything he said he was going to do. But that seemed normal to Elaine, since her mother was an alcoholic and never followed through with anything, either. Just as Elaine had always rescued her mother, she also tried to rescue her husband. She felt guilty leaving him.

Besides, Elaine had never been alone before, and she was afraid. She described herself as a chameleon, changing colors with each person she came in contact with—even me. She tried to be a perfect client. And now in her early forties, she had no idea who she really was. She felt a deep void inside that she didn't know how to fill and was deeply frightened by it.

Elaine's self-discovery program started with these basics—spending as much time completely alone as possible and writing about her likes and dislikes—from her favorite color to her favorite music; angry feelings she had repressed toward others in her life; what she believes in (her values); what she remembers enjoying from her childhood but no longer takes time for now.

She began to recreate parts of herself that she had known and loved. She began to pull away from others who were using and abusing her—especially her mother and her husband. She divorced her husband and told her mother she would not spend time with her if she was going to drink. She began to make herself the most important person in her life and to take better control of it. Her behavior was now based on what she wanted rather than simply reacting to others like she had in the past—such as arguing with her husband just to prove a point. She began to care about pleasing herself rather than worrying about pleasing others. In the past, she had changed her major in college from music to business, to please her parents. In breaking her emotional dependence and learning to rely on herself and her choices, she began following old interests like taking piano lessons again.

These "alone" exercises soon became ingrained in her, opening more and more doors through which to discover herself. She rediscovered a part of herself that she only remembers knowing as a child, playful and creative. When she looked back through memorabilia and talked to her family, she began to resurrect her long-buried love for dance. She recalled the feelings of accomplishment that came with winning several spelling bees. She gave herself permission to rekindle her youthful passion for animals. These were all parts of her that she had given up to be what others wanted her to be. She slowly and gradually filled that inner void, and she found out that there was a likable person inside her with whom she had lost touch. She began to admire herself and feel alive. In fact, she even began to enjoy being single. She had more time to discover herself—her likes and dislikes. She began to listen to and hear the special meanings in song lyrics. She started to enjoy the cold, crisp air of winter, when she once saw it as unpleasant. She liked doing what she wanted at her own whim and no one else's. She stopped following others' rules and began to enjoy a daily life of little freedoms—from spending a day in bed when she wasn't sick to working on a project all night long; from going for a drink, or even to Mexico, on a moment's notice to closing off the world for a weekend and hibernating. She began to balance her passion for eating with an exercise and nutrition program. Elaine learned to juggle a rigid schedule at work with unstructured, unplanned, nurturing time alone at home. She began to travel wherever and whenever she wanted and to spend time with whomever she liked. Her life alone became exciting, exhilarating, and full. The void disappeared. She told me that she had found an inner thread that she could now hold onto . . . it was her identity.

5

Step Three:
Forgive Yourself
for Not Being Perfect

The third step in becoming a self-reliant woman is ridding ourselves of guilt and forgiving ourselves for not being perfect. Most people can forgive others much easier than they can forgive themselves. They say, "I know he didn't mean to do it," or, "She has a lot on her mind these days." They understand why others behave certain ways, but these same people are often their own worst enemies. Take Alicia, who's seeing the married man. Each time she comes to see me, she feels bad about herself if she has seen him again. Granted, it would be better if she hadn't seen him. But she thinks she's failed when she can't stay away. I told her that I was involved with a married man once and asked, "Does that mean I'm a bad person?" She said no. She understands how I could make that mistake, but *she* knows better and is still doing it. I told her that I should have known better too, but I had to feel the pain and learn the lesson, and so does she.

I remember feeling like Alicia did. Part of what sent me to Aspen (and certainly what caused me to let men treat me badly when I was there) was the guilt over ending a relationship with a nice man named Greg. He said I taught him to love and then abandoned him. I believed him and thought I was a terrible person for what I'd done. Because I felt guilty and had trouble forgiving myself, I allowed men to psychologically abuse me the way I felt I'd psychologically abused Greg.

It's common for us to understand why *other* people do what

71

they do, more often than we understand what we do ourselves. We believe that "knowing" something should give us the ability to change it. But our intellect doesn't control our actions as much as our feelings do. We can't change our feelings on demand, although we think we should be able to. We must instead process our feelings. Alicia needs to break off with her married man, but she will probably regress a few times until she's felt enough pain to really want it to stop. She has to work through her feelings, not override them or control them. Alicia needs to understand that and forgive herself for not being perfect.

Guilt is a very destructive emotion. Maybe it is helpful for Alicia to feel enough guilt about hurting her married lover's wife to get out of the relationship, but the majority of her guilt comes from feeling stupid for being in the relationship in the first place. Guilt is nothing new for Alicia. She's felt guilty for a variety of reasons most of her life—guilty for being female, guilty for being smart, guilty for being overweight, guilty for not being organized, guilty for not being a morning person—guilty for being who she is that isn't who her family or bosses wishes she was. Too many of us fall into this trap.

Nobody's Perfect

It's difficult to get rid of guilt when we've been criticized all our lives, and when those criticisms still spin around in our heads like a tape that won't stop playing. Often when we start to feel good about ourselves, someone will say or do something that pushes one of our buttons and reminds us that we're not perfect. These "buttons" are made up of all those criticisms on the tape that was created when we were children.

People push our insecurity buttons by saying something like, "I can't believe you did that! Are you really that stupid?" Then we think, "My mother used to say that about me, it must be true." Because we're so afraid we're stupid or ugly or "bad," we work extra hard trying to please this person, letting him or her manipulate us because of our insecurities. Our pervasive guilt about who we are allows this to happen because of our feeling that we "should" be better than we are. Until we can accept our humanness, especially our shortcomings, we can never allow others to get close to us.

People love to tell other people what they should and shouldn't do. It gives them a sense of power—a sense of righteousness. And it's easier to try to run someone else's life than run their own. These self-righteous people think in black and white terms. They are rigid and insecure about their own thoughts. They have never sorted out their own values and are therefore threatened by yours. They are dependent on others' approval and want you to remain that way too.

The term "selfish" is used by others to manipulate and control. Anytime we're not choosing to do what is best for someone else, that person will accuse us of being selfish to try and convince us to do what he or she wants. The best counter to this manipulative accusation is to feel good about being selfish and say, "At times I *am* selfish, and I'm glad that I go after what I want instead of always trying to win someone else's approval!"

But sometimes we get intimidated because we see people who we think look and act perfect. Often, emotionally avoidant people do this. Don't believe it. These people are great actors and actresses who never show their insecurities or emotions to anyone and end up putting a bullet through their heads or getting in their cars and driving off, never to be seen again. Don't let them intimidate you. They are just as insecure as you are, if not more.

Values

We have to demand that others accept us as we are. We can't let anyone lay his or her value judgments on us. We can't let others play God with us. And in return, we can't play God with them.

I grew up in a small town in the Midwest where, before you could do anything you wanted to do, you always had to consider, what will people think?—"people" being every person in town. Those expectations of how I should act made my life miserable. Those "shoulds" kept me in a marriage in which my husband was verbally abusive. Those "shoulds" kept me listening to my mother's whining, enabling her to stay in her bad marriage. Those "shoulds" kept me from enjoying my life. Those "shoulds" caused resentment, created guilt, and put responsibility where it didn't belong. What have the "shoulds" done to you?

When we were small children, we trusted our thoughts and feelings. We knew when we felt angry or sad, and we expressed these feelings naturally without thinking about whether we should or shouldn't. Then we were told by our parents and others in society, "You shouldn't feel that way," "What do you mean you don't love your mother?," "Don't you talk to your brother like that!" We learned to trust our parents' moral dictates—you *should* respect authority, you *should* obey your husband, you *should* always be polite to others—more than our own. Are the people telling you these things always able to follow them themselves? I doubt it! Then don't let them force these perfectionistic values on you.

When we behave in a way that is different from the way we believe, especially when it ends up being harmful to someone, we get angry at ourselves, and send confusing messages to others. We think, How could I have done that? It's hard to forgive ourselves for these mistakes. What we have to remember is that our parents taught us how we "should" behave and what we "should" believe and how we "should" feel. If we would have behaved according to our real feelings, we might have acted differently. It is the teachings of our parents that make us so confused. We need to be angry at them for teaching us behaviors and beliefs that don't really work. We must tell ourselves, "It was all I knew at the time. I was naive. I was programmed and I couldn't help it then."

But, now as adults, the responsibility to change is ours—now that we are aware of the problems, we must not continue following our parents' teachings or stay stuck in blaming them. We must work through these issues to be able to let go of both the blame and the guilt of not being perfect.

What "Shoulds" Do You Follow?

Start by separating your wants from the "shoulds" in your life. Most of us attempt to hide our real feelings, pretending instead that we feel the way we think we "should" feel. Hugh Prather states in his book *Notes to Myself:* "The configuration of most situations implies, through tradition, a corresponding emotion, e.g., your wife goes out on you; therefore you are enraged (when actually you might be aroused). I often respond the way I 'should' feel rather than the way I do feel. Confusion or indecision is a good sign this is happening."[1]

Below are "shoulds" that many of us were taught. See if you

can write a rebuttal to each one. (Example—"I should be nice to my mother, *except* when she's harming me.")

Were you taught that:

I should be nice to my mother, except ——————————— .
I shouldn't go out alone at night, except ——————————— .
I shouldn't yell at my children, except ——————————— .
I should love my parents, except ——————————— .
I should respect my teachers (doctors, lawyers, experts),
   except ——————————————— .
I should keep my house clean, except ——————————— .
I should save my money for a rainy day, except ————————— .
I should go to church, except ——————————————— .
I should get married and have children, except ——————— .
I should have a good job, except ——————————————— .
I should be on time, except ——————————————— .
I should be thin, except ——————————————— .
I should work hard, except ——————————————— .
I should be polite and considerate, except ——————————— .
I should never tell a lie, except ——————————————— .
I should do unto others as I want them to do unto me,
   except ——————————————— .
I should be ashamed for feeling however I feel,
   except ——————————————— .
I shouldn't get angry with my brother(s)/sister(s),
   except ——————————————— .
I shouldn't talk to my father like that, except ——————— .
I should always respect my elders, except ——————————— .
I should never be selfish, except ——————————————— .
I should always be considerate of others, except ———————— .

Now go back and decide what you really believe. Can you argue your point with someone who believes the opposite? Try.

Become aware of all the "shoulds" in your conversation. Each time you use the word "should," stop for a moment and ask: "Do I really believe that? If not, who taught it to me? Who is this person to run my life? Is he or she perfect? What I really believe or want to do instead is ——————————————— ."

Should you be polite to the phone salesman who keeps calling at the dinner hour? Should you respect the doctor who recommends surgery you don't feel is necessary? Should you keep your house clean at the expense of spending time with your children? Start to evaluate each "should" situation when it comes up, and stop and ask yourself how you feel about it and how you want to handle it.

Values Clarification

When I was a school counselor, an important part of my job was spending time with teenagers, trying to help them sort through their values. It's very difficult, however, for teenagers to resolve value issues while they're still living at home. When teenagers realize that they believe differently from their parents, they don't know what to do except rebel. They need to be able to talk openly to their parents about their differences, but most parents won't allow it.

However, as adults, we can and need to. Our physical security isn't threatened by our parents' anger when we're adults, so we should have more courage to discuss our differences with them. Because most of us are still dependent on their approval emotionally, however, we are afraid to do this. To rid ourselves of the perfectionism in our lives, we must defend our values to those who taught perfectionism to us.

For instance, you may seldom go to church, though you think it's a good idea to attend. Then your mother calls and asks if you went. You say no and feel guilty. Instead, you need to tell her that you're an adult now and that to you, getting enough sleep this weekend was more important than going to church, and you don't want any flak from her about it. Then let it go and don't feel guilty.

Values Clarification Exercises
Answer the following:

1. Are the following true for you? If not, what do you believe?
   People should be honest no matter what.
   You should always be nice to those who love you.
   Money is the best security.
   The important thing is not whether you win or lose, but how you play the game.
   It's not good to mix business with friendship.
   A penny saved is a penny earned.

People who get to the top have hurt a lot of people along the way.

If you have your health, you have everything.

God helps those who help themselves.

In business, anything goes.

2. Ask yourself:

What do I believe in?

What would I like to see changed in the world?

What thoughts or ideas arouse passion in me?

What makes me feel proud?

What's really important to me?

What would my regrets be if I died tomorrow?

Who in life do I admire? Who do I believe are the villains in our society today?

What would I do with my life if I found out that I had only one month to live?

If someone had just left me a million dollars, what would I do with it?

What is the most beautiful thing I have ever seen? Do I try to see it often?

What would I like put on my tombstone (''She was ____ '')?

Is there anything in life I believe in enough that I would die for?

When was a time that I felt at one with the universe? What happened or what made me feel this way?

3. Put the values below in order of importance to you. (There is no right or wrong order. These are your values.) Add any values of yours not listed.

money	friendship
love and sex	religion/morals
leisure	politics
work	family
maturity	character traits
death	intelligence/education

Look at your list. Do you live your life according to what's important to you, or according to what's important to other people in your life?

4. Make a list of all the responsibilities you have. Put at the top

of the page, "I have to _____ ." Finish the list before you continue reading. Now see how many on your list you can change to "I want to _____ ."[2] Except for a few "have to's" such as making a living, try to spend as much of your time as possible doing what you want to do. And don't feel guilty for doing what you want in your life.

These exercises can help you discover what is really important to you. They helped Barbara realize that making money wasn't as important to her as it was to her father.

Barbara had lived her first twenty-seven years trying to win her father's approval. She lived by his values instead of her own. Because her father thought she was stupid, and because she had always been good at sports, she had decided to get her college degree in recreation. Her degree didn't seem to matter anyway, since all her father really wanted was for her to marry after graduation.

After working through these exercises, she began to get in touch with her own interests and desires. She had never married, so she had chosen several careers in the past, like real estate and sales, because she felt pressure from her father to try to make good money if she wasn't going to marry it. Unlike him, she realized that she admired people who helped others more than she admired the rich.

She decided to go back to school for a degree in occupational therapy so she could help others deal with some of the frustrations she had been dealing with herself.

You'll know you are healthy and acting with integrity when your beliefs match your actions. Find out which beliefs are keeping your behaviors from changing. Separate your unique interests and beliefs from your parents', friends', lover's, or others' interests and beliefs. Don't let anyone push their beliefs or "shoulds" on you. Know that "I believe these things" and behave accordingly.

How many things are you doing now because someone else wants you to do them, or because you want approval badly enough to sacrifice your own needs? Do you want to live your life according to someone else's script or your own? Often we don't even know the difference. Those "shoulds" may be keeping you in a job you hate. They may be keeping you from playing golf on Saturdays or taking a day for yourself in bed or following an interest in comic books. Stop following someone else's script and figure out what you need to do to get on track to become the person you want to be. Remember, only you have the answer. There are no real boundaries—only the ones you create or allow others to create for you.

False Beliefs

Others telling us that we should behave differently than how we *do* makes us anxious. Sometimes, we use these false beliefs to support our fears. If we want to stand up to others but are afraid to, we might hold onto the belief that it is unfeminine to do so, and then our belief becomes our excuse. If we're afraid to ask for what we want, we may hold onto the belief that it's selfish to do so. If we want to be successful, yet we're afraid to try to be, we may hold onto the belief that hurting others is the only way to make it to the top. These beliefs become our excuses, and we have to let go of them to be able to change our behavior.

For instance, most people believe that *you should never abandon a friend.* "Good people," we've been told, "don't leave their friends." And if you *do*, you'll be sorry, because "you can never tell when you may need them later."

So we put up with the depressing friend who often calls in the middle of the night or the lonely neighbor who constantly drops in on us during the dinner hour. The result? We feel angry and resentful towards them but pretend we aren't. We'd like to tell them how we feel, but we use the aforementioned belief as an excuse not to confront them, because we're really afraid to.

Many of us believe that *merit has its own reward,* that if "I'm good at what I do, I shouldn't have to work at letting others know that." Many women use this excuse not to market themselves in business. So do some women who are overweight and/or don't take pride in their appearance. They think, I'm a good person; a man should be able to see past the way I look and know that.

Many women believe *that's just the way men are.* This false belief keeps us putting up with men's abuse and from asking them for what we want.

We often believe that *there is just one right and wrong way to do things.* We're afraid that we'll be punished in some way if we don't do "it" right, so we procrastinate or become immobilized.

We believe that *we shouldn't hurt others.* When we believe this, we don't do what is necessary to take charge of our lives.

We believe that *failure is bad.* When we hold onto this belief, we use it as an excuse not to risk and move forward.

We believe that *there are some perfect people who do everything right.* When we believe this, we constantly feel inadequate. We use it as an excuse not to try, and to psychologically beat ourselves up.

We believe *it's good to give to others,* when in reality, giving and giving to others only helps them learn to take.

We believe that *problems will go away if we just ignore them.* This false belief keeps us from facing problems head on and taking control of our lives. It keeps us in denial.

We allow false beliefs to hold us back. We must rethink these and other beliefs and see which ones we are simply using as excuses. Remember that rebelling against a belief is not the same as rethinking it and changing how we feel about it. If you're rebelling, you're being controlled by someone else's belief system—not your own.

To get rid of a false belief, try to remember who taught it to you or who is still promoting it in your life. Go back to that person (often a parent) and tell him or her that it doesn't work for you, you don't agree with it, and that you believe differently. Chapter Eight, "Step Six: Confront Your Parents," will help you do this. You cannot override the belief with your intelligence. Confronting the person(s) who taught it to you is the only way to completely erase it from your subconscious. This is how you "unbrainwash" yourself.

People who say they care about us will be threatened and will try to hold us back from changing our beliefs. They will be more comfortable if they can convince us to continue to think like they do, like we're "supposed to." If we say nothing, we are taking a passive stance and allowing them to believe we agree with them. If we scream and fight and tell them they're wrong, they won't hear us. Instead, we need to tell them that they may choose to live however they please, but they have to allow us to do the same.

You have one of two basic choices. You can do what everyone expects of you, follow society's rules, be accepted, and live a life dependent on others' approval, *or* you can accept the fact that you can't please everyone all of the time, understand that being respected is as important as being loved, and make your life the way you want it to be.

Strengths and Weaknesses

To take charge of your life, you must accept that you aren't and never will be perfect. But you must also accept your strengths and weaknesses for what they actually are. For instance, I'm good at. . . . I'm not good at. . . . If you don't accept your imperfections, you can't accept yourself as you truly are, so you will have to maintain a facade.

Do you believe that there are certain areas that you are weak in? Are you afraid you aren't smart enough? Attractive enough? Nice enough? We all feel insecure about something.

Most of us have been given intelligence tests, and some of us were classified as having learning disabilities or math or reading problems. Our inadequacies have been pointed out again and again, but few of us know about our strengths. Many of us don't know the difference between a real weakness and something we've been criticized for. Again, take Barbara. Her father always told her she was stupid. She believed it for years. It wasn't until she graduated from college *and* passed a real-estate exam that she decided he must be wrong. She thought she probably did have a learning disability or a reading-comprehension problem. After years of feeling like something was wrong with her, she recently found out after extensive testing that the only thing wrong with her is common "test anxiety." She no longer feels stupid or inadequate.

Through the psychological evaluations I've given, I've learned that people who score in the same intelligence range are usually extremely different from one another. Some are very high in one area and low in another. And some people are average in everything. Those with a variety of strengths and weaknesses are by far the most interesting and, I believe, most likely to be successful—if they're able to focus on their strengths.

For every weakness, we usually have a strength that balances it. Once we realize what our strengths and weaknesses are, we can defend our self-worth.

When I was married, my husband always intimidated me because I had trouble remembering details. He would say, "You mean you didn't know that?" It pushed a button in me from my past—a fear that I wasn't smart enough—and I would feel insecure. But now that I am aware that I have a strength that balances that weakness, when someone says, "I can't believe you don't know that!," or asks me to play Trivial Pursuit, I say, "I'm not good at remembering details because I have a more conceptual mind." It shuts them up and I walk away with my self-esteem intact.

Most of us focus on our weaknesses too much. Make a list of some of your weaknesses. Then go back and write out a corresponding strength. Don't stop until you come up with a strength for each weakness. The following are examples of this process:

Weakness	Strength
Controlling	Good leader
Can't remember people's names	Usually remember what people are really like
Overly concerned with looks	Attractive
Unattractive	Focus on more important things
Insecure	Understand others' insecurities
Cocky	Confident when others aren't

We All Make Mistakes

There isn't a person alive that hasn't hurt someone, whether intentionally or not. We all make mistakes and our mistakes affect others. When we do make mistakes we may need to clean them up to rid ourselves of the guilt.

Christian teachings and Alcoholics Anonymous are big on this. They teach repentance as, "Admit [ted] to God, to ourselves, and to another human being the exact nature of our wrongs." (Step 5 of the twelve steps). The problem with this kind of repentance is that a true understanding of the problem does not usually take place, therefore, the issue is not resolved and no change in behavior occurs. "Knowing" we shouldn't do something doesn't keep us from doing it. We must understand *why* we hurt someone to be able to keep from hurting them again. Then—and only then—do our hearts have enough warmth for us to be able to truly be sorry and forgive ourselves.

We most often hurt others because we've been hurt ourselves and never dealt with our own hurt and anger. If we tell someone we're sorry before we've dealt with why we hurt them and what we were feeling at the time, we can't be sincere. Our hurt, turned to anger over what this person or someone else has done to us, makes us injure others.

For instance, when I left Greg, I told him I was sorry for hurting him, but the guilt didn't go away. I didn't understand at the time why Greg—or any other man—wasn't "enough" for me. I thought it meant something was wrong with me. Then, ten years after I'd left him, he tracked me down in Aspen, confronting me, and telling me how I had screwed up his life. At first I felt terrible. Then I began to remember why I had left him. Here he was blaming me for his not moving forward in life when he had always been stuck—even back then. He never took risks, he just talked about them. Obviously he had continued to stay stuck for ten more years, using me as his excuse this time. I had always felt held back by him. I now saw that I had good reason to leave him. It wasn't my fault. Once I remembered that, I wrote him a letter expressing my anger and was able to forgive myself.

Just as Greg and I couldn't move on until we expressed our anger, you can't forgive others until you confront the issues with them, or you will continue to wonder deep inside if you deserved their treatment. Once you deal with the problem and come to a resolution, you not only convince the offender that you deserve to be treated better, you also convince yourself.

When you feel guilty, you can clean up your mistake by saying: *"I feel terrible about what I've done to you. I really didn't mean to hurt you. I am sorry I hurt you. The reason I did what I did is _____ . But that's no excuse. What can I do to make it up to you and earn your trust again?"*

Elaine did this with her daughter, explaining to her why she had given her up for adoption. Elaine, now forty-three-years-old, became pregnant out of wedlock when she was twenty-five and decided to give her daughter up for adoption. Her family had kept her pregnancy a secret. When she began to clean up her past, she first went home and confronted her parents about the incident, but she was still afraid to begin the search for her daughter, who by then was eighteen.

The real family healing began when her daughter found her. They spent days together, talking and bonding. Elaine explained to her daughter what the situation was like when she had been born and why she had given her up. She told her that she had had so many problems of her own then, that she feared she couldn't do a good job of raising her. She also told her that she loved her and wanted to make up for the past.

Elaine's first step in accomplishing this goal was to go back to her family and let the old secret out of the bag. She planned a "coming out" family reunion so that everyone could meet her daughter. Many family members were upset by Elaine's actions, but she stood up to them and did not allow them to make her feel guilty or to treat her daughter badly.

Though most of us may not have a "mistake" in our past as traumatic as Elaine's, we all have issues to deal with. I didn't realize that I had guilty feelings about my sister until she got cancer.

When I read that one of the personality characteristics of cancer patients is passivity, I realized that my sister had always been a doormat, especially in her relationship with me. I was the older sister and always dominated and controlled her. I'd never thought about how that might have affected her.

I wrote her a letter recounting incidents from our childhood in which I had overcontrolled her, and apologized for each one. Then I explained why—that I had felt abused by mom and dad, and that I had unfairly and unknowingly taken my frustrations out on her.

I told her I thought she married a man like her sister (me) and apologized for setting her up to be controlled by him. Then I concluded with:

> I'm telling you this because I want you to understand why I did it, that I never meant to hurt you, and that I intend to stop be- having that way. I want to talk with you about this and to make it up to you by being as supportive and noncontrolling with you

as possible. I really do love you so much. I'm sorry that it took cancer for me to realize what I did to you.

I was not, and am not perfect, but I have learned to forgive myself by cleaning up any relationships I needed to, growing and moving on from my past mistakes. I have forgiven myself for not being perfect, and you can do the same.

6

Step Four:
Understand Why
You Are
the Way You Are

I remember waking in the middle of the night to the sound of my parents' fighting. The noise level from their bedroom would be rising. I was scared, but I was afraid that if I didn't do something, it would get worse—it had in the past. I always got up, went into their bedroom, and talked them down. When I didn't, all hell broke loose. I felt very powerful. This was my first job as a therapist—at the age of ten.

As the years passed, my parents and my younger sister began to look up to me more and more, and they often gave me more credit than I deserved. I soon fell into a trap of trying to live up to their high expectations of me. I started pretending I was stronger than I really was. My family looked to me for answers, so I gave them answers. I became more and more controlling with them and with others.

I carried this behavior into adulthood. As time went on and through therapy, I realized what a responsibility I was carrying and how this attitude was affecting my present relationships.

I was having difficulty with men I dated and in my friendships with women. It seemed I was happy only when I was running the show. John Bradshaw described my attitude perfectly in a column from *Lear's:* "Sharing has always been hard for me. I've been a loner all my life, never knowing how to belong unless I'm the leader, the hero, the star. It's hard for me to belong just as a participant."[1]

I never learned to share. As a child I demanded things be done my way or I "took my marbles and went home." Because my parents usually gave me control over their lives, I certainly wasn't intimidated by my peers. When men broke up with me, they often said, "I'm tired of letting you run my life." My biggest complaint about female friends was that they were never there for me. What I didn't realize at the time was that I was never vulnerable enough to let them be there for me. When I confronted one friend about not coming to see me when I was in the hospital, she said, "What could I possibly have done for you? You're the one with all the answers!" At the time, I was incredibly hurt and didn't understand what she was trying to tell me. Now I do.

All I knew then was that I didn't like my life. I was over-stressed and had too much responsibility—I was a school counselor and spent my free time counseling friends, boyfriends, and my parents, which was a full-time job in itself. Rescuing others from their problems helped me prop up my ego. I felt insecure but didn't realize it and would never have admitted it, because I covered my feelings of insecurity with a facade of a superiority complex. I was constantly busy proving I was right about something.

Once I began to understand why I was the way I was, I began to understand why I was behaving as I did. Then I was able to realize that my parents trained me this way; and that I would have to retrain myself before I would be able to change the way I related to others. Understanding why I am the way I am helped me understand that my problems weren't inherent in me and could be solved.

Examining Your Past

"I Can't Remember"

Many of my clients say they can't remember what happened to them in their pasts. They have a few vague memories, but they don't remember specific incidents, what their relationships were like with their families, or the feelings they felt back then. This is not uncommon. When something is painful, we often block it out. The more we have blocked something out, the more probable it is that it was extremely painful and is important to uncover.

Women who have been sexually abused are often the most blocked. One of my clients was in therapy for three to four months before she remembered that she had been sexually abused by her sister. She was shocked when she realized it. Part of her was trying very hard *not* to remember.

If you're blocked about your past, you may also be trying to forget. Or it might be that your childhood was so void of emotion and you repressed your feelings so much that it's difficult for you to get in touch with it now. We often begin to block our feelings during a major crisis like a death of a loved one. The feelings often seem too painful to handle, and no one seems to know how to help us process them. You may have started blocking your emotions when you were abandoned by a lover or experienced a failure in school—or were embarrassed by a comment or situation. Maybe you were severely punished or criticized each time you shared your feelings, so you learned to block them regularly.

Dr. Kevin Leman, coauthor with Randy Carlson of *Unblocking the Secrets of Your Childhood Memories,* says, "It's not the events from early childhood that are important, it's what we remember about them. These memories give us important clues about the kind of adults we have become. . . . The earliest memories are the *real* you . . . not who you think you are or would like to be."[2]

Uncovering Your Pain

If you are blocked about your childhood, it can help to gather information from your family members. Reach out to siblings or aunts, uncles, cousins—anyone that can help you remember. Even comments written in my yearbooks and old letters helped me get a clearer picture of what I was like growing up. Sometimes it can help to look at old pictures of yourself when you were a child. Do you look happy? Tired? Stressed? Try to remember how you were feeling in each one.

My sister was helpful. When I told her I had a lot of buried anger at dad that I was starting to get in touch with, she said, "Well, I'm not surprised—after all he did to you!" Then she began to remind me of things I had forgotten. She helped me piece together the story of why I was angry at him.

As you figure out the story of your life, it is extremely important that you don't approach it in a logical manner. Many people try to follow the program without feeling the pain, but it doesn't work. It's denial. Your locked-up emotions from the past are the reasons you are repeating destructive patterns in relationships. All the times that you felt hurt, rejected, or unloved cause you to crave love so desperately now—or to close off for fear you'll never get any. You must uncover the pain, or you can't process the information enough to work through the issues.

For instance, if you discover that your mother was pregnant with you prior to marriage—and now you realize why your parents never celebrated their wedding anniversaries, don't just understand that intellectually, ask yourself, "How do I feel about that? How does that information change things? What does it do to my level of trust with them?" Then discuss your feelings with your parents to extricate the emotional pain that this has caused you all these years.

At first, it may feel too overwhelming to go back into your past and find every painful experience and work it through. But it gets easier as you go along. Dr. Leman says:

> "The memory must be yours alone, not family stories that have been repeated so many times that you're not sure whether you actually remember the incident or were just told about it. *How to tell:* There should be a feeling attached to the memory. The memory must involve a very specific event—not something that happened every day. If you can't remember a specific event, trigger memories by thinking back to where you lived as a child. Close your eyes and wander through the house until you get to your bedroom. You should find something there that will help. *Also:* Think back to early teachers, family vacations, holidays, the first time you rode a bike, bedtime, etc.
>
> Attach a feeling to the clearest part of the memory, then study that feeling. Does it recur with any consistent pattern today? Under what circumstances?"

Don't be afraid of what you may uncover. Use your journal or workbook to record your feelings and thoughts so you don't forget anything.

Finding and Facing the Skeletons in Your Closet

It can be scary when we start to take an honest look into our past.
In fact, it may feel sacrilegious, since part of what we've been
taught is to "Honor thy father and thy mother"—no matter what.
But if you hold onto your Pollyanna outlook of having had a
perfect childhood and of never having felt "negative" feelings,
you're probably lying to yourself. We all feel pain, anger, hurt,
and rejection. Besides, you will never be able to understand why
you are the way you are until you look at your true feelings.

As you process this, you may try to defend your parents by
saying, "I'm not that upset at them for anything," or, "My parents didn't do anything terrible to me!" But, telling you not to
feel your feelings, or criticizing or ridiculing you when you did
something they didn't like, or taking away a pet, or not discussing
a relative's death with you, or never spending enough time with
you can leave deep emotional scars. It doesn't matter if they—or
you—justify what they did. It's how you felt about it at the time
that counts. All of us felt victimized in some way, if just by being
in a submissive position as a child.

We all have feelings of inadequacy we developed in our past.
Once we find out what caused these feelings, it's easier to get
beyond them. You have to figure out how and when your feelings
of inferiority were created. Perhaps the birth of a sibling and your
subsequent loss of parental attention made you feel worthless;
maybe you experienced lack of attention or neglect; or maybe it
was the brunt of your parents' constant criticism that has been
heavily imprinted on you. You need to get in touch with the
feelings of rejection you've suppressed and discover what caused
them.

Alicia was constantly reminded during her childhood that she
wasn't the perky, petite, blonde cheerleader that her mother had
always wanted. Alicia's mother was always trying to "beautify"
her tall, brainy, brunette with elaborate hairstyles, putting her on
diet pills (even though she wasn't overweight), making her wear
a girdle, buying her contact lenses even though Alicia didn't really want them, and pressuring her to have the "right" kind of
friends. She inflicted the idea on Alicia that the natural and real
her wasn't okay. Alicia rebelled against her mother during ado-

lescence by eschewing makeup and boyfriends and gaining weight to exert some control over her own body. Her rebellion, although it may have satisfied Alicia's need for revenge, didn't make her feel any better about herself. She still felt she wasn't "good enough." Now Alicia sets herself up to chase exclusively after men who aren't available to her, proving to herself what she thinks she knew all along: she really *isn't* good enough. By carrying old parental-rejection baggage around with her, Alicia assumes a priori that any man with any sense will reject her after getting to know her.

In therapy, Alicia relived many of her bad moments with her mother and described her accompanying feelings of anger, hurt, rejection, and abandonment. She realized, after a time, that her mother's insistence that she be more like a cheerleader had more to do with her mother's insecurity about her own self-worth, self-image, and lack of popularity in high school than a belief that Alicia wasn't good enough. As she discovered these realities, her feelings of inadequacy began to dissipate. She began to understand what had happened to her and why she had been treated that way. But understanding it was only the beginning. Her next step was to work it through with her mother.

It can be frightening to take a good, hard look at the skeletons in your closet. But you must go back, unweave the story of your life, and take the time alone to ponder the questions you have about why you are the way you are.

Use your journal or workbook. Write your thoughts down so you won't forget them. Our minds often try to protect us by blocking out self-revelations, keeping us in denial. Each family has its own "secrets." For some families, the secrets are big, like Elaine's child out of wedlock, someone's infidelity or abortion, or an alcohol or drug addiction. It's these secrets that make us feel crazy. Secrets impair our perceptions.

Don't be surprised if your family resists you as you try to uncover these secrets. As you come near the truth about your past, expect them to say, "Why do you have to dig all of this up now? What difference does it make anyway? You're just trying to cause trouble. Let it be." Remember, most people are in complete denial of their feelings, and as you piece together the injustices they did to you, they will be very uncomfortable. Dragging out garbage in your own life may trigger issues from their lives to come to the surface. They *have* to fight you because they want to stay in denial.

When this happens, the problem may be a discrepancy between what you remember and what your family remembers. You may say to your father that in your recollections of childhood, he was never home. He may reply, "That's not true. I was home all the time." Your father doesn't want to admit that he wasn't there for you, so he denies it, keeps it a secret—even from himself. Trust yourself. Because the problem caused emotional pain in you, your memory is probably clearer than his. Realize that he has worked very hard to block out negative things about himself.

Who Victimized You?

Along with your childhood memories of your relationships with your parents, look for other people and incidents that have affected your life. Usually the people whose approval you've wanted the most have had the power to hurt you the most.

Recognize that when you think, "That sounds like my dad," or "She's treating me just like my sister did," it probably means this current person in your life is victimizing you in a familiar way. When a movie makes you cry, use it as an opportunity to find out more about yourself. Ask yourself, "What's going on here? Why did that upset me so much? Who or what in my past triggered that feeling?"

In your journal, make a list of everyone who ever victimized you in any way—parents, siblings, other relatives, teachers, clergy, past lovers, bosses, etc. By "victimized," I mean anyone who ever made you feel that you were not good enough, anyone who ever made you feel that you were less than them, anyone who ever put you down or hurt your feelings, even if they didn't know they were doing it at the time.

Every person and issue that hurt you has left an emotional scar that keeps your love addiction alive and your self-esteem low. Low self-esteem is a key element in keeping you from becoming self-reliant. Working through these issues will raise your self-esteem and will facilitate the process of taking charge of your own life.

Teachers Who Victimize

Many teachers criticized us and made us feel stupid. My sixth-grade teacher did the opposite but it still hurt. It was his first job right out of school. He was young and attractive and I was an impressionable young girl. He was friendly and flirtatious, and I felt sure he cared about me as much as I cared about him. That is, until the day he got married. I was crushed. I thought I wasn't good enough. I had just reached puberty, and my father had pulled away from me at the same time. I felt abandoned by all the men in my life. I felt so ugly and unworthy that I withdrew from everyone and went into my own fantasy world for months.

Abandonment by a Friend

Friends can also have a great effect on us, especially a friend we really care about who walks out on us. A client of mine hadn't realized just how much one of her friends had affected her until recently. She came in to see me because of problems with her husband. She had developed a hard, cold defense of "I don't need you." Much of it started with her mother, but she remembers a traumatic incident involving a friend's rejection of her. The friend's father had criticized her, and her friend took the father's side instead of defending her. She was very hurt but acted like she didn't care. This resurfaced in her "I don't care" defense that she uses today in most of her relationships.

To process your hurt and anger take your list of victimizers—whether friends, teachers, or ex-husbands—and begin a letter to each one telling them how hurt and angry you are about what they did to you. Chapter Eight will teach you more about writing constructive confrontational letters. Mail your letters if you can.

Discovering Your Story

In the third person, write out the drama of your life. In doing so, be sure to include the answers to the following questions.

1. Who did your family *say* you were most like—your dad, the old maid aunt, a long-lost cousin? Did you interpret it as good or bad?
2. Who in your family *are* you most like? Why?
3. What was important to you when you were a child? Why?
4. What conversations and behaviors were forbidden? Why?
5. Who were you afraid of? Why?

6. As a child, what techniques and defenses did you use to protect yourself? Rebelling, withdrawing, acting like it didn't hurt?

7. What happened the first time you tried to fight back? Did you stop or continue? Why?

8. How did your sisters and brothers treat you? Did they control you, lean on you, hit you?

9. Who was your savior? Who believed in you when others didn't? Who made you feel special?

10. Who were your positive and negative role models?

11. What role did women play in your life?

12. What did you learn about men as you grew up?

13. What is the theme of your story?

14. What was your character in the family—Cinderella, a fairy princess, the mama, the clown, the black sheep?

15. As a child, were you driven by fear? Guilt? Resentment? How did these emotions hold you back from happiness? Do they still?

16. What were you taught about dependency, being sweet and nice, expectations in life, achievement and success, authority, femininity?

17. How did you try to get what you wanted in life? Waiting and hoping, manipulating and seducing, intimidating and controlling?

18. What makes you behave so passively or aggressively now?

19. What makes you push others away or desperately cling to them?

20. What happened in your past that makes you carry anger around now?

21. What secrets do you keep from your family?

22. What are your best and worst school memories?

23. What's the moral of your life?

24. What horrified your parents?

25. Who took your power away?

26. Who and/or what keeps you feeling boxed in?

27. When did you first lie? What was it about? What did you learn about lying? Telling the truth?

28. Who made you feel small? What did they say or do?

29. What were you most ashamed of as a child?

30. What were your most important life events?

Is your story the great American novel? Is it sad? Exciting? Do you feel sorry for that little girl? What does she need now? Can you see how she was a defenseless child who didn't feel loved and nurtured? Can you understand why she sometimes got angry and acted out? Can you help her? Make a decision to take care of her now—above everyone else.

What Happens Now

When the picture becomes clear, it may frighten you. Understanding why you are the way you are often creates feelings of anger toward your parents and others for what they did to you. Don't feel bad or frightened for having these feelings. They are a normal and natural reaction.

Many of my clients drop out at this point because they become so uncomfortable. Sometimes people stay miserable and unsuccessful intentionally, just to punish their parents for what they've done. Many people don't want to move forward because they really don't think they deserve to be happy. Some feel guilty if good things start to happen to them. Some are getting too much out of being depressed to want to change. Almost everyone is frightened by the prospect of changing.

Fear often keeps us from completing this step. We're afraid we'll hurt our family. We're afraid we'll be punished for thinking these thoughts. We're afraid of how our lives will be different. We're afraid of failing. We're afraid of winning and not deserving it. We're afraid we'll have to take responsibility because we will no longer have an excuse for being unhappy.

Fear can paralyze many people. They often say, "What I don't know won't hurt me," but it's not true. It *does* hurt you. With this attitude, you live your life too unaware to take control of it.

The answer to why you are the way you are today is in your past. And the way to get beyond your past is in the next few chapters.

7

Step Five:
Get in Touch
With Your Feelings
and Communicate Them

The clues were all there but I ignored them. On our first trip to Mexico, Kevin turned to me and said, "It's great seeing you so happy about the trip. I wish I could get that excited about things." Later as I was breaking up with him, he said, "You act like I'm holding back my feelings. What you don't realize is that I don't ever *have* any feelings." I felt sick that I'd spent three long years trying to get this man to feel for me without realizing just how emotionally blocked he was. I finally really heard him and got the courage to walk away.

Kevin wasn't the only seemingly unemotional* man in my life. I'd been through a series of men like him, beginning with my father. I'd tried again and again to get each one to open up and feel *with* me and *for* me—to no avail. This was the form my love addiction had taken. I believed that since I was such an extremely emotional person, I could rescue these unemotional men; by doing so, I would prove what a good person I was. What I didn't realize was that you can't save someone who doesn't want to be saved. I was not as emotionally in touch with myself as I thought I was, and I was using Kevin as a means to avoid dealing with myself.

Most women see themselves as very emotional and men as very unemotional. The truth is that most women are more dramatic than men and sometimes more in touch with how they feel, but

---

*All people are emotional; many people just aren't in touch with or just don't know how to express their feelings.

seldom are they any more "emotionally honest" than men are. Women get in touch with their feelings and then often proceed to tell everyone in the world about them, except the person they need to tell—the person who caused the feelings.

Step Five is getting in touch with all of your feelings and learning to communicate them in a healthy, direct, powerful way.

The previous chapter, "Understanding Why You Are the Way You Are," may have already put you in touch with some of the feelings you have suppressed over the years. Hurt and anger about what others have done to you usually start coming to the surface as you realize how your past is affecting your enjoyment of the present. You may also experience sadness about feeling unloved, neglected, or criticized as a defenseless child. If you are not starting to get more in touch with your feelings as you've been working through the program, you may not be allowing yourself to feel. When we are not in touch with our feelings, our communication becomes unclear, indirect, confusing, and sometimes abusive. Instead of communicating, we often whine, threaten, preach, manipulate, judge, rescue, avoid, tease, question, criticize, or blame. These responses block communication and push people away.

When we were small dependent children we learned that talking about feelings was "bad." If mom was right when she told us that we would get burned if we touched the stove, we thought she must be right when she said, "Don't talk like that, don't feel that way, don't be selfish." We learned, in fact, that sometimes we have to do things that don't feel right to us in order to please mom and dad and win their love and approval. We learned to sacrifice our own feelings and needs as a trade-off for their love. This is how our dependence on approval began. Most of us believe we should do the same with the men we love.

Trusting Your Feelings

Deep inside yourself, you know when something feels right or wrong, even though you may block those feelings. When someone insults you, you know it doesn't feel "right." But your brain overrides your emotions and you try to control yourself by saying things like, "He's not worth it," "That shouldn't upset me," or "She didn't mean it." To take charge of your life you must learn to turn off the control tapes, admit your feelings, and then express them. In fact, it will feel *right,* though scary, to stop the person from insulting you by saying, "I'm insulted and I will not allow you to talk to me like that. Stop it now!" Expressing your feelings and setting limits with the person will help you keep your self-respect intact.

How many times have you walked away from a situation and wished you'd said something different? The next time you do this, call the person back and say it. It will help break your patterns. Saying what you feel instead of what you think you "should" say develops self-trust and self-respect.

Avoiding Feelings Hurts Us and Others

When you put off feeling pain, depression, sadness, or anger, it simply intensifies. The sooner you deal with issues and the feelings they create, the more quickly "negative" feelings dissipate and the sooner you'll be able to feel good again.

We usually try to stay in control of our emotions. We've been taught that "strong" means not showing emotion. We think that if we're strong, we should be able to control ourselves, i.e., not fall apart. We certainly want someone who feels like murdering to stay in control and not follow his or her angry feelings. However, we fail to understand that keeping feelings of anger under control for a very long time without working them through causes them to build inside until the person completely loses it and commits murder or suicide.

Luckily, most of us deal with our angry feelings before we reach this point. But holding angry feelings in also causes us to be sarcastic, revengeful, bitchy, and/or abusive.

Repressed anger makes people behave abusively. On the other hand, people get depressed when they turn their unexpressed anger inward. By teaching us not to express our anger, society forces us to do the very thing that will cause us to harm ourselves or harm others in the long run.

When we don't express an emotion, it comes out in other ways. Women who are afraid they aren't good enough may act self-indulgent or narcissistic to make up for their feelings of inadequacy. Women who become hysterical or overly dramatic are trying to make up for the lack of emotional expression they get from men. Men often don't call back when a sexual experience has been especially good, because the more intimate the experience, the more frightened of their feelings they are, and they don't know how to deal with their fear.

Men beat their wives because they were never taught how to express anger verbally. Men and women are unfaithful because it's easier to find someone new to relate to than it is to confront problems with intimacy in an ongoing relationship.

People lie when they know they'll be punished for telling the truth. People kill others when they feel so victimized that destroying the perpetrator seems to be the only way out.

Most people don't choose to be bad or to intentionally hurt others; they just don't deal with their feelings or problems, and it finally catches up to them. Not expressing our feelings also distances us from those we say we love. We often hold feelings back for fear of hurting and then losing someone; but by holding them back, we ensure such bad communication that we usually end up losing that person anyway.

For instance, before Tom and Peggy came in for counseling, Peggy often woke up crying and feeling depressed. She tried to stay in control, so she ignored her feelings, got dressed, and went on about her business. However, on weekends she was less able to hide from the situation and often cried all day, especially if Tom was off playing golf. She knew there was a problem with her marriage but feared bringing it up, even though she hadn't been happy for years. Instead of talking to her husband and letting him know how she felt so they could work on the problem, she had an affair. This simply made her feel worse. By the time they came into my office, she and Tom had drifted so far apart from their poor or nonexistent communication, their marriage was irreparable. In my office, she finally did what she should have done the first day she cried about her marriage. She talked to her husband, shared her feelings and asked him to share his, and tried to come to a resolution. But it was too late.

When you hold in unexpressed feelings of any kind—love, anger, hurt, fear, etc.—you damage your relationships. Most people "know" when there is something wrong in a relationship, even if they're not sure why. Poor communication can kill a relationship, just as it did Peggy and Tom's.

When you don't acknowledge pent-up fear, anger, and frustrations, you allow the other person control in the relationship, and you lose your power. Unexpressed communication allows the other person to believe that he or she is right and you're wrong. You are unconsciously allowing that person to have little or no respect for you, because you accept negative opinions and feelings without defending yourself. By not speaking up about our feelings, our desires, our needs, we set up a win-lose situation. We lose, they win—again.

Expressing Your Feelings

Anger is probably the most difficult emotion to express, and many of us don't believe we *should* express it. We fear it because we've usually only seen it in its explosive stage. Healthy anger is not explosive. It is not meant to harm someone. It's protective—it simply and clearly lets someone know they are hurting you and that you want them to stop. The sooner you can express anger, the better. When you hold it in, it continues to destroy relationships.

Most of us don't believe that we can love someone and still be angry at them. Anger is only temporary unless it is repressed and allowed to turn into resentment. Unexpressed anger blocks good, loving feelings until the anger is resolved. But expressing anger as you feel it keeps relationships clean, so that loving feelings can continue to come through.

Without the use of anger, we have no power. Without power, we feel we can't protect ourselves without being manipulative and/or abusive. We fear intimacy because we fear not being able to protect ourselves.

When you find yourself wanting to avoid a feeling or a problem by abusing alcohol, food, drugs, work, sex, or by sleeping too much, realize that these are simply distractions to cover up your fear of dealing with your emotions. We can distract ourselves quite easily. You may want to go to the office and work because you feel unloved at home and are bored. You may feel you need a drink because you feel so stressed. You may want to sleep excessively because you want to escape from feeling bad about yourself, or ''feeling'' your feelings. You may continue to eat when you should feel full because emotionally you feel empty. Don't beat yourself up if you avoid in these ways from time to time, but if you do one or more regularly, you are avoiding taking charge of your life. Instead of accepting temporary solutions to feel better, begin to search for a long-term answer to your problems.

Talk to yourself. Try to figure yourself out. If you're usually tired, you may be depressed or bored. Ask yourself why. If you can't sleep, you may be anxious. Try to discover what you are nervous about or afraid of. If you're confused, you probably have several feelings to sort out.

Take the time to allow your mind to wander. Allow it to search for the answers. If you can get yourself into a meditative state of consciousness and aren't afraid, your mind will gradually reveal your feelings, desires, and what you need to do. You have more answers about you and what you need to do inside of you than all the experts in the world. You have to begin to listen carefully to yourself and trust the answers you get. You may need to use some of the alone-time techniques discussed previously to get in touch with these feelings.

Visualize yourself handling the problem the way you wish you could. Imagine not being afraid. Imagine feeling successful. When you start trusting yourself, you won't be able to ignore the right thing for you to do or say, because it will feel uncomfortable if you do.

"What If I Don't Know How I Feel"

There are times when you just don't know how you feel and can't express your true feelings to a friend or colleague. When this happens, you can simply express that you are confused, or that you feel several different things at once, or that you don't know for sure how you feel. Tell him or her that you need some time to get in touch with your feelings, or try to express as much as you do know at that moment.

You can also allow your body to help you discover your feelings. If you say you don't "really" feel angry, check out your body and see if you find any anger in the way you are standing, in the feelings in your stomach, in the tension in the back of your neck.

When you know something is bothering you, but can't access your feelings and/or don't know who you're upset with, ask yourself:

- What's really going on with me right now?
- What happened right before I started feeling bad that could have triggered these feelings in me?
- Was an old button from my childhood pushed? Who pushed it in the past? How is that childhood incident similar to what just happened?
- Am I feeling bad about myself? Why? Who caused this?

It may take several days or weeks to get in touch with what you're feeling. Don't give up, and don't get distracted and hide your feelings from yourself. And don't assume that you have to have your feelings perfectly figured out, either. Sometimes if you start talking about surface feelings first, the submerged, deeper ones will be uncovered, and the more comfortable you will become at looking for them *and* expressing them. Then the process becomes easier. Sometimes talking to others can help you get in touch with your feelings; but don't use others as a replacement for expressing yourself to the person that you're upset with.

As soon as you are in touch with your feelings, it's important that you take action. If you're angry at yourself, you may need to make some resolutions—start that diet or clean your apartment or do that project. If you feel guilty because of something you did to someone else, apologize and get the situation resolved as quickly as possible. If you're angry at someone else, confront that person as soon as possible. If you feel sad, cry. But don't drown in self-pity. Self-pity needs to gradually turn into anger at the situation. Some women cry and cry and never get to the anger stage. The sooner you can process all of your feelings from hurt, sadness, embarrassment, etc., to anger, the sooner you can take charge of your life. It's very important to get to the anger stage, because anger motivates you to take action and make changes.

Beyond Your Wall of Anger

Many gorgeous, successful women never have men approach them, and they're not sure why. They usually think it's because they've become so strong and independent that men are intimidated by them. What is often the case is that they have held onto unresolved anger, which has created a sharp edge to their personalities that keeps men from approaching them. They have developed a jaded attitude that they aren't even aware of. Many of these women, and I used to be one of them, feel they've gotten where they are today in their careers because they stopped being soft and quit trying to have relationships with men. This attitude comes from feeling victimized in the past and having not fought back. Now they feel it necessary to build a defense that will not allow a man close enough to hurt them. Even when one of these women wants a relationship with a man, she doesn't know how to let him get close to her. The solution lies in eliminating the buried anger.

These women are afraid to be vulnerable around men. They feel that each time they try to, the man either takes advantage of their softness or disappears. So to protect themselves, they try to appear overly independent and without needs. Their independent, cold attitude not only attracts fewer men, but usually only those men who aren't looking for a close relationship. Their wall of anger sets them up to fail.

Old anger at men must be purged. One way to work through resentments of all kinds is, as I mentioned earlier, to write letters to those who have hurt you in the past, expressing the hurt and anger, and letting them know that you would never let them or anyone else hurt you like that again. Purging the old anger will help you to trust yourself and to be open with men again. As you set limits, you will begin to believe that you can keep others from hurting you, so you can risk being vulnerable again. Fear of intimacy is fear of what you will let a man do to you, because you don't know how to stop him. Once you have the strength to set limits, you'll know that you won't let a man hurt you. It will then be safe to become approachable again.

Becoming Approachable Again

After you've purged the anger, you may still have difficulty knowing how to act. To learn how to be approachable you can try to relearn the feminine softness you probably had in your teens. Try and remember what you were like during your prime dating years. Try to recall the soft, flirtatious you before you developed the wall of anger. This doesn't mean that you should act like a weak, helpless little girl. You should choose the parts of your past flirtatious feminine ways that you want back and discard the others. For those of you who did not date much, did you fantasize? If you did, try to remember your fantasies. If not, choose an ultrafeminine role model to copy. Picture yourself as the sexiest, most sensual, exciting female imaginable. If you are out of touch with this part of yourself, buy tapes and books on feminine dressing and flirting to get back in touch with it. It's there inside of you and you can find it, even if it's been repressed for years.

Take Alicia, for instance. Although she didn't date much in her teenage years, she fantasized about being a stripper and actually played with scarves and belts and stripped in front of her bedroom mirror. Of course, she did this behind locked doors when no one else was home. Although at the time she felt guilty and thought that something was wrong with her, through therapy she has realized that this behavior was an important part of getting in touch with her sexuality and femininity during adolescence. Although she was embarrassed to tell me about her fantasizing, she was relieved to know that what she did was normal and healthy. You may still need to experiment like she did.

Being approachable also involves being emotionally vulnerable. Get in touch with those old soft, warm feelings again and realize there is nothing wrong with them! Many people think that showing vulnerability means being weak. A woman who shows and talks about her feelings incessantly without taking action (and when talking about them makes you feel you "should" fix things for her) is weak. A healthy woman, on the other hand, can let others see her humanness—the soft, tender parts of who she is, her sensitivity, even her problems, yet she sends the message that she can handle her life and is not asking you to fix anything for her. She doesn't go too far and expose more about herself than the person she is relating to does. She may open up first but will withdraw to protect herself if the other person doesn't self-disclose. She doesn't ask to be rescued. That's the difference between being soft and being wimpy.

Being vulnerable—allowing someone to know the "real" you—is the only way to create intimacy in a relationship. How much do you let others know about you?

Self-Disclosure Questionnaire[1]
Decide *who* you tell what to and mark these statements accordingly. Then look them over and find out who you let in and who you don't.

M—male friend   L—lover   P—parents
F—female friend   S—stranger   O—others, e.g., ministers, siblings

WHO DO YOU SELF-DISCLOSE TO?

ATTITUDES AND OPINIONS
1. My personal opinions and feelings about religious groups other than my own, e.g., Protestants, Catholics, Jews, atheists.
2. My views on the government—the president, government policies, etc.
3. My personal views on drinking/drugs.
4. My personal views on sexual morality—how I feel that I and others ought to behave in sexual matters.
5. My personal standards of attractiveness in women/men.

TASTES AND INTERESTS
1. My favorite foods and beverages and the way I like them prepared.
2. My likes and dislikes in music.
3. My favorite reading matter.
4. The kinds of movies that I like to see best; the TV shows I like.
5. The kind of party or social gatherings that I like best, and the kind that bore me or that I wouldn't enjoy.
6. My favorite ways of spending spare time, e.g., hunting, reading, cards, sports events, parties, dancing, etc.
7. What I would appreciate most for a present.

WORK
1. What I find to be the worst pressures and strains in my work.
2. What I find to be the most boring and unenjoyable aspects of my work.
3. What I enjoy most and get the most satisfaction from in my work.

4. What I feel are my shortcomings and handicaps that prevent me from getting further ahead in my work.
5. What I feel are my special strong points and qualifications for my work.
6. How I really feel about the people that I work for and/or work with.

MONEY

1. How much money I make at my work.
2. Whether I have savings, and the amount.
3. All of my present sources of income—wages, fees, allowances, dividends, etc.
4. My total financial worth, including property, savings, bonds, insurance, etc.
5. My most pressing need for money right now, e.g., outstanding bills, major purchases that are desired or needed.

PERSONALITY

1. The aspects of my personality that I dislike, worry about, that I regard as a handicap.
2. What feelings, if any, that I have trouble expressing or controlling.
3. The facts of my present sex life—with whom I have relations, if anybody.
4. Sex—knowledge of how I get sexual gratification.
5. Sex—problems that I have.
6. Whether or not I feel that I am attractive to the opposite sex; my problems, if any, about getting favorable attention from the opposite sex.
7. Things in the past or present that I feel ashamed and guilty about.
8. The kinds of things that make me furious.
9. What it takes to make me feel very depressed.
10. What it takes to make me worried, anxious, and afraid.
11. What it takes to hurt my feelings deeply.
12. The kind of things that make me especially proud of myself, elated, full of self-esteem or self-respect.

BODY

1. My feelings about the appearance of my body—things I do and don't like.

2. How I wish I looked; my ideals for overall appearance.
3. Any problems and worries that I had concerning my appearance in the past.
4. Whether or not I now have any health problems, e.g., sleep, digestion, gynecological, heart trouble, allergies, headaches, etc.
5. My feelings about my sexual worth—whether I feel able to perform adequately in a sexual relationship.

Self-Disclosure Is Necessary for Intimacy

Who do you let into your world? Who do you keep out? Do you let many men in? Do you make sure they share equally with you? Do you expose too much or too little to them? Ask yourself these and other questions to discover how much you self-disclose and to whom.

Sidney Jourard, in his book *The Transparent Self,* suggests that if one does not gain the courage to be herself with others, it ''. . . often results in sickness, misunderstanding, and alienation from self. . . . People's selves stop growing when they repress them. . . . Alienation from one's real self not only arrests personal growth, it tends to make a farce out of one's relationships with people.''[2]

Without expressing our feelings to others, we can't know ourselves, and without knowing and loving ourselves, it is impossible to have healthy relationships with others.

Four Steps of Healthy Communication

In Chapter Two we discussed dependency roles and how most of us behave in either one of two ways: victim or persecutor. These roles are modeled after our parents and come from denial of feelings. To break out of these roles, all we need to do is communicate our real feelings. For instance, when we feel victimized, we are feeling hurt. We need to express that hurt to try and stop the victimizer. If the victimizer doesn't stop his behavior when we say we're hurt, and tries to take advantage of our vulnerability, we need to move to the angry stage. Sharing the anger we feel and asking him to change should stop our victimizer; if it doesn't, it's time to tell him you're leaving if he doesn't stop and then leave. On the other hand, when we're in the pleasing role, we're feeling guilty about something we've done. Instead of trying to please others at this point, we need to express our guilt, sincerely apologize, and ask how we can make reparations. If our victim says he wants nothing, believe him and let it go—without feeling guilty.

Below are four steps for developing healthy communication. They have worked for me and my clients, in all areas of life from personal to professional. When you use these four steps, you will not be behaving in a dependent or avoidant way. You will not be pleasing. You will not be acting desperate. By following all four steps, you will clearly express your feelings and wants and take responsibility for your life. You will show the person how you are in charge, whether or not he or she comes through for you.

Step One: "I Feel _____ ."

Express your feelings. Start using "I feel _____ " statements. Begin by telling another person how you feel and what the behavior is that caused you to feel that way. Say, "I feel (angry, sad, hurt, happy, uncomfortable, etc.)," and then name the behavior that made you feel that way. For example: "I feel angry when you show up late for dinner." (Note: Do not say, "I feel *that* _____ ." This puts you in an intellectual mode, not a feeling one.)

If you're in an argument with a man, a common mistake is to attack him ("you're inconsiderate," "you're stupid") instead of saying how *you* feel. These are *your* feelings, so you need to own them by saying, "I feel _____ ," rather than criticizing or judging. You will put him on the defensive if you accuse with "You're . . . " However, he might become defensive no matter how you express yourself and try to intimidate you when you let him know how you feel. It's an emotional risk you need to take, anyway. If he does react with "You're crazy, you have no right to feel that way," or "You're overreacting," ignore the response, realizing that he is trying to manipulate you and get you off track. Remember that your feelings are valid. Restate them once again, tying them in with the behavior that caused them. Afterwards, you should respond to his "You're overreacting" comment by telling him that you're insulted or angry, and that you don't want him to ever pull that again!

Step Two: "I Want _____."

State your wants as clearly as you can. Just as children need to hear, "I want you to eat your peas," instead of, "Finish your dinner," adults need to hear clear, direct messages. "I want you to call when you're going to be late" doesn't leave a man guessing about the woman's expectations. Neither does it leave much room for argument.

If you are angry because someone showed up late, try saying: "I *feel* angry when you're late. I *want* you to be on time from now on or call me if you're running late." Unfortunately, your needs might not be that simple. If you want several things, try something like: "I *feel* humiliated when you don't respect me and I *want* you to do several things: Pay attention to me when I'm talking to you or inform me that you're too distracted to listen. Talk more respectfully to me, consider my feelings more often, and listen to my feelings when I try to tell you how humiliated I feel."

You may think, "Isn't this too much to ask? It seems like I'm trying to change him." But you really aren't. You are only trying to change the way he treats you. You may think, "Do I really deserve this?" You are not asking too much. You are simply asking to be treated with respect. You can ask for anything you want. The person you ask can always say no.

Many people get this far in their communication but no further. They continuously let someone know their feelings and wants but never go on to use any power to get what they want. If you state what you feel and want regularly but with no power, others have probably stopped listening to you long ago because they consider you a nag or a "whiner"—someone who complains repeatedly without ever doing anything about the problem. This is what Alicia did on a regular basis with her friends. You must go further.

Step Three: "Will You _____."

Ask for a commitment. Your request may still go in one ear and out the other. That's why you have to ask, "Did you hear me, and will you do what I asked?" Ask this person to repeat your request in his own words and then to answer it. You are checking to see if he heard you; if he didn't, you will repeat your request until he does. Like a kid being called on in class by a teacher, if he knows you'll hold him accountable, he's more likely to listen.

Ask for a commitment from him to change the way he treats you, such as, "Will you call the next time you're going to be late?", or, "Will you start treating me with respect by at least listening to my feelings?" You may even ask that he repeat the agreement back to you. You may find out the person hasn't been listening to you, you may run into resistance, or you may get a half-hearted commitment: "I don't know if I can, but I'll try." If the person hasn't heard you, begin again with step one. If he resists, get ready for step four; if you get an "I'll try, but...", let the person know that you'll be glad to point out to him when he is doing something that bothers you so he can stop the behavior. Then follow through.

Step Four: "If Not, I Will _____ ."

You must have a plan. You must give an ultimatum and go through with it if you do not get what you want. The person might not agree to your request or, more likely, he will agree but not act on it. He might even respond with, "So what? I don't care. What are you gonna do to me?" You must let him know what will happen if he doesn't give you what you ask for. Without this step, the rest of your attempts to gain equal power in the relationship are wasted. You must impose a consequence. We think nothing of imposing consequences or penalties if someone doesn't keep a business promise. But we were taught by our mothers to never give men ultimatums or we might lose them. Without the power to do this, we lose our self-respect. In the first three steps of communication, you expressed how you felt, what you wanted, and you've asked the person if he will give you what you want. Now it is time to use power to insure that you get it. When the other person resists and doesn't want to give you what you ask for, you then respond with, "*If not, I will* _____ ." You may use something as simple as, "*If not, I will* eat dinner without you," or something as drastic as, "*If you don't* start treating me with the respect that I deserve, I *will* leave you."

Ultimatums are a show of your strength and power. You have no power in your communication without the ultimatum. However, don't give any ultimatums you can't keep. Ultimatums should not be used out of spite or to get even. Use them to take care of your own needs. Ultimatums allow you to take responsibility for your own life and to rid yourself of dependency on the other person. You let the person know that if he doesn't work with you, you will do whatever is necessary to handle the problems in your own way. At first, ultimatums usually generate a range of negative feelings—from discomfort to anger—from those you use them on, because they're used to having all the power. However, after the initial shock wears off, people usually begin to respect you more once they see you follow through and mean what you say. Most people will test you the first time or two, so start with small issues to gain their respect, such as, "If you're late, I'll go to the movie alone." After you follow through on small issues several times, he will begin to believe you. He will know that you mean business and will believe that you will follow through with bigger issues. Then when you say, "If you don't, I'm leaving you," he will, if he cares, be more likely to treat you the way you want. Be a person who deserves respect—one who communicates feelings, expresses wants, asks for a commitment, and follows through with what you say.

By following the four steps, you will be setting limits with others about what is and is not acceptable treatment of you. As you do this, it will improve your relationships and raise your own level of self-worth.

Remember, the Four Steps To Healthy Communication are:

"I *feel* _____ "

"I *want* _____ "

"*Will you* _____ "

"*If not, I will* _____ "

Effective Communication

To communicate effectively, you must use drama. We often say what we want in a squeaky little voice or with no impact. As with actors, using emotion, intonation, and facial expression is necessary to make an impact on the person with whom you're communicating. Many of us have squelched our emotional expression to the point that we don't know *how* to express our feelings. If you have an important message to get across, you may want to practice it in front of a mirror. When you say you're angry, do you look believable?

Communicating effectively with power involves risk. Without it, we end up stuck in unhealthy relationships that hurt us. By risking, we at least have a possibility of winning. When you communicate in a healthy way, others will either respond to you by relating back to you in a healthy way, or the relationship will end sooner and not be dragged out. Either way, you win. When you are comfortable with yourself and with being alone, the risk will not be as frightening. You will be more willing to communicate how you really feel and to drop the "dead wood" or bad relationships from your life.

Although this four-step method does not guarantee that you'll always get what you want, it teaches you to communicate with power, to develop back-up plans for yourself, how to meet your own needs, and how to walk away from issues or relationships with your self-respect and self-worth intact. That's self-reliance.

8

Step Six:
Confront Your Parents

Lana's father flew in from Michigan to meet with her in my office. I was a little nervous, as she had described him to me as a con artist. But, when I met him, I found him instead to be a fascinating, funky old man. Lana had written him a very angry letter. He had responded with a letter of his own, filled with intellectualism and defensiveness. Lana didn't respond to it. He then called and told her that he would do anything to repair their relationship. She asked him to fly out and meet with her in my office. She hadn't seen him in nineteen years.

It took Lana a long time to get the courage to confront her father. She had dropped out of therapy twice before when I pushed her to write the letter to him, once for more than a year. She kept insisting that she didn't want a relationship with him.

Why Confront?

Everyone who comes into my office is usually just as resistant as Lana was when I talk to them about confronting their parents. They can't understand why it's necessary. They ask, "What difference will confronting my parents make? I already understand what happened to me and why." Most want to know, "How will hurting *them* help *me*?" They believe that knowing why they are the way they are should be enough to help them change. But it isn't. Changing the way we relate is an emotional process that

113

requires communication of emotions. You cannot do it by yourself where no risk is involved. You must do it within a relationship.

Most of the hurts our parents inflicted were not *intended* to hurt us. But, if we allow *their* hurt, we'll allow others to hurt us too. And if we don't let others know they've hurt us, they'll quite likely do it again.

In her book *Toxic Parents,* Dr. Susan Forward says, "Many people—including some prominent therapists—do not believe in confrontation. Their rationales are quite familiar: 'Don't look backward, look forward'; 'It will only cause more stress and anger'; or, 'It doesn't heal wounds, it just reopens them.' These critics simply don't understand."[1]

What they don't understand is that just as a rape victim must confront her rapist in order to heal herself, we cannot heal ourselves without confronting those who abused us—no matter how minor the abuse is perceived to be. Without parental confrontation, we hold onto the anger and cannot move forward and take charge of our lives.

Our parents abused us and fostered our emotional dependency by:

- teaching us to deny our real feelings, especially anger.
- teaching us to be fearful of taking risks.
- never accepting our imperfections.
- teaching us to never confront our problems.
- trying to keep us dependent on their judgment of how we should live our lives.
- providing us with only two role models: victim or abuser.
- never allowing us to feel loved unconditionally.

Debbie, a forty-year-old Aspen dropout, thought she had a very normal childhood. She had everything—a stable, religious family, plenty of material things, a great social life, and a college degree.

However, at forty, she appeared in my office feeling like her life was hopeless. What had happened? Not only had she received the normal dose of parental abuse as described above, but she was given a large dose of religious doctrine as well. Because she was not the way her parents wanted her to be, Debbie felt that she was a bad person. She had started hiding her true identity from her parents at a young age. As a child, she was secretive about her normal curiosity about sex and her desire to have fun. But as she got older she pretended more and more to be different than she really was. She felt worse and worse about herself. The worse she felt about herself, the more love addicted she became and the more she allowed abusive behavior from men. By the time a friend sent her to me, she had turned to prostitution and drugs and was totally alienated from her family. Debbie was never able to talk to her parents about anything important, and she never felt loved by them. When I called them to ask them to come to my office and work this out with her, they said they would only pay for and visit an alcohol-rehabilitation center, as they felt sure that alcohol was the real problem. They probably still believed that the day she committed suicide. If Debbie had been able to confront her parents, she'd probably be alive today.

Break Destructive Patterns in Relationships

Most women who come to see me have been trying to change for years. They've read every self-help book on the market and have been to many therapists. They have analyzed their problems and may know that they are involved in destructive patterns in their relationships. They may even realize that they are from dysfunctional families. Some know they're still emotionally dependent on men. Some have even been able to break their dependencies temporarily—long enough to get out of a bad marriage or end a destructive relationship. But few have been able to break their emotional dependencies permanently. They often get into other bad relationships and repeat their patterns without being aware that that's what they're doing.

That's what happened to Lana, and that's what brought her back to therapy the last time. She had fallen in love with Doug, a doctor in Los Angeles. To her surprise the relationship was becoming increasingly abusive. In the past, when a man didn't do things her way, she walked out. This time, however, she began to believe the things that Doug was saying about her. He told her she was arrogant and spoiled. That pushed a button in her because her mother used to say the same things. She believed Doug and was trying to be what he wanted, until one night when his abuse finally became physical. She was appalled at how she had let the abuse get so out of hand. This time it took very little to convince her that her parental issues had to be resolved before she could put an end to the pattern in which she either abused men or they abused her. Doug was treating her the same way she had often treated men—coldly, critically, and threatening to abandon. This is also the way her father treated her, so it felt "normal." Her father's abandonment of her had made her feel that she deserved such treatment.

As I talked her back into finishing the program, she stated again and again that she thought it was useless to try to get through to her father. She was convinced that he was impossible to deal with. She was just as convinced that healthy relationships with men were impossible. The confrontation with her father proved her wrong.

Until we are able to confront our parents and set limits with them, we will not be able to do so with a man in a love relationship. *We can never have a relationship with a man any healthier than the one we have or had with our parents.* Our parents were our first relationships and leaving those relationships imbalanced sets us up to have unequal relationships forever. It's easy to think about what an equal relationship is supposed to be like and completely understand equality intellectually, but it's difficult to pull it off when we have had no practice and no role models. *We* must become role models for ourselves and for our children, so that the pattern does not continue.

Learn to Resolve Conflicts

Those who begin the program but quit at this step because they become so frightened, often get stuck in their hurt and/or anger. If they get stuck in hurt, they usually beat themselves up for not being able to change now that they understand the problem. Then they get more depressed. If they get stuck in anger, they blame, punish, abuse, and use their parents—which is much worse than confronting them. Some people don't want to let go of the blame.

When trying to talk themselves out of the confrontation some of my clients argue, "I'm responsible for my mistakes, not my parents." It's true, you *are* responsible for changing your life and making it the way you want it to be, but you are not responsible for your need to be dependent and the feelings of low self-worth your parents created in you. Accepting the blame would be like agreeing with your parents that you are inadequate, that you were born "bad."

It is their fault. You were born an innocent, loving person with a full range of emotions *you* wanted to express. They stopped you. As you begin to feel the anger at your parents, you will blame them. It is necessary to blame them to relieve yourself of guilt and self-blame. If you blame yourself, you will forever feel bad about the way you are.

The goal is not to try to hurt your parents and/or harm their self-esteem. Instead, it is to hold them accountable for the beliefs and actions they taught you that didn't and don't work. The goal is to eliminate the blame. We eventually stop blaming them as we process the hurt and angry feelings toward them through confrontation. In learning to confront them, we learn to take a conflict to its resolution while maintaining self-respect *and* respect for our parents. Doing so will therefore equalize our relationships with them and ultimately with others.

When we have differences of opinion with anyone, we need to be able to discuss our differences with them openly and without fear. When we believe something different from our parents (or others) and don't express ourselves, it's like silently saying that we agree with them.

If We Can Stand up to Our Parents, We Can Stand up to Anyone

Our parents have told us negative things about ourselves for years, things that continue to affect our self-esteem. When Barbara's dad told her she was stupid, she tried to prove him wrong by getting a master's degree and experimenting with different jobs. What she needed to do was accept that she's not perfect, but not accept her father's evaluation of her. She had to remind him of his imperfections and reject his belief that intelligence is related to street smarts. It not only took her "telling" him he was wrong but also aggressively forcing him to listen to her, before she was able to let go of this belief about herself.

For instance, Alicia's mother taught her that she should cater to men to get them to like her. She doesn't agree with that, yet she hasn't told her mom that she thinks she's wrong. Since she hasn't asserted her opinion, she wonders from time to time if her mom is right. So one minute she caters to men and the next she hates herself for doing so. Alicia needs to resolve this with her mother by telling her that she doesn't believe the assertion, by telling her that following the belief has not worked but has negatively affected her life, and demanding that her mother respect her beliefs now. Alicia doesn't have to change her mother's behavior, but she does need to demand that her mother be vulnerable enough to admit that teaching her this belief about catering to men has harmed Alicia. But even if her mother doesn't admit this, Alicia will be clearer about her own value system simply by confronting the issue. It forces her to sort and process what she really does believe. She and her mother might even agree to disagree, but Alicia will no longer allow her mother to judge her by her own standards.

Our parents have a greater investment in us than anyone else. Because of this, they are more likely to hang in there while we demand equality. If we've let a man control us for years and then demand equality, he's more likely to walk out on us than our parents are. Therefore, confronting our parents puts us at the most and least risk. They are the most likely to try to continue to control us and the least likely of all our relationships to leave us.

Most of the women who come in to see me, however, are terrified that their parents will abandon them if they confront them. They think they could handle a man's walking out more easily than their parents not speaking to them for the rest of their lives. It *is* scary, but more often than not the anticipation is worse than the actual confrontation is. And most parents *will threaten* abandonment, just as many of them threatened to withhold their love from you when you were a child if you didn't obey. However, it's usually just a power play. You must be willing to call their bluff by accepting their temporary—and sometimes permanent—abandonment to make your point and to break your emotional dependency.

Most parents will probably use one of these two manipulative techniques to back you down: guilt to make you feel sorry for them, or anger and a threat that they'll end the relationship. If you cave in to your parents when they try to stop your confrontation, you will forever remain a child emotionally. As long as you are afraid of your parents, you will fear others in society, and there will always be someone who will be able to use your fear to manipulate you and abuse you. Once you can stand up to your parents, you will be able to stand up to anyone. It takes strength, and in standing up to them, you will become stronger than most of the people you know. Confronting your parents is the scariest thing you will ever have to do in your life.

Your Relationship With Your Parents Will Improve

Parents are the most intimidating people in our lives. They are the people whose approval we most long for. That's why successful confrontation of parents and/or others who have physically or psychologically abused us breaks emotional dependence permanently.

The reward for your confrontation is not only your increased self-esteem but usually a better relationship with your parents in the long run. Most of us have a love/hate relationship with our parents. We love them, but hate the way they treat us. Anger often covers the love. Before I confronted my mother, I used to talk to her in a condescending tone of voice and say, "Yes, mom," like it was all I could do to put up with her. Now, none of that is necessary. If I don't feel like talking, I tell her and call her back when I do. Our relationship is still not perfect, but when we do have a problem, we talk it out. Recently she said, "I really am sorry for involving you in all the problems your dad and I had as you were growing up." And I replied, "Look what it did for me—it made me a great relationship therapist!" Before I confronted her, I was too angry to feel anything positive about my childhood or her. Now the relationship feels more loving and less needy on both sides.

A Successful Confrontation

After much pressure from me, Lana finally wrote the following letter to her father, excerpted here.

Cliff,
I've always needed a father. Someone to look up to. Someone to love and support me unconditionally. I spent my early years trying to do what I thought you wanted, to make you proud of me. You

never gave me that. Consequently, I have spent a lifetime moving from one unhealthy relationship to another, trying to make men proud of me, or I have been totally emotionally unavailable, like you.

You taught me that emotional abuse is normal. You badgered Mom until she lost control and yelled and cried and then you said, "Your mother is nuts, look at her, she's hysterical," with a satisfied, all-knowing smile on your face. Because I never wanted that to happen to me, I chose not to be like mom—a woman who suffers from hystrionics. I chose the only other option I had, to be like you.

I chose to be strong (on the outside), decisive, cut and dry, unemotional and controlling, just like you. I am a good-looking, smart, sensitive woman who went into early war because you and mom forced me to bear arms (shields from the hurt and pain) way too early in life. I was cheated out of my childhood and I am really angry about it. The decision to be emotionally absent like you has affected my life for thirty-four years. When you left mom, you used me as a tool of manipulation against her for a while, and then I never saw you again.

Because I got your attention while you were using me, I felt guilty and have spent years trying to make it up to Mom and Mike [brother] by taking care of their needs. I had to create cancer in my body to make me see my self-destructive pattern.

I have always wanted and have probably been searching for a "daddy" in the men I dated. Someone to call for support, share my victories with and cry with when sadness fell upon me. I still want that.

If you and I are to establish a relationship, I will require the following:

1) Openness to discussing our early years.
2) No judgment or "little girl" guidance.
3) You must be willing to be completely emotionally present and *honest*.
4) I need to hear that you feel remorse about what happened.

The ball is in your court. If I hear from you I will assume you are ready to start the process. If I don't, I wish only the best for you in the remainder of your life.

Please write only if you desire to build a relationship with me. I am frankly not interested in a rebuttal or explanation of why things were the way they were.

Lana

Lana felt sure that she would never hear from her father, and that was fine with her. In fact, the only reason she changed the ending of the letter and told him the ball was in his court was at my urging. She wanted to write him off, like she usually did with the men she dated. I told her that for her to have intimacy in a love relationship with a man, she needed to risk intimacy and being her real self with a man—preferably her father.

When she discovered a message from him on her answering machine, she called me in a panic. "He says he wants to work this out with me. What do I do now?" She was scared. She didn't call him back for two weeks. He finally called her back. That's when Lana asked him to come to my office and he agreed.

When her father arrived, I spoke with him alone first, explaining the process. We discussed how he and Lana's past communication hadn't worked very well. I asked him to try not to be judgmental or defensive. He told me his side of the story and reluctantly talked about his own hurt. I asked him to share it with Lana. He said he didn't know if he could.

Lana came in prepared. She expressed her anger, describing incidents from the past when he had hurt her. She told him how she had felt abandoned by him ever since he had divorced her mom. She confronted him with his treatment of her mother, including his many affairs.

He said he was sorry about many things. She asked why had he done them, and he tried to explain. He agreed that his excuses didn't make his past actions right, and he promised that he would never treat Lana abusively again.

He told her how hurt he was that she had testified against him during a lawsuit her mother had filed regarding child support. He said that was why he had never contacted her again. She reminded him that she was only fourteen at that time and felt torn between him and her mom. She reminded him that he did have financial responsibilities. She reminded him that she was just a little girl then and that he was the adult—he should have been the one to maintain the relationship.

He told her that he was so hurt he couldn't contact her because he feared more rejection. He cried. He told her he was sorry. He agreed that she was right and that he had made a mistake. She said she'd never heard him admit that he was wrong about anything before, and she liked that.

She said it would take time for her to rebuild her trust in him. He said he had the time. Lana and her father have a relationship now that she never thought was possible. Because he lives in another state, they don't see each other often, but they're staying in touch. But most important, Lana now understands that her father does love her and always has. She now sees his humanness and the reasons he did what he did. She now knows how to hold a man accountable. She now believes she is lovable and worthy of being treated with respect.

Impossible Confrontations

In Dr. Susan Forward's book *Toxic Parents,* she mentions that there are some "impossible confrontations."[2] I don't believe that there are any confrontations that are truly impossible. Even if your parents are in a coma or have Alzheimer's disease, you can say what needs to be said. If your parents are deceased,* you can write your feelings in a letter and read it at their gravesite, or you can role play. Most people are so frightened of confrontation that they look for excuses so they won't have to confront. This section contains some of the most common excuses.

There have been very few times that I've ever agreed that the consequences could be so bad that I thought a client should not make a confrontation. One was a woman who needed to confront her abusive ex-husband who had pulled guns and knives on her when they were married. I agreed that she should not make contact, but write the letter as if she would. Anytime you actually fear for your life or safety, do not confront, or do it in a safe way with others around. One man swears to me that since his confrontation with his abusive father, his father has put a contract out on his life. It's difficult to believe, except that his father is a multimillionaire who has never been challenged by anyone, and who certainly has the money to do it. The client isn't sorry he

---

*If your parents are dead, you can confront them in a letter and/or through role playing. You must mail the letter and follow up if your parents are alive, however, because they are presently affecting your life psychologically.

confronted, even though he's obviously been written out of his father's will. However, he has reached his goal—he now has a healthy relationship with a woman he adores. To him the trade-off is worth it. Some clients fear that their parents will have a heart attack when confronted, and it did happen with a client's father once. But these are the worst possible cases, and they are few and far between. The more common "worst possible" cases are parents' disowning their children and never speaking to them again. But usually the parents do this only for a few months or until the next family crisis.

It would be good, however, for you to prepare for the worst thing that could happen and decide how you would handle it if it did happen. This will not only have you well prepared, it will also help you overcome your fear and be able to take the risk. *Without taking the risk, you can't have the best thing that could happen—a warm, loving relationship with your parents and/or with the opposite sex.*

Common Excuses:

"I've Already Done It and It Didn't Work!"

When Barbara first started therapy she insisted that she had already confronted her father. She came into my office because she couldn't get over her last boyfriend, Eric. She said that Eric "acted like his shit didn't stink." Remember that Barbara's father always called her stupid as a child. Eric continued to make her feel that way by "helping her"—helping her to be smarter and to move up in the world so that she would be good enough for him and his family. Two years after he left her, she can't stop obsessing about him. When she told me that she had confronted her father, yet she couldn't stop obsessing about Eric, I knew something was wrong.

Barbara's confrontation at that time consisted of telling her father that calling her stupid had made her feel inadequate all these years—which was good. But his response was, "I didn't mean to make you feel dumb. I don't think you're dumb. And if you still feel that way, that's your problem."

He made her feel dumb and intimidated all over again. So she dropped the ball. What she needed to do—and finally did do—was to tell him that he's the one who created the problem, and that she expected him to help her work it through. Their problem went much deeper than the word stupid. Her father is and was extremely neglectful and abusive. She had to do a more total confrontation with him about his past behaviors. She had to ask him to stop criticizing her and to treat her more like the intelligent adult she is today. She had to let him know that as long as he continued his "it's your problem" attitude, she wasn't interested in having contact with him.

Once she confronted her father and showed him that she believed in herself and felt as good as or better than he is, she was able to give up her obsession for Eric and other men like him. She has since met a warm, loving man and is now building a healthy relationship with him.

"I Don't Want to Be Close to My Parents"

This was Lana's excuse to avoid the confrontation with her father. Clients like Lana who have repressed their anger for years are often the most resistant to confronting their parents. It's taken a long time for them to repress their anger sufficiently, and they really believe that their parents are not affecting them anymore. They'll say, "I no longer let mom get on my nerves. She lives a thousand miles away, and I just put up with her." Or, "My dad and I are pleasant to each other, and I don't want any more than that." Their parents are out of their lives and they like it that way. This behavior is emotionally avoidant and, like Lana, these women will remain avoidant in their relationships with men if they do not work out their problem with their parents.

When we are not and cannot be our real selves with our parents, deep inside we believe that being our real selves is not okay. Women afraid of intimacy use "I don't want a relationship anyway" as an excuse, because they fear closeness and love as much as they fear harm. And to those afraid of intimacy, closeness and harm often mean the same thing. It's very important that they work these issues through with their parents so they can create and maintain true intimacy with others in their lives.

"You Don't Know My Parents"

Over and over I hear, "But you don't know my mom/dad!" Each person thinks her parents are worse than any others—more intimidating, more closed, more critical, even more pathetic.

Lana and Barbara both said this about their fathers. Barbara's father was truly and admittedly a con artist. He was extremely controlling, overpowering, manipulative, and critical—even in my office and even to me.

I could see why Barbara had trouble confronting him on her own. It took both of us confronting him at once for him to back down. He would give some ground and then ten minutes later pick up where he had left off, as if he hadn't heard a word we had been saying. We worked together four to five hours over a two-day period, and he still didn't "get it" until Barbara finally screamed at him on the phone a few weeks later. She told him he was acting abusively again and threatened to stop talking to him altogether if he continued to do so. He finally changed.

"I Can't!"

Many of my clients get to the point of confronting their parents and move no further. They seem paralyzed with fear. The fear is understandable, but the longer they procrastinate, the worse it gets. There are several ways to get around the fear. First, try to make yourself start by writing a confrontation letter. Just putting down words will help you. Remember that no one can *make you* mail it. Second, talk to others who will give you their support.

The third way to overcome your fear is to have the confrontation in your therapist's office. But if you do, be sure that your therapist really supports what you are doing, is strong enough to handle your parents, and won't allow your parents to psychologically abuse you while you're there.

You Need to Confront Your Parents Until, and Unless,

- You no longer edit your conversations around them.
- You do not allow them to criticize or judge you.
- You feel loved, accepted, and respected by them.
- You do not feel the need to keep secrets from them.
- You no longer feel obligated to call them, see them, or do things for them.
- You no longer feel like a child (or parent, if you've reversed roles) around them.
- You no longer think their past criticisms of you are true.
- You no longer lean on them for emotional or financial support.
- You've expressed your resentments from childhood to them.

- You can express your full range of emotions to them—from tears to rage.
- You have worked through the blame and can now take charge of your life.
- They treat you the way you want to be treated.

Preparing for the Confrontation

The most successful confrontation with your parents is one in which they understand and accept your feelings, are sorry for what they did, and, as Lana's father did, agree to treat you differently in the future. But you can have a successful confrontation even if you don't get a positive response from them. What's important is what happens inside of you as you confront your parents, and that you have the courage to stand up to them. That is the real victory.

Find the Crack in Their Armor

Most of us don't get close enough to our parents to know that they feel as insecure as we do. We've learned to look up to them, respect them, and allow them their secrets. The problem is that their secrets make us believe they are perfect and we are not. Their secrets make us fear that our perceptions of events are wrong. When we say that we saw mom with a man, but she says it's not true we fear we're crazy. Our parents hide behind masks of confidence, we believe them, and feel intimidated.

Your parents are locking you out and keeping you from seeing their humanness because they think they have to be ''strong'' for you. They don't understand that sharing their humanness is the only thing that can help raise your self-esteem and connect you to them. It's the only thing that can help you accept your own imperfections and make you feel loved. When they aren't real with you, they end up losing the one thing they fear losing the most—your love.

You must talk to your parents and dig for information before you can realize that they have the same human imperfections they criticize you for. Don't let your parents get away with pretending that their lives are perfect or that their teachings worked for them. They might say that their lives are good, that they have no regrets. But remember, most of them had goals to simply ''get by.'' My mother used to say that sacrificing for a husband and children was the right way to live. She always called me selfish. I pointed out that it was her selflessness that not only allowed dad to treat her so badly, but which also made me more selfish. Now she tells me how smart I am to not be married not have children and not follow in her pattern.

As you ask questions of your parents, be ready to see and hear information that may make you uncomfortable. Also, be ready to take your parents off their pedestals, leaving you with no one to look up to—except yourself. Discovering their flaws is extremely painful, scary, and difficult, but it must be done for you to become your own person.

Take a Realistic Look at Your Parents

Ask yourself these questions:

1. Have my parents' lives been perfect? Would I choose to live my life just like theirs?
2. Have their values worked for them? If they followed ideas like "Turn the other cheek," didn't they often get stepped on? If they were aggressive go-getters, don't the emotional and family sacrifices they made seem too costly to me?
3. Don't both mom and dad have regrets about their lives? What fantasies have they left unfulfilled?
4. Why should I let my parents' evaluation of life and of me act as the guide to live my life by? Which of their beliefs are valid for me and which aren't?
5. Why do I still pretend that I agree with them, or why do I rebel against them when I don't necessarily feel that way?
6. How often do my parents avoid dealing with problems? Isn't that wimpy instead of strong? Why do they do that? What are they afraid of?
7. How often are my parents just pretending to be happy? Why won't they be honest with me?

When you see yourself following in your mother or father's footsteps, talk to them about it. Ask them if they had their lives to live over again would they live them the same way. Challenge their answers. Ask them if they would choose the same path in life for you that they chose for themselves.

For instance, if you're dating a man who seems abusive to you, your mother may say she can see how bad he is for you and tell you not to put up with him. But did she put up with abuse in her relationship with your father? Where does she think you learned this behavior? Hold her accountable for her teachings so that you will see the pattern more clearly and be more likely not to follow it. Ask her to admit her mistakes and imperfections and to not expect any more from you than she did from herself. Ask the same of your father.

Once we see how afraid of life and emotions our parents really are, it's easier to see that we are stronger than they are because we will face up to these issues in our lives. Then we will realize that by confronting them we are doing them a favor. They are hiding behind masks of fear, and our confrontation may release them. Lana's father said that his relationship with his wife improved after Lana's confrontation with him.

We don't realize that deep down inside everyone desires closeness and intimacy. A client of mine recently accused her parents of not caring and her mother said, "I don't want to intrude in your life. You're entitled to your privacy, and I promised myself never to interfere in your life like my parents interfered in mine." My client's mother had passed down the opposite pattern from her own mother, but this pattern left my client feeling unloved. Most parents want to break out from behind their walls and connect as much as we do, but they're afraid of our rejection and we're afraid of theirs. We don't reach out and neither do they. Finding the crack in your parents' armor will help both them and you to be able to accept each other's humanness and to stop pretending to be something that none of you are. It will help everyone to be real with one another.

Take Baby Steps

You may want to practice confronting your parents with others, with a therapist, or at home alone. You could start with a present issue or with small issues. For instance, say that you will be visiting them soon, and you want to stay at a friend's house part of the time, but you know it will upset them. Practice confrontation by using the four steps of healthy communication to deal with this issue. You can start slowly by telling them that you want to stay with your friend two nights, but you aren't doing it to upset them. Ask them to understand. If they get angry, go deeper and tell them, "I feel upset that you're trying to make me feel guilty. I want you to hear and respect my desires. Will you? If you won't, I will stay a shorter time, not come home at all, etc." (whatever you decide).

It is possible to begin this confrontation stage by starting with someone besides your parents, if it seems easier. You can start with friends, lovers, bosses, or whomever to gain practice. However, you will move much faster if you begin with your parents. Once you handle your fear of them, no one else will intimidate you as much.

Make Clear Agreements

Making clear agreements means setting limits up front. It's important that we do this with our parents whenever possible. For instance, when we know how they might respond to us, we can make an agreement in advance. For instance, Barbara now tells her father, "I'll share this idea with you if you promise not to 'rain on my parade.'" She protects herself in advance by making this agreement.

In business, we make clear agreements all the time—I give you this, and you give me that in exchange. But somehow in our personal relationships, we fail to do this. Women are especially guilty of giving, giving, and giving and then saying, "Why didn't I get anything back?" Parents often do the same with their children, and then resent them. If we let someone know what we expect up front, he can warn us if he doesn't plan to give it to us. Then we can make a better decision.

In any negotiation, both parties must communicate clearly. They must state what they feel, want, and what they will do if they don't get it.

Sometimes a man will take us out to an expensive dinner and, even though it is unspoken, expect sex in return. I've often said to a man, "Sure, I'll go out to dinner with you as long as you know not to expect sex at the end of the night." Then there is no obligation. He can withdraw the invitation or take me out with no expectations. Expectations left unspoken are the reason for most fights.

When clear agreements are made early in a relationship, those relationships are more likely to be successful. Any issues with your parents from the past or in the present that you resent need to be resolved and new clear agreements made.

Identify Your Accusations

You must prepare this confrontation as well as you would prepare for a court case that you are determined to win.

1. Start by making a list of all the injustices caused to you by your family. Go back to your journal and review your notes from previous chapters, especially "Understanding Why You Are the Way You Are." The list can consist of the main issues you have to deal with and/or small incidents that have caused you great pain.
2. Then think about and list the values they still push on you that have harmed you so far in your life.
3. Tie in your present problems to these incidents and teachings.
4. Then write a first draft of the confrontation letter; do not worry about organization. Let it flow and include everything you can think of. Make this draft as vicious as you can make it to purge as much of your anger as you can.
5. Finally, write a final confrontation letter you can live with. Make it more direct, but don't leave any major points out.

Actualizing the Confrontation

Many clients prefer to do the initial confrontation verbally, but I usually recommend the first confrontation be by letter. You can get your grievances out all at once and your parents are less likely to intimidate you or stop you in your tracks in a letter.

I have found that those clients who insist on an initial verbal confrontation are often setting themselves up to fail. They tell me, "You don't know my parents; they'll never get it." Then they confront, are shot down within the first few minutes, come back, and say, "See, I told you it wouldn't work!"

Five Steps of Confrontation

You have learned the four steps of healthy communication. For confrontation, we simply need to insert an extra step—"This is how what you did to me has, and is, affecting my life."

FIVE STEPS OF CONFRONTATION*

1. I feel/felt hurt and angry when you _____.
   (You probably have many feelings and issues to bring up under this first step).
2. This is how it affected, and is still affecting, my life.
3. This is what I want from you now.
4. Will you give it to me?
5. If not, this is what I'll do if I don't get it from you.

Setting Limits

In your confrontation, setting limits about what you will and won't accept is key to not being victimized by your parents. When we tried as children to set limits regarding the way our parents treated us, they often said, "Who do you think you are?" We were not able to set limits since we had no other options. We didn't have the power to say, "I won't let you treat me that way!" But as adults, we do.

Think about how your parents overstep their boundaries with you. Are they critical? Judgmental? Do they pay too much attention to how you look? Does your mother clean your house without your permission? Do they go through your things? Do they come over without calling? Begin to develop new ground rules with them. By setting limits with our parents about how they can and *cannot* treat us, we will begin to be able to do it with others. Our parents, of course, also have the right to set limits with us.

Take an Emotionally Aggressive Stance

Many clients work on their confrontation and present it, but it has no effect at all because they take an intellectual approach instead of an emotional one. To do it right, it cannot be a logical presentation. We must be completely emotional and not be more concerned about our parents' feelings than our own. We must behave aggressively and not be afraid to show our full range of emotions—anger, hurt, sadness, fear, and frustration.

*(These five steps also work when confronting others besides parents.)

Your normal reaction around your parents is probably to follow their instructions and submit to them or to rebel. If you confront them unemotionally, you're playing by their rules. If you do this now, you can't possibly win. When your parents tell you that they "don't want to hear it" or begin attacking you, you must cross over the line of calmly and intelligently talking to them and become aggressive. You may need to say something like, "Sure, do what you always do, shut me out and avoid the problem! Not this time! I'm not stopping. And if you throw me out, I won't be back until and unless we finish this conversation." When Barbara's father called her stupid in my office, I modeled aggressive behavior for her to shut him up. I said, "And you're the smart, together one? You've admitted you've ripped people off to get where you are today, and you've been through five marriages, yet you call *her* stupid?" He backed down each time I became aggressive. By the time he left my office, he not only respected me but couldn't stop telling me how "taken" with me he was.

Abusive people like to be "put in their place," but few people are able to put them there. They respect only those who do. Barbara was able to do it with her father after watching me.

Those of us who have felt victimized have a difficult time defending ourselves, much less aggressively attacking our victimizers. But it's not until we are able to cross over this line and take the risk of showing enough intense anger to make a counterattack that most of us can break out of the victim mode and successfully get through to our parents. I am not talking about sarcastic jabs or anger in the heat of passion. I mean delivering a clear, direct picture of how you see your parents and their faults without backing down. You must equalize the relationship by showing your parents that their lives are no more perfect than yours, that they have their own problems and insecurities, that their teachings have not even worked for them, and that you will no longer allow them to be the authority over how you should live your life. Until and unless you are ready to go this far, you will fail in the confrontation with your parents.

If you want, you can begin your confrontation in a warm, loving way, reminding your parents that you love them and are trying to improve the relationship, but if this doesn't work—and it most often doesn't because they won't give up their power easily—

you must be prepared to attack them to break down their defenses. This is a war, and your self-esteem is at stake.

Identify What You Need/Want From Your Parents

In your confrontation, you need to tell your parents what you want. Many clients say, "I don't want *anything* from my parents," or, "I don't know what I want from them." Here are basics that most of us need/want from our parents, though you will also have your own particular "wants."

1. Unhook the Rejection

The rejection from our parents has damaged our self-esteem and caused us to choose relationships with people who will hurt and reject us as they did. To release ourselves from this negative spiral, we need our parents to unhook us from their rejection.

Tell your parents not only what you *don't* want, but also what you *do* want from them. What most of us want is for them to finally tell us:

> "I don't think you're bad, or stupid, or ugly. When I called you that, it was my problem, not yours. There's nothing wrong with you as you are. I was insecure. I was angry at the world. I took it out on you. I shouldn't have. And I'm really sorry. I don't want to hurt you, and if there's anything I'm doing now to hurt you, let me know what it is and I will stop it. I love you and always have and will do whatever is necessary to be sure you know that from now on."

2. Vulnerability

We need our parents to show us their weaknesses so that we can know they are human and not any better than we are. We need them to be honest about their fears. We need to hear stories of their childhoods and their own struggles in growing up.

3. Emotional Honesty

We need our parents to tell us how they really feel about us and their relationship with us. We need them to communicate their concerns, but in a supportive, nonjudgmental way. Saying, "I feel

concerned and upset when you work yourself to the point of ex-
haustion,'' is more helpful than, ''You shouldn't work so hard.''
We need them to treat us with the same respect they would give
a friend.

4. Support and Encouragement to Take Risks
Failure is something our parents can't protect us from. We need
them to realize this and to encourage us to try new things, even
if we might fail. Risking, failing, and learning from mistakes is
how we will improve our self-esteem and learn to trust
ourselves.

5. Open Communication
When we share our negative feelings with our parents, we need
them to listen and encourage our expression of feelings. We need
them to share their thoughts and feelings with us. We also need
to hear them tell us they're sorry if they hurt us, explain why
they acted the way they did, and ask if there is anything we want
them to do to make it up to us.

6. Unconditional Love
We need them to let us know that they love us no matter what,
even if they don't like what we do. We need them to tell us that
our imperfections and/or mistakes don't make us unlovable any
more than theirs make them unlovable. When we no longer feel
their control, the resentment will be gone, and we can love them
for who they are as well.

Write Your Letter and Follow Through

Using the information you've learned so far in this chapter, write
out the final draft of your letter. At the end, either instruct your
parents to call you when they're ready to deal with it (but be
prepared to wait a long time—they'll probably wait until they
think you're ''over'' your problem), or tell them you will follow
up with a call or visit in a week or so. Mail the letter. Then don't
let them off the hook the next time you talk to them, or you will
be making a fool of yourself by backing down.

Remember that when your parents do contact you, they may
have some counter complaints against you. Do not let them be

abusive to you, but allow them to express their feelings if they will "own" them (i.e., by saying "I feel _____ when you _____ "). After one of my many confrontations with my father, he called and said, "I've got a few things I'm angry at you about too, like the time you took your mother to a lawyer to divorce me." I had to accept his anger and tell him I was sorry for hurting him—which I was.

It can help to let your parents know that they, too, will get something out of cleaning up their relationship with you. You will be able to be a warm, loving daughter once you are rid of your anger. They will be able to ask for the same respect from you that you are asking for from them. Later on you will all be able to enjoy visits together more and will feel closer and less lonely.

Remember that a confrontation doesn't have to be perfect, and if it doesn't go well the first time, you can have more than one try. Also, if you feel that you hurt your parents too much, you can clean it up by apologizing for their pain, but don't take back your comments. Don't be afraid to take the risk. It can change your life.

Alicia's Confrontation

Alicia covered four of the five steps of confrontation in her letter to her mother. She saved the last one, "If not . . . ", for a confrontation with her in my office. Her letter is excerpted here.

> Dear Mom:
> There are things you have done, and still do, to me that really get me down. I'm tired of being labeled the "crazy" one or the one with all the problems because I'm emotional and feel things so deeply. I'm tired of feeling like everything I do isn't good enough. It makes me angry because I try to please you, and it's never enough, and that leaves me feeling inadequate and depressed. Being thin, wearing makeup, and having a clean house does not guarantee me a happy life, husband, and kids.
> I'm always afraid to say anything to you because I don't want to hurt your feelings. I don't want you to get angry at me or criticize me. I get afraid that if I really am myself with you, you'll put me down.

I need you to understand that what happened to me in the past is still affecting me. I look for approval from everybody—still trying to get yours and Dad's. I try to please everybody in the hopes that if I do enough, people will love me and accept me. I'm so afraid of rejection and abandonment that I'll do anything to keep a man around who's not good for me. I think part of the reason I haven't married is because I didn't want to take orders from a man and do everything he wanted me to do, like you did with dad. The way I saw it was that men had all the rights and power, and women were just there to support them. I feel stifled in other relationships too. I don't let people see the whole me.

I need you, but not in the way you think. You are the only mother I will ever have. I can't replace you. I'd like you to see and appreciate the good parts of me—the generosity, the kindness, the caring and compassion, the warmth, the humor. You don't seem to value those qualities in me and that hurts.

I've questioned why I can't have a healthy relationship with a man. There are many reasons, but one of the most important is that I never had a healthy relationship with anybody in my family. I would really like to have a good, solid, loving, and fun relationship with you. I would like to be accepted for who I am, warts and all. I wish appearance didn't matter *so* much in this family and in this society.

I want you to be supportive and understanding at *all* times. At least try to understand my fears, loneliness, and sadness. Do you think you can try to like me for just being me, because I'm worn out trying to be something I'm not.

I want you to come out here and work this through with me in my therapist's office. Will you?
Love,
Alicia

Her mother did come to my office and they began to work it through, although Alicia's confrontation didn't work quite as well as Lana's.

Parental Rebuttals

"You're Crazy"

If we come from a dysfunctional family, our parents are basically psychologically unaware. And most parents want to stay that way, because they are experts at denying their feelings. When presented with our angry feelings toward them, their normal response is "You're crazy! You're overreacting!"

Usually, our parents will tell us that what we say happened to us in our childhoods is absolutely not true. They *did* have a different perspective than we did—we can give them that. When they criticized us about the way we looked, they say that they meant no harm and were doing it "for our own good." They may not have meant harm, but we still feel pain from it and need to express the pain. They've blocked out these negative memories so that they can function more effectively; they don't want to believe that they hurt us.

"After All We've Done For You"

"How could you say these things to us after all we've done for you?" All parents want to think of themselves as good parents, so they only remember the good things they did for us—the food they put on the table, the bicycle they bought us at Christmas, the time they sacrificed to buy new clothing for us. They remember the "things" they gave us and think that should make up for the way they treated us. What mom doesn't, and won't, remember is how many times she took her anger out on us, when she was really angry at dad. Dad won't remember how he overprotected us from boys because of what he did to girls in his youth. Neither will remember how they called us stupid when we accidentally spilled a glass of milk.

But they didn't know how we felt. They really didn't know that they hurt us. We didn't tell them. We couldn't. We couldn't take the risk of losing their love, their protection, and their approval. If we ever tried to tell them, they said, "You shouldn't feel like that!" We were made to feel bad, wrong, and/or crazy for our feelings and who we were.

Be ready for their comebacks and don't get into a power struggle. Instead, tell them that these are your feelings and perceptions, and you expect them to listen to them and respect them.

"I Have the Right to Judge"

When I confronted my father, I told him I didn't need his criticism and judgment anymore. I wanted his support instead. He replied, "What? You want me to lie and pretend I think something's a good idea when it's not?! Besides, I'm your father and it's my duty to try and guide you to do the right thing. It's the way I show you my love, and it's my right as a father."

Many parents believe it's their responsibility and God-given right to tell us how to live our lives—even when we are adults. Let them know you need them to be your friend, not your parent, and that you will accept nothing else.

Confronting Our Fathers

Our fathers impacted us in very special ways. They were the first males in our lives.

What Our Fathers Did

· Never let us know them, because they hid their emotions.
· Faked strength, leading us to believe that men can actually take better care of us than we can take care of ourselves.
· Taught us to have low expectations of men.
· Taught us that intimacy means being controlled.
· Taught us that men are insensitive, when they're really just afraid of their emotions.
· Set us up to search for men that don't exist—men as strong as we thought our fathers were.
· Either avoided or became too interested in our sexuality—sending us our first negative message about femininity.
· Overprotected us, which keeps us from risking and keeps us looking for someone else to take care of us.
· Taught us to fear men.

I decided to confront my father first, since it was him that I felt the most anger at and who I felt was affecting my relationships with men the most.

Before I dealt with my father, to me, you only let men into your life to overpower, criticize, judge, and tell you how to live. I couldn't see any reason why I would want to do that.

Most of our fathers don't have the first clue about how to communicate. They've been taught to protect, take care of, and control women and children. The idea of talking to us with the respect they would show a male friend is often incomprehensible to them. *But you can get through to them.* It's just that most of us never have had a role model or the courage to stand up to them ourselves. We've never let them know that we're insulted by the way they talk to us, and that it is no longer acceptable.

Most men have never had a female—any female—ever stand up to them, ever hold them accountable. Our mothers, in fact, taught us the opposite.

Hold Dad Accountable

Anne, thirty-four-years-old and divorced, recently stood up to her father against her mother's wishes. Since then, Anne and her father have developed a great relationship. Anne's mother is now jealous. To get even, she continually reminds her husband that he was a terrible father all those years and that he'll never make up for that. Anne's mother doesn't see that Anne did what she herself should have done years ago. She doesn't understand that Anne's confrontation caused her father to respect her and, therefore, improved their relationship. Guess who's next on Anne's confrontation list?

Demand Intimacy From Your Father

Tell him how you feel about the fact that he may have "provided" for you but was never emotionally there for you. Tell him it's not too late, and that you want him to be there now. You want to know about him—his weaknesses, problems, trials and tribulations. You want him to share his feelings about life with you—business, family, friends, politics. Ask him to stop taking care of you and treating you like a child, and to instead treat you like a friend—an adult friend. If you can develop an intimate partnership with your father—the most intimidating man in your life—you will not be easily intimidated by other men.

Creating intimacy with your father begins with demanding that he be emotionally honest about his life and his relationships. For instance, say, "Dad, if working that hard is the key to a good life, how come you don't seem happy, and why did mom end up leaving you?" Holding dad accountable includes asking him why he sent your brother to an expensive East Coast school instead of you. It includes asking him to share his fears and regrets in life.

Without this interchange, our fathers still hold power in the relationship, and we're likely to give power to the next man we meet. Once we break through our fathers' facades and see them as real people with the same needs, feelings, and fears as we have, we'll be able to hold other men accountable.

Tell your father that his old ways of treating you—judging and insulting you—are no longer acceptable. Let him know you love him but will not accept the relationship as it has been. Demand an equal relationship with him. When he says, "I'll never stop being your father," say, "Fine, but you can no longer *treat* me like a child. You must treat me with the same respect that you would give one of your friends. If not, I won't talk to you or spend time with you."

One letter or confrontation may not do it, but don't give up. Continue letters and discussions. Let him know when he's talking to you in a judgmental or insulting way. Ask him to stop it, or you will hang up or leave.

Sheri tried to explain to her father that she can never have a relationship with any man healthier than the one she has with him, and she asked him to work it out with her. Below are excerpts from her letter to him.

Dearest Daddy,

First of all I want you to know that the reason I have not visited you on my last two vacations is that I'm afraid of you. I'm afraid of relying on you and being emotionally abandoned by you again. Let me explain.

I remember a little girl who was adored by you. But as I grew older you were wrapped up in your own life, and I ran loose. I spent a lot of time alone and lonely for your love.

Our relationship has directly impacted my relationships with men. I want the attention of a man so bad that I become obsessed with him to the point I lose myself, and I stay in relationships that don't work. I'm now attracted to men who are emotionally unavailable to me, like you were. I always try to force a relationship, instead of allowing things to happen naturally. I cease to function when things don't happen my way. I call in sick to work, become reclusive, go into an emotional coma, and I lose sleep because I can't control or second-guess what a guy will do.

Because I feel I lost your love, I fear I'm not good enough to love. I'm ashamed of who I am, so I fear letting the real Sheri out for fear I'll be rejected. I settle instead for being needed and do things I said I would never do to try to win a man's love and approval.

I know some of the things I've said here are going to hurt, and I'm sorry—I'm not bringing all of these things up just to hurt you. I want and need you to come to me, to get to know me, to tell me I am important to you. When you make excuses to me about not coming to see me because of money and layovers, it hurts. It makes me feel unimportant. I am grateful that you are a hard worker and you were a good provider, but I feel I don't know you very well, and I want you to try to get to know me. We can't change the past, but we can become friends, can't we?
Love,
Sheri

Sheri's father had no idea she felt like that and he was eager to work out the relationship with her.

Unlike Sheri's father, who abandoned her, Alicia's father was overprotective. Now she longs to attach to a man like him, who will take care of her, although she knows she's smarter than most of the men she meets. Lana, as we know, had never gotten over her real father's abandonment, even though she had a warm, loving relationship with her stepfather. Peggy and Kay say they had perfectly normal relationships with their fathers but admit to never really knowing them. And both of their fathers treated their mothers in very degrading ways. Valerie's father was overly controlling and physically abusive, which taught her to fear men.

Vicki, a forty-year-old single woman who appears to have no interest in men, had quite a few problems dealing with her father. It was difficult to hold him accountable when they had hardly spoken since her mother's suicide. She finally wrote him a vicious letter, telling him how upset she was, not only about the way he had treated her, but especially the way he had treated her mom before her death. She got no response. Three months went by, and she did nothing. Then, with the help of my support group, she confronted her boss and an old boyfriend. She decided she might as well handle dad; after all, she was on a roll. Her father was in the middle of another divorce and had reached out to her under the guise of asking her to do some work for his business. It gave her the opportunity to say "Not until we resolve our personal problems." She asked him to meet in my office. He agreed.

During the session, Vicki and her father cleared up a lot of misconceptions. He explained his side, that he felt that Vicki's mother had turned her against him after their divorce. Though Vicki told him she *had* felt that it was all his fault, she now better understood his side. Vicki felt her father never loved her as much as he loved her sisters. He always gave them things, but not her. He said that he didn't think she needed anything. They realized how much alike they are. She pointed out that he always rewarded ineptness by rescuing the weak, and that he had done that with her mom, her sisters, and the younger woman who was now divorcing him and taking him to the cleaners. Vicki asked him why he didn't admire her strength. He said he'd never understood that he was rescuing. He felt that Vicki didn't need him and he didn't know how to relate to her. He had never seen her point of view before. He admitted that he used to think he was always right, but now he was "mellowing in his old age, and could try to understand her now." He asked, "Can I drop by your house for a cup of coffee sometime and just talk?" As they left, he was reminiscing about when he used to help put her hair in pigtails. He told her he was really glad they were doing this.

Confronting Our Mothers

As there are issues particular to our fathers, there are also some issues that are particular to our mothers.

How Our Mothers Contributed

· Didn't protect us from our fathers' criticisms, anger, etc.
· Kept emotional distance between us and our fathers, i.e., "Don't tell your father."

- Taught us "That's just the way men are" by never holding our fathers accountable.
- Taught us that women are weak, by allowing our fathers to control them.
- Taught us to fear men, because they were afraid.
- Taught us to sacrifice for and please men.
- Often depended on us for nurturance, instead of nurturing us.

Since Vicki confronted her father, she's now looking at her mother differently. Why was she so weak? Why did she take her father's abuse? Why wouldn't she get help? Vicki always took care of her mother, defended her against her father, and, after the divorce, let her mother live her life through her. Her mother was never really a mother to Vicki. She leaned on her instead of taking care of her. I asked Vicki to make a list of what a perfect mother would have been like. She said, "Protective and nurturing." I said, "Imagine being a little girl again. Don't you wish your mother would have said to her frightened little girl, 'Honey, don't be afraid. I'll take care of you. You're safe with me.'" Vicki cried and admitted that she never felt safe or nurtured as a child.

Many of us didn't feel nurtured by our mothers. Though they may have cooked and cleaned for us, many of them were so weak that they leaned on us more than they gave us support. When our fathers wouldn't or couldn't make them happy, many of them often tried to put that responsibility on us.

Lana's mother was jealous of her. She continually told Lana that she was spoiled and selfish, and reminded her of all she had sacrificed by raising her without her father's support. This worked to make Lana feel guilty. At the age of thirty-three, she still felt responsible for her mother's happiness. She was supporting her mother financially and emotionally by catering to her every need. Lana was appalled when she realized just how far her caretaking had gone when, after she was assigned a big account, her mother got excited and said, "Great, now I can live in the style I always felt I deserved." Lana realizes she's been so busy acting as a caretaker to her mother that she's had no time for relationships with men.

Hold Mom Accountable

Lana decided to confront her mother in person. She told her, "Yes, I am now selfish—in fact, in the past I've been too selfless, and I've decided to stop taking care of everyone else—including you!'' She cut off both her mother and her brother financially. She started worrying about her own happiness instead of her mother's. Lana's mother has learned her lesson and has become more nurturing with Lana. Their relationship has equalized.

This happened with my own mother. I told her, ''Mom, I want you to start being my mother for a change. I want you to ask how I'm doing, to remember who I'm dating, and ask about my life. I want you to show an interest in me.'' It was awkward for her at first because she was used to complaining to me about *her* life. I didn't realize at the time that I had been keeping her dependent on me and making her feel more inadequate by allowing her to lean on me while demanding nothing from her.

Stephanie had a different problem—her mother was cold and unemotional. Stephanie found herself becoming more and more like her mother, and it frightened her. She is a thirty-four-year-old attractive, bright woman from a wealthy background.

Stephanie's past was filled with family secrets. She exposed all of them and followed the five steps of healthy confrontation in an eighteen-page letter to her mother, which is excerpted here:

Dear Mom:
I want to tell you how I feel about many things in my life.

First and foremost, I feel sad. Sad because we never had a real family unit—one that was open and honest and shared true feelings.

I also feel a lot of anger and pity. Pity because of your narrow-mindedness, and anger because you are never honest and you've concealed secrets about your affairs from Dad for years. And secrets from me about my being adopted. We learned ''keep everything a secret. Support the game.'' We became afraid. We played the game. *Don't talk.* I learned quickly. I learned not to talk, and I learned not to trust.

I feel you don't respect me, because of the way you hide information from me and wouldn't tell me about my real father until my therapist forced you to.

Lastly, I feel hurt. Hurt that you never let me get close to you.

I want our relationship to be different than it is now, but I also want it to be different than it has ever been before. I want to have a one-on-one adult relationship with you, with equal respect shown to each other. I want you to appreciate me and my strengths. I want you to be caring in your thoughts, attitudes, and behavior. True caring. Caring about how I feel.

I want us to be a real family. *Real families don't act like ours!* Real families are honest with one another. Real families show true feelings and they communicate those feelings. Real families don't hide their problems and don't live a secret.

I have one more wish, but this is probably the most difficult for you. I want you to be a more vulnerable person and not in constant control. You would be so much softer and nicer to be with if you would show true emotions. Being vulnerable means crying when you're sad, laughing when you're happy, telling someone you feel angry when you're upset at them. Not accusing them or talking behind their backs, but telling them how you feel. Being vulnerable doesn't make you weak. On the contrary, it makes you strong because you become human and believable. That to me is strength.

Will you be open and honest with me and try to promote communication on an honest and feeling level? Will you try to treat all of us as equals and not play favorites or pit one against the other as you have done in the past? Will you promote the idea of us becoming a "real" family, through communication and genuine loving and care?

And—will you love me completely without qualifying that love? I want it that way, I wish it that way and, if not, it's easier to have nothing. I will just go on imagining. I will not have the superficial relationship we had in the past. It's time for everyone to grow.
With much love
Stephanie

Stephanie's high-society mother was shocked. Like Vicki, Stephanie received no response to her letter for months. Then her mother sent her a birthday card and present as if nothing had happened. Stephanie responded with a note thanking her for the present and card, but demanding a response to her letter. She still didn't hear from her. Later, when visiting her sister (who lives near her mother), she and her mother slowly and gradually began to talk, but Stephanie had to press the issue more than once.

Confronting Both Parents at Once

Valerie could see that she behaved with her husband, Ken, the same way she had always behaved with her father. Both men were extremely intimidating, and Valerie was afraid of them. When Ken was upset with her, she withdrew, just as she had done with her father when she was a child. In therapy, with my help, she stood up to Ken and told him how she really felt about his dominating, chauvinistic attitude. She told him that she was afraid of him, and that every time she would try to communicate with him, he acted like "It's my way or the highway." They were able to work out most of the issues in their marriage, but I told her that she wouldn't be able to maintain her power in the relationship if she didn't confront her father. Valerie disagreed and dropped out of therapy. A few months later, she returned.

She had regressed and lost power in her relationship with Ken. They were both behaving much like they had in the past. Again, I helped Valerie resolve issues with Ken. And once again I talked to her about confronting her father. This time she believed me but said she didn't have the courage to do it. She said she would confront him in her own time. For now, she felt she didn't need any more therapy because things were better with Ken. I insisted that she make an appointment each month with me, so I could check in and see if she had dealt with her father yet. Finally, after Valerie's brother almost committed suicide, and she knew that her parents had affected him as much as they had her, she wrote a letter to both of them. Her letter is excerpted here.

A letter to my Mother and Father:
I've never told you how it really hurts me that you virtually abandon Bill and me whenever we're hurting emotionally and need you to talk to and listen to us. You always put everything in terms of how it's hurting you—not how it's affecting either one of us.

I hate that I feel obligated to call you, yet you never call me. I spend hours listening to you lament about your illnesses, and you never ask about what I'm doing, let alone how I might be feeling.

I want to feel angry at all of this, but I feel mostly sadness and fear. I want our family to be more supportive and loving to one another, but I fear we never will, and that makes me sad.

I know that my lack of confidence, my low self-esteem, my fanatical perfectionism, and my rigid nature come from trying to prove myself, mostly to you, Dad. I was always trying to prove to you that you could be as proud of me as a daughter as you could have a firstborn son. As it turns out—and isn't it diabolic—you're just as distant—if not more so—from Bill as you are from me. Sometimes I remember how scared I always was to express myself to you. I could never express anger or disagreement! Boy, if you only knew how horribly that affected me throughout my marriage to Ken—I couldn't speak up to him—and I can't even tell you how scared I am in the world of business.

I've never felt like I have had a solid, supportive home base to turn to with either of you. I feel like you don't want to hear any of my problems—you say it's because you don't want to interfere. I don't buy that. I think you really don't care.

I'd like to get rid of worrying about how I talk to you, about the fact that we're not that close, about all the stuff that's way back there that affected how I turned out as an adult.

I am depressed and frustrated. I still try to please everyone. As I turned forty this year, I've had more sadness and depression than I want to have, and I'm ready now to grow above this stage. I want to find the thread of self-confidence and sureness, not go fat and thin whenever I begin doubting my self-worth and abilities. I will no longer let you badger me and make me feel like I should call more, do more, and be more responsible for keeping our family together.

I want you both to know how much I do love you deeply in my heart, and how much I want to know you now as people rather than just my parents.
*Valerie

Confrontation as a Way of Life

Once you confront your parents, you won't be as afraid to confront others. Many of us feel as unloved and abused by ex-husbands and old lovers who have hurt us as we do by our

*Not much changed in their relationship until she got angry and wrote a follow-up letter a year later.

parents. Siblings, relatives, bosses, even children—nearly anyone we come in contact with—have the power to victimize us and hold us back from feeling good enough about ourselves to become self-reliant. Go back to the list you made in Chapter Six of everyone who has abused you, and decide who you will confront next.

It's possible to get so energized by making confrontations that you start to look forward to being verbally attacked by others so you can use your new skills. Confrontation can and will become a way of life. At times in the future, it will be necessary to express anger, set limits, and let others know you will not allow them or anyone else to treat you badly. Without this skill, you will either be victimized on a regular basis or have to wear a macho shield as protection.

Confrontation, however, will become less necessary as your attitude changes from feeling victimized to feeling self-confident. A self-reliant woman will usually set limits in advance, so she'll seldom have to confront once she's cleaned up her present relationships. But when and if a situation calls for confrontation, she will have developed the know-how to use the skills of constructive confrontation.

Effective confrontation enables you to create and maintain high self-esteem and also enables others to maintain theirs. In addition, you will be increasing your self-respect, as well as gaining the respect of others.

The model you have learned in this chapter will enable you to set boundaries with men so that you will never again have to lose yourself when you love someone.

9

Step Seven:
**Complete Your Adolescence
Through Risk-Taking
and Experimenting**

Fifteen years ago, when I was living in St. Louis, I was deeply depressed. A male friend who was concerned about me asked, "If you could do anything in the world, what would you do?" My answer was, "Move to Aspen and be a ski bum." "Do it," he said. "I can't afford to," I replied. Knowing that I was severely depressed, he said, "You can't afford not to!"

I had become disillusioned with life at the age of twenty-seven. I had been through two long-term relationships—a three-year marriage and a three-year living together relationship. I had been through two unsatisfactory careers—teacher and school psychologist. I was living my life the way I thought I "should" live it and felt imprisoned by the world I had created. I had grown up (or so I thought), graduated from college, married, worked hard in my career, and awakened one day, wondering if this was all there is to life. I felt empty.

A few times in my past I had felt temporarily secure—for a while when I was married, and when I made tenure as a teacher—though I had seldom felt happy. Each time I arrived at what others considered security, I became bored and walked away—and everyone thought I was crazy. I began to wonder if they were right.

The risks I had taken up to then had been minimal—I had changed jobs or left a man. This time I decided to take a big risk and leave it all behind—friends, family, career, and the part of the country I grew up in. My friends, family, and coworkers told me I was just running from my problems. I told them they were wrong. I sold most of my belongings and left for Colorado.

I was crying hysterically—from both fear and exhilaration—as I drove that night on icy snow-covered roads to Aspen over Independence Pass. I was driving by myself in my loaded-down sports car at 11 P.M. No one in Aspen was awaiting my arrival, and no one in the world knew where I was. I felt very alone. I was scared to death. Independence Pass became symbolic for me as I rejected my old life and moved on to my new hedonistic lifestyle. I had no idea what was ahead.

I had with me my teacher-retirement fund of one thousand dollars and not another penny or any way to get more money (my family made it clear that they would not support my move to Aspen). What I didn't know was that I was about to experience the adolescence I missed during my teen years. Developmental theory says you have to crawl before you can walk. As stated in Chapter Four, you also have to complete the adolescent stage of life before you can be happy with who you are as an adult. I was about to do that.

Fear of Moving Forward

If you've worked through the program so far, you may feel somewhat lost at this point. You may feel frightened and vulnerable because you've given up your defenses and many of your dependencies. You may feel like you know what not to do, but not who you are or what you want. Although the most difficult step of the program is over—confronting your parents—deciding how you want your life to be has just begun.

You now have no excuse not to take charge of your life. You can no longer feel sorry for yourself or blame your parents. You can no longer expect someone else to make you happy. No one is holding you back now.

You must experiment with new ideas and interests and take the risks necessary to create a different life. The road of challenge lies ahead, and you must be willing to give up the rest of your dependencies and false securities.

If you know what you want in life and aren't trying to get it, then your fears are keeping you from it. If you don't know what you want, then you need to keep sorting and experimenting until you figure it out. Either way, it's time to move forward, experiment and experience new things, overcome your fears, sort out your values, and become the person you want to be.

No Vision of Self

Men were taught at an early age to visualize their future, whereas women were taught to have no vision of themselves in the adult world. Research on tennis and other sports shows that to be extremely successful, one must be able to visualize oneself as successful in that act. Sports psychologists stress, in fact, that a player sit and fantasize about playing a game well—and winning. Normal male development encourages men to see themselves as an expert in some area. Little girls are taught to look for a male expert to marry. When I told my father I wanted to go to college, he said, "I'm not paying for you to go away to college to find a husband. You can find one right here."

Create a Vision

Close your eyes and fantasize your life the way you'd want it to be if it were perfect. You can live anywhere you want to live—in a beach house, a ranch in the mountains, or a city high-rise. In your fantasy you make the kind of money you want, work at the perfect job—whether it's as a top executive at IBM or training horses on a farm. You are with the man of your dreams or with no man at all—whichever you prefer. Get a very clear picture. How are you dressed? Who are you with? What are you doing? Don't read further until you do this. Close your eyes and create your fantasy now.

Why aren't you living that fantasy? Many people believe that it's totally unrealistic to think they could ever have their fantasy come true, but it's not. Several of my fantasies have come true— including this book—and yours can too. Answer the following questions to move you closer to accomplishing your fantasies.

1. Are *you* holding yourself back? Why?
2. Are you letting a man, a parent, or a child hold you back?
3. Is following someone else's "shoulds" holding you back?
4. Why aren't you doing what you say is important to you?

5. Which parts of your present life do you love and not want to change?
6. Which parts of your life do you hate the most?
7. What are the main differences in your fantasy life and your real life?
8. What would you have to do to make your fantasy come true? Make a list.

Now that you have a better idea of where you want to be, you need to explore and experiment to make it all come true!

Assert Your Values

You began sorting your values in earlier chapters. Now it's time to stand up for the values that are important to you. You may have started standing up for them when you confronted your parents. Now stand up for your values by living them.

You may feel anxious or stressed by the idea of all the changes you need to make, and that's natural. Most people think that stress and anxiety come from things outside themselves. Too much work or too many life changes certainly create turmoil, but it is the inner turmoil that causes the stress. Inner turmoil usually comes from confusion between what you want to do and what you think you should do, or from trying to do both. You often can't please others and please yourself at the same time, so you must make a clear choice to please yourself, to have control over your life. It's time to set limits and say no to those who put "shoulds" on you, and to catch yourself from falling into the same old traps.

Don't let friends or family pressure you or make you feel bad about your choices and decisions. We're all entitled to get what we want out of life—according to our own values, not someone else's. Your main goal may be to make a million dollars. A friend may say he thinks you're being too materialistic or call you a yuppie or say you're not being humanitarian enough. He's entitled to live his life with those beliefs in mind but not to impose them on you. If he makes a derogatory comment to you that feels judgmental, don't let him get to you or make you feel bad. And don't try to be more humanitarian to please him. Instead, simply remind him that what's important to him isn't necessarily what's important to you, and that you want him to stop putting his values on you. Stand up for what you believe.

For instance, my client Karen, a thirty-year-old attorney, inherited a lot of money when her father died. She went out and bought tons of clothes, a Mercedes convertible, and a four-wheel drive vehicle. Then she traded in the Mercedes for a Jaguar. Brian, her boyfriend at the time, criticized her decisions and called her selfish. He said she should use the money to help others (I think he had himself in mind) or that she should at least save it. He made her feel wrong. He imposed his values on her. She came into my office asking if I thought she was being selfish. I said no. I told her I thought she deserved the money and had a right to spend it however she pleased. Her father had criticized her all her life; at least he left her money to have fun with after he died.

Brian was married. I questioned her about *his* values. Who was *he* to make a judgment about what was right or wrong for her, when he had his own life so screwed up? She agreed with me and went back and told him so. She learned how to stand up for her values, tell him what she believed, and let him know he had no right to impose his values on her.

There is no right and wrong in what we do, except when we cross over the line and intentionally harm someone else. You may feel that it's wrong to spend money on clothes and dining out when you have tons of bills to pay. Or you may believe that enjoying life comes first. As long as you deal with the consequences of spending the money, it is not wrong for you. And no one has the right to tell you that it is.

Accepting Change in Ourselves

Psychologist Abraham Maslow, in his "Hierarchy of Needs,"[1] says that our values change as our needs change. He says that we can't worry about love when we don't have food on the table, or a roof over our heads; we can't worry about self-actualization when we don't feel loved. That's why many of us are not "self-actualized" and don't have our lives as we want them to be. After dealing with love and approval issues with your parents, you should now be ready to move closer toward self-actualization.

Some people think that they should be one way, remaining consistent in their beliefs and values throughout their lives. But this isn't natural. As we grow both emotionally and physically, our needs and desires change. As we achieve one thing, we want another. We always want "more" and we always will. If you're poor, you probably want money. If you have money, you may want friends. If you have friends, you may want a better job. If you have a good job, you'll probably want nicer clothes, etc. This is normal.

Our values and priorities change as we grow older. For teenagers, a social life is quite important. Later—with responsibility for a family—jobs, more money, and a home naturally become more important. As adults, we often fight change. Midlife crises are often caused by a change in our priorities after we've lived our lives too responsibly for too long. Social life, fun, excitement, and missed opportunities often emerge again as priorities when we've lived our life too long by someone else's "shoulds."

Life is a process of growth and change, of continually moving from one thing to the other, of learning and changing with the new information. To change with life, we need to ask ourselves regularly how we feel, what we want, and what we need to do to get it. Then we need to follow our desires regardless of who tries to hold us back.

Change is both scary and exciting. And it can even be sad. We must give up the old part of ourselves to move forward and become stronger. Parents often don't want their children to grow up. The rich have trouble when they become poor. Most of us have trouble growing old. When I moved to Denver, I had trouble giving up my identity as an Aspen ski bum, which had made me feel special. We often have to mourn the loss of our old selves before we can move forward and find our new selves.

There comes a time when the old ways aren't working anymore, and we're holding onto them simply because we feel secure in them. Change gives us a new opportunity to get what we want in life.

Daring to Be Different

Others in our lives want to keep us where they are psychologically. When we start to grow, they feel threatened and abandoned. When I first started dating Alan, my girlfriends spent a lot of time trying to remind me that men were real jerks. They were uncomfortable seeing me happy with a man when they weren't. His friends were even worse. They were in bad marriages, as he used to be. The happier he became, the more they told him to watch out for me, because I probably had something up my sleeve. The more they tried to break us up, the more we bonded against them. Our motto became "We aren't going to let anyone mess up this deal."

As you change and grow, your friends and family and other members of society will not make it easy on you. They will say things like, "That's not like you! I thought you had it more together than that! I think you're really losing it!" You have to use their comments to clarify the new you instead of letting them hold you back. Tell them, "I'm not losing it, I'm just finally learning to take care of myself and go after what I want. And it feels great!"

Most of our society is *outer-directed*. Most people are concerned about what others think of them, about what others believe is right, and about where they "should" be in their growth and development, e.g., "I should be mature enough to handle that!" *To become a self-reliant woman, you must be inner-directed.*

In his article "Changing Values: The New Emphasis on Self-Actualization," Joseph T. Plummer says,

> Tradition-directed groups value security and sustenance. By nature, they are static societies that change very little. Similarly, outer-directed groups value belonging and success, looking to others for ideas about what is acceptable behavior. Status within outer-directed societies is obtained by following the rules and owning the material goods that society acknowledges as valuable.
>
> Inner-directed individuals, while aware of the expectations of others, often decide not to behave in accordance with those expectations. They value personal expression and creativity and strive for self-actualization. Inner harmony is often more important to them than social harmony. These individuals often have ideas about how to improve the well-being not only of themselves, but of others.[2]

The inner-directed people Plummer speaks of are those who have the courage to be different, to go against society and its beliefs, to follow their own feelings and ideas, and to stand up for those beliefs and ideas.

If you decide you want to work on a boat for the rest of your life or live among the homeless, you have the right to do so. Don't let anyone talk you out of it. My parents told me that I was crazy—after all my education—to give up a good job as a school psychologist to be a ski bum in Aspen. I could understand their line of reasoning, but I wasn't happy as a school psychologist in St. Louis. When I told them that, they said "happy" wasn't the issue. How the hell was I going to support myself? I said, "I don't know, but I'll figure it out. That's not what's important to me. Happiness is!" When other people aren't happy, they think that's normal and that you don't have the right to expect to be happy either. They'll tell you how they've suffered and how you should expect to do the same.

Barbara told me that no matter what she was doing, her father always tried to "rain on her parade," and she didn't understand why he would do that. During his visit in my office when Barbara and I confronted him, he criticized her for swimming, working out every day at the club and skiing on weekends. He said, "It must be nice! I don't get to do that!" He said that instead, he had to work hard and felt that's what Barbara "should" be doing. He admitted that he was jealous. His jealousy tried to keep her from enjoying her life. Barbara and I told him that maybe he should change his life; instead of making money such a priority, he should learn to have more fun. Nobody was making him "suffer" instead of enjoying his life. Valuing money vs. fun is not the issue—following your own beliefs is. Barbara was being different from her father. She valued fun more than making money and was able to "dare to be different."

To respect ourselves, we *must* match our actions to what we say we believe. We must do this—take a stand—for ourselves and our identities. Most people fear alienation from others when they take a stand that's different from the norm. In taking a stand, we give up pleasing others. You must choose between being true to yourself or staying addicted to others' love and approval. Alienation from yourself is, in the long run, a far worse alternative than alienation from others.

Completing Adolescence

Though I didn't grow up rich, my life had been relatively easy. I had graduated from college and was hired as a teacher at the first job I applied for. I had always had men seeking out my company. I made enough money to pay my bills. Then, at twenty-seven, everything changed. Nothing seemed easy anymore. I was no longer following the script and I felt lost. I had no job, no money, no boyfriend—and a lot to learn.

I was to find that in this new situation, my *old* values no longer worked. I had always prided myself in keeping my word, especially with job commitments. In Aspen I began to take jobs and quit them within two weeks. I had ten different jobs, hated them, and quit them all in the first four months I was there. I worked as everything from a night dispatcher at the Aspen Police Department to a nude model for sketching classes. At the Aspen Police Department, I was required to sign a two-year commitment. Again, two weeks later I decided to quit. I was sick of working nights, had caught a cold, and the hours were messing up my skiing. I went in to quit and the police chief reminded me of the commitment I had signed. I found myself behaving like a rebellious, cocky teenager and saying, "So what are you going to do to me? Force me to come in? Sue me?" They did nothing, of course. In fact, a year later I was dating the same police chief who had tried to pressure me into staying.

I was testing my values the way I should have at sixteen. I learned that I had to do what was best for me and face any consequences. This is not what "good little girls" are taught to do.

In the past I would have worried about my boss's approval and whether I was a "bad" person for what I was doing. I would have been more concerned about what others would think and what was right or wrong from their viewpoints than worry about myself. But not this time. Besides, Aspen has its own hedonistic value system. The town's motto seems to be "Do whatever you want, just don't intentionally hurt others." That was very freeing for me.

Besides work and commitment values, I also experimented with sex. I had decided to remain a virgin until I married. My sex life with my husband was terrible, and I had regretted my decision. Like most women, I usually thought I was in love every time I had sex. I began to envy the fact that men seemed to be able to walk away after sex without a second thought. I decided to learn to separate love and sex myself, so I would stop giving men power over me because of sex. I made up for lost time and went from having numerous one-night stands to three sexual experiences in one day. That didn't make me feel any better.

Next I decided to experiment with alcohol and drugs. My family didn't drink much, and neither had I. But now I began to drink every night. I also tried marijuana, cocaine, and LSD.

I rebelled in every way. I stopped wearing makeup, gained weight, let my hair frizz, and wore tattered jeans. I went to nude Valentine parties and began wearing fresh flowers in my hair every day. It wasn't the sixties, but it certainly felt like it to me! It was *my* "hippie days."

I tested almost every value that I'd ever been taught. I finally got tired of drinking, always looking for the next man, and having no substance to my life. I started getting clearer about who I was and what I wanted to do . . . and this wasn't it.

I began to develop a new fantasy. I wanted to be thin and attractive again, to have a business that made money, to enjoy the excitement and challenge of a city, to have a beautiful home in the country, to *actually* date several interesting men at once (in Aspen, we seldom had real dates, we just hung-out together), and to write a book. I was ready for the next chapter of my life.

"Go for It!"

I'm standing at the top of a difficult run on Aspen Mountain and my ski instructor yells, "Go for it!" I feel paralyzed by fear and yell back to him, "I can't!" He yells, "What other options do you have?" I'm panicked. I don't move. He yells again. I consider sliding down on my behind. Finally I turn the skis and make it to the bottom. I'm relieved.

All my life I'd been taught, "Don't fall," "Don't hurt yourself," "Be careful." My parents had taught me not to take risks because I might get hurt.

Parents often try to keep their children (even adult children) from taking any risks they're afraid to take themselves. Sometimes parents don't want their children to grow beyond them. More often they're holding us back because *our* failures hurt them as much or more than their own do. In talking with Barbara's dad, he said this was certainly true for him. They can't stand to watch us fall down, because they feel responsible when we do. But if we don't learn that it's okay to fall and pick ourselves back up, we never grow and are never able to take control of our lives. This is especially true for women. We learn that someone will always be there to pick us up, and we don't have to do it ourselves.

We are taught to opt for security ("Save your money, you never know what might happen"). We want our parents and others to say to us, "I know you can handle it," but they don't. They fill us with fear—fear of being broke and starving, fear of rejection, fear of looking stupid, fear of finding out how incompetent we really are, fear that we will be failures. Fear paralyzes us so that we can't take charge. When we don't take charge, our greatest fears end up coming true.

In one of my many letters to my father, I confronted him about his teachings on risk-taking. I wrote, "Just because you've been afraid to take risks all your life, you shouldn't try to hold me back. When I was in high school, you tried to hold me back by telling me not to go away to college. Then when I divorced, you told me that was a mistake. You tried to keep me from quitting my job and moving to Colorado. You wanted me to be like you—stuck in the same job and small town for the rest of my life. Think about what my life would be like if I had followed your advice . . .and you tell me you're supportive. That's not support!"

Once Stephanie had confronted her high-society mother, she realized how much her father had affected her. His values were her values. She had followed in his footsteps in many ways, especially trying to develop a good business mind. However, after several years as a manager in one of her father's companies she began to reject the corporate world and adopted a more hedonistic life-style. She rebelled against her prejudiced upper-class background and moved in with a black artist for a time, adopting his values. However, that wore thin as she became frustrated with his pauper-like life-style. Next, she had an affair with a wealthy playboy who became the authority in her life. As she changed men, she changed priorities and values, continually switching one set of values for another. When you asked Stephanie what she wanted in her life, her answer reflected whatever the present man in her life wanted. She trusted men more than herself.

Once she realized this, she decided she needed to finish her own adolescence. She pulled away from men altogether, moved to Maui, and began to examine her own values. She tried a variety of jobs. She took a long-awaited trip to Europe. She had dreamed of becoming a country and western singer, so she signed up for voice lessons. She began to experiment and try to decide who she was and what *she* really wanted from life.

Risk-Taking

Many women, especially married ones, are bored and don't know what to do. They blame their husbands and their jobs, when the real reason for their boredom is that they're afraid to take risks. When I ask these women to fantasize their lives as perfect, their fantasies are always extremely different than their present realities. Sometimes they're living in another part of the world, sometimes they're a famous artist. I ask them to at least take the risk of sharing their fantasies with their husbands or other people in their lives that they believe are holding them back. That way they can at least verify whether others really are holding them back, or whether they are just paralyzed by fear as I was on the ski slopes.

Which Risks to Take

If you are married, list all of the characteristics that your husband has that you like or admire. If you are single, do the same with your "fantasy man." Make the list as long as you want and prioritize the qualities you list. Do this now before reading on.

As I said in an earlier chapter, the major reason women lose their identities with men is that they often choose men they think make up for their own personal inadequacies. Is this true in your relationships?

Go back and look at all of his qualities. Put a check mark by those qualities that you also have yourself. For instance, if you want him to be attractive, are you attractive? Do the same with the other qualities. Those qualities with no check marks are the areas in which you are dependent on him or want to be. You may think, "Since he makes a lot of money, I don't have to worry about making money." Or, "He's smart, so I can always ask him how to handle a problem." These are the areas that you must work on and develop within yourself, the areas in which you must take risks.

The greater he has to be in areas that you are weak in, the more insecurities you have about who you are. We usually get along best with, and can be the closest to, people who are most like us—those who have similar interests, believe the way we do, have similar personalities, have the same financial and class status, have similar strengths and levels of career expectations. If you don't take risks and grow in your weak areas, you will easily give your power away to someone you believe is stronger than you, rather than finding an equal partner. Until you work on your weak areas, you are half of an addictive relationship waiting to happen.

ARE YOU A RISK-TAKER?

The following quiz may help you decide. Be sure to be honest, as the risk-taking answers are obvious.

1. If you inherited $10,000, you would
   a) use it to start that business you've always wanted.
   b) save it.
   c) neither.
2. If you're at a party and see an attractive member of the opposite sex, you would
   a) find a way to meet him.
   b) wait to see if he approaches you.
   c) neither.
3. In exercise, you
   a) push yourself to try new sports or exercise programs.
   b) do the same exercises over and over again.
   c) never exercise.
4. You know a male coworker with a lower position than yours is making more money than you, you
   a) confront your boss, asking for a raise.
   b) try to prove your worth to him so he'll give you a raise.
   c) quit your job and file charges of discrimination.
5. When a close friend says something that hurts you, you
   a) let him or her know it hurt you.
   b) ignore it and act like nothing happened.
   c) end the friendship.
6. After a fight with a lover or spouse, you
   a) say you're sorry and try to work it out.
   b) wait for him to apologize.
   c) pretend it didn't happen.

7. In sports, you
   a) mountain climb, ski, backpack, hang glide, or participate in other slightly dangerous activities.
   b) participate but not in dangerous areas.
   c) don't do anything athletic.
8. When you want to connect with someone you've just met, you will
   a) make the first call.
   b) hope he calls you.
   c) wait to see if you run into him again.
9. When you don't like something your sexual partner is doing, you
   a) tell him.
   b) grin and bear it.
   c) stop having sex with him.
10. When dealing with your finances, you
    a) sometimes push your financial limits.
    b) keep track of every penny.
    c) don't deal with finances at all.
11. When you have a business or career problem, you
    a) confront it as it arises.
    b) see if it clears itself up.
    c) blame your boss or fire the person you think caused it.
12. When you have thoughts and ideas you believe in, you
    a) tell people what your ideas are.
    b) keep them to yourself.
    c) feel your ideas are not worth talking about.
13. Sexually speaking, you have had
    a) many partners.
    b) few partners.
    c) don't want to discuss it.
14. Socially, you
    a) look forward to and involve yourself in social situations where you'll have the opportunity to meet new people.
    b) wish you were dating someone new, but do nothing about it.
    c) date too much.
15. When it comes to money, you
    a) enjoy it and spend it the way you want.
    b) feel guilty when you spend it.
    c) have no money to spend.

16. Five years from now in your career, you
    a) know where you want to be and are taking steps to get there.
    b) know where you want to be, but take no steps.
    c) don't know where you want to be.
17. When your lover or spouse is not meeting your needs, you
    a) tell him.
    b) think "so what else is new?"
    c) get them met elsewhere.
18. When it comes to danger, you
    a) sometimes do what others say you shouldn't do, such as leaving a building alone late at night, driving fast, etc.
    b) always play it safe.
    c) constantly put yourself in jeopardy.
19. When you are upset about personal problems, you
    a) confront them as they arise.
    b) figure they'll go away in time.
    c) scream, yell, and cry.
20. Sexually, you are
    a) eager to try new sexual positions and/or sex in new places.
    b) bored, but wish you weren't.
    c) just not interested.

Scoring

The more As you chose, the more of a risk-taker you are. If you answered with mostly Bs, you probably opt for what appears to be the "safe" way. If you answered most questions with C, you either avoid issues or take inappropriate risks. In what areas do you risk and in what areas do you avoid risk?

Financial risk-takers choose A answers to questions 1, 10, and 15.

Emotional risk-takers choose A answers to questions 5, 6, 17, and 19.

Social risk-takers choose A answers to questions 2, 8, and 14.

Physical risk-takers choose A answers to questions 3, 7, and 18.

Sexual risk-takers choose A answers to questions 9, 13, and 20.

Career/business risk-takers choose A answers to questions 4, 11, 12, and 16.

In which areas do you seldom take risks? Take several sheets of paper and write down the six risk-taking areas above (or create your own headings) at the top of the pages. On each sheet write down several goals in each area, such as, "I want to change jobs by the end of the year," under Career/Business. Most of us need to take a few risks in every area, but start with your weakest areas. Now, under each goal, list some risks you could take to reach that goal, such as send out resumes to other companies, look at ads in the paper, etc. Write down as many possibilities as you can, even if you think you would never do them. Now, put them in a hierarchy from the easiest to the most difficult. See Alicia's Overall Risk-taking Chart on page 166. Plan to do the easiest one first. If that one still seems too difficult, think of a step that is even easier. For instance, "sign up for an art class" could be made easier. You could first go to the library and get books on art or send away for catalogs describing art classes. Promise yourself you will start this week.

You may want to break each area down further into steps like Alicia did. She took the physical area and broke it down further into areas that were of concern to her. They included weight, skin care, eyes, nail care, and smile (teeth). (See her Physical Risk-taking Chart on p. 168.)

Evaluating Risks

When you start to take a risk and you are frightened, ask yourself, "What is the worst thing that could happen to me?" Then ask, "Can I handle it? If so, how?" Next ask, "What's the best thing that could happen? Is the best thing worth the trade-off against the worst thing?" If so, do it. If not, don't.

Some women, however, overrisk in one area or overrisk in inappropriate ways to avoid taking risks in the areas they really need to risk in. For instance, many of my Aspen friends continually ski more and more difficult runs and hike steeper mountains, so they are great physical risk-takers. However, they never take risks in areas like how to make more money or how to stand up to a man. They consider themselves risk-takers because they risk in certain areas. However, to become secure in yourself, you must move out of your range of comfort and try new things in all areas, especially those you are weak in.

Many women today feel that they're running out of time and try to take all of their risks at once. They overrisk in their weak areas, trying to save time.

That's what Peggy did at first. After obtaining her real-estate license, she decided she should immediately open her own office. With no experience in the field, she borrowed a large sum of money, rented three offices, installed several phones, set up an expensive bookkeeping system, and hired an accountant along with a full office staff. Then she waited for clients. But she had none. She didn't take her risks gradually, making her mistakes and learning from them, so she went under after only a few months. She failed because she *risked too much too soon.* She's back working for another realtor now. It's important to evaluate your situation realistically, but don't let the fear hold you back so that you don't risk at all. You just have to be smart about it.

Taking Baby Steps

Taking risks can be scary, but not if you take them slowly. As I said earlier, you must crawl before you can walk. If you take baby steps, you can feel a sense of success as you move forward.

Taking "baby steps" means that if you want to hike to the top of a mountain, but are afraid, you don't go out alone and head for the top the first day. Instead, you begin experiencing the mountain gradually, gaining information for your ascent, walking part of the way up and back, taking hikes with friends and overcoming your fears as you gather more information. Relationships need to be handled in the same way.

Once I moved to Aspen, I decided to work through the physical fear my mother had ingrained in me as a young child. In the area of physical risks, I chose to "backpack alone." Baby Step number one was going backpacking with friends many times until I knew the ins and outs of doing it.

ALICIA'S OVERALL RISK-TAKING CHART

Goals

Steps	Career	Financial	Social	Physical	Emotional
Goal	Become psychologist; write book; write articles.	Have control of bills; follow budget; have money saved; buy home.	Have new friends like new self; involved with healthy man.	Maintain ideal weight within 5 lbs; walk every day.	Self-reliance.
8	Take job in field and/or create own business.	Begin to invest; check into house-buying options.	Ask for & give commitment to intimacy & relationship.	Develop new eating habits for life; sign up for scuba lessons.	Stop seeing married lover.
7	Interview for jobs in new area and/or explore business opportunities.	Open savings account; check & communicate opportunities.	Bond with a man as I communicate openly & require same from him.	Take in old clothes and/or buy a few new ones for new body!	Write confrontation letter to married lover.
6	Combine business skills & psychology skills to find/create a new position.	Prepare taxes and clean up problem with IRS.	Express self and take emotional risks with one or more men.	Stroke self for weight-loss and sticking to walking program.	Write letters to brothers and deceased father.
5	Work part-time and go to school part-time, taking courses in area of interest.	Control frivolous spending; update wardrobe, plan vacation, etc. instead.	Meet some of the men from the dating services; socialize with women like me.	Take aerobics class at gym; investigate scuba-diving lessons.	Confront friends and equalize relationships or end them.
4	Take night classes in psychology.	Operate on a cash basis; cut up credit cards; keep bills current.	Talk to men at work and out in public; find places to meet women.	Start diet program; take daily walks; join gym.	Finish letter to ex-boss and mail; express real feelings to married lover & friends.
3	Send for information on colleges and different areas of psychology.	Devise a regular budget; join 401K plan at work.	Investigate and join dating services; go out with the "girls" at least once a week.	Sign up for weight-loss plan; investigate gyms in area; plan walking program.	Mail letter to ex-boss.
2	Identify specific areas of interest. Talk to and interview people in the field.	Pay and/or negotiate bills now in collection.	Attend new social events; plan at least 1 time per week to be around men in a social setting.	Talk to dietician and health professionals about best approach to take to lose weight.	Write letter to Mom.
1	Investigate all areas of psychology specialties and possibilities and length of school involved.	Collect money from friends; formulate payment plan for creditors; gather bills together.	Stop letting friends lean on me and drag me down; start going out more where I can meet men.	Read diet books and decide which plan to use; investigate activities I can do outside.	Write out anger in general at men, family, friends, life, etc.

Career   Financial   Social   Physical   Emotional

Baby Step number two was attempting an overnight backpacking trip all alone at a familiar camping spot nearby. I checked and rechecked my pack to be sure I hadn't forgotten anything. As I was hiking up the trail, I ran into a couple who said, ''We should warn you that there's a bear on the trail ahead. We don't think he'll bother you, but since you're alone, we thought you might be afraid.'' Yes, I was afraid! I immediately turned around and headed down. A bear was my greatest fear. Was I going to chicken out? No, I finally decided that I would stay. I wouldn't camp where I had planned, but instead several miles lower and closer to the trailhead. I pitched my tent, built a large fire (I had heard that bears don't like fires), and took pots and pans in the tent with me (I also had heard that noise scares them away). I looked over my shoulder regularly as I sat by the fire that evening, and had trouble going to sleep. But I did it! I had accomplished the next step. I actually backpacked to this spot several times again before trying anything else.

For Baby Step number three, I made plans to go alone in an area nearby that required hiking down a somewhat dangerous, steep pitch. On another hike, I had seen this spot with a small ledge next to a waterfall, but getting down there would be difficult. When I reached the steep area, I became very nervous. My heart started beating fast and I was perspiring. I thought maybe I had made a mistake. My fear told me to first scout it out without my forty-five pound pack. I walked down, sometimes slipping, hardly able to breathe because of my fear. Then I went back for my pack and sat awhile next to the steep grade, shaking. I started to walk away when I caught myself—a man wouldn't walk away, he'd trudge right down there. It angered me to think I was such a wimp! I asked myself, ''What's the worst thing that could happen? I could fall and hurt my leg and not be able to get out of there. But someone would come tomorrow or I could probably crawl out if I really had to.'' Neither of these alternatives sounded appealing to me, but they also did not sound like the end of the world. I took some deep breaths and headed down. I had to stop at times because of my anxiety. But I made it! I camped by the waterfall and was fine until the time came to climb back up. Then I had to deal with my fear all over again.

Finally, Baby Step number four was to go alone to a new area, much farther away, in questionable weather. Halfway up the trail, the rain started. I crawled under a large pine tree, read my book,

ALICIA'S PHYSICAL RISK-TAKING CHART

Goals

Steps	Weight	Skin Care	Eyes	Nail Care	Smile (Teeth)
Goals	Maintain ideal weight within 5 lbs; exercise 3× per week!	Follow skin-care program every day; luxurious bath 1× wk!	Wear contacts regularly, and makeup!	Have long, healthy nails that are manicured weekly!	Have great smile—teeth are straight, white, and in great shape!
8	Treat self to night on town in glamorous new handmade evening gown!	Treat self to professional facial and makeover!	Buy contacts in several different colors!	Treat self to professional manicure and pedicure!	Have any bonding done that is necessary.
7	Alter old clothes; buy few new ones; develop new life-style eating habits.	Wear makeup every day in my colors!	Buy new contacts.	Admire nails and use hand lotion every day!	Have cap put on second front tooth; have teeth polished.
6	Stroke self for weight-loss and sticking to walking program.	Soak in tub at least 1× per week in herbal bath; use loofah 1×/week.	Get fitted for contacts.	Give self strokes for not biting nails; buy a pretty scarf!	Have cross-bite fixed. (Braces if necessary).
5	Take aerobics class at gym; ask buddy to join me on walks.	Clean face every morning and night, following chosen skin-care routine.	Decide on contacts best for me.	Give self manicure and polish nails 1×/week—even if short and stubby.	Have front cap replaced; practice good flossing and brushing.
4	Start diet program; take daily walks; join gym.	Buy any new products necessary for makeup, daily skin care, and bath.	Make appointment with opthomologist.	Buy anti-nail-biting product and use!	Have teeth cleaned; make initial appointment for cosmetic dentistry.
3	Sign up for weight-loss plan; investigate gyms in area; plan walking program.	Decide which skin-care routine to follow and determine which products I need.	Read information on new types of contacts; ask doctor for recommendation.	Buy nail products and paraphernalia necessary for weekly manicures.	Talk to dentist about cap and possible cosmetic dentistry.
2	Talk to health-care professionals and dietician to devise best weight-loss program for me.	Look through skin products and makeup I currently own; discard old makeup; find out my "colors."	Buy new prescription sunglasses and long-distance glasses.	Research materials to find out what nail products build and strengthen nails.	Find and read literature on current orthodontic procedures for adults.
1	Decide to lose excess poundage; read diet books; read exercise plans.	Investigate skin-care products for my sensitive skin—both for face and body.	Get eye exam and new prescription.	Make decision to stop biting nails; buy book on nail care.	Make dental appointment for semi-annual checkup.

| Weight | Skin Care | Eyes | Nail Care | Smile (Teeth) |

and ate cherries until it stopped, telling myself, "You don't have to go all the way to the lake if you don't want to, you could camp right here if necessary." Then I headed on to the lake, frightened as lightning flashed around me when I hiked over the pass. On the other side, I got lost. I searched and searched for the lake as it got darker and darker. Finally, I saw a man who told me how to get to the lake. After asking him the way, I thought, I shouldn't have told him where I'll be, he might harm me. I worried as I hiked as fast as I could. At the lake it was dark and raining, so I skipped dinner, eating an emergency protein bar I'd brought along. Luckily, I was so exhausted that I slept like a baby. The next day was fine until, halfway back, I encountered a hailstorm. I continued to hike as the weather changed back and forth from rain to rocks of ice. I was worried about hypothermia, and I walked faster and faster, trying to keep my body temperature up. Upon reaching the car, my fingers were so numb from the cold that I could hardly move them to find my keys. I was soaked, but really proud of myself!

Each of these steps was a learning experience that prepared me for the next and gave me confidence in myself. Each step was necessary for me to obtain the next one. After that, I regularly backpacked alone in the woods, almost without a thought to all the terrible things that could happen. After all, I had already proven that I could handle most crises.

Fear can be overcome rather easily if you are willing to take a risk, learn from it, and then take the next risk.

Experiment With New Behaviors

Try some of the following exercises:

- Do something you've always wanted to do but never did for fear of looking foolish.
- Do something you've been told you shouldn't do (even though you never understood why you shouldn't do it).
- Do something you consider very "unlike" you.
- Follow up on an interest you've had for a long time.
- Try wearing a different style of clothing than you've ever worn before—a sari, a sequin dress, tight jeans.
- Argue the opposite side of points you believe to see how it feels.

- Find a trail or path that looks interesting and follow it.
- Don't do what you usually do after work. Be spontaneous. Ask yourself, "Where do I want to go and what do I want to do right now?"
- Try not to listen to anyone's problems for a day or a week.
- Don't do the laundry or some other chore you always do on a regular basis.
- Try wearing your hair differently, maybe in a ponytail or pulled back on top of your head.
- Try dancing all night or staying up all night for no other reason except that you want to.

Take all the risks necessary to find out who you really are and who you want to be. You need to go at your own pace. You may choose to risk in one area at a time or to take risks in every area all at once. It depends on your sense of urgency in having your life be different. However, it is important that you begin to experiment with risks in your weakest areas to put balance in your life.

Over the years many people have been envious of my days in Aspen. I certainly enjoyed them and they helped me grow. I tell everyone that I would never give up those experiences, but I also would never repeat them. I certainly don't recommend that everyone complete their adolescence the way I did.

You don't need to completely drop out. One of my female clients simply took a "week-long adolescence" break. She called me in crisis one day when she felt she couldn't stand her life the way it was any longer. I was still living in Aspen at the time, and she lived in Denver. I told her to take time off from work and come up to Aspen for a week. I found her a place to stay, gave her maps of trails, lent her my bicycle, and prepared various assignments for her, from writing confrontation letters to experimenting with her image. Each day was a new adventure. Her favorite exercise was going into a second-hand store and trying on a variety of clothes, from sexy dresses to torn jeans to fur coats to hats. These exercises helped her reform her identity and image.

For your behavior to match what you say you believe, you need to experiment with who you are and who you want to be. A self-reliant woman is one who looks forward to the next step or stage in life, instead of fearing it. Excitement and fear are close emotional relatives, and how you see a situation depends on whether you view the world like a glass that's half full or half empty.

10

Step Eight:
Take Responsibility and Control in Every Area of Your Life

Many women arrive at the last step in the program and still can't take control of their lives. Although the other steps can be done in any order, this step must be done last. You must at this point have the information and knowledge about yourself and life to create your own script. If you aren't ready, you may have to go back and see which steps you really haven't completed—like Alicia and Vicki.

Confront Yourself

When Alicia began to let go of her relationship with the married man, she panicked when she realized how out of control her life had become. For Alicia, letting go of the fantasy that this man would someday leave his wife for her meant she was a failure and that the last two years of her life were a painful farce. She also had to face the fact that he never really loved her. It became clear that she had been blinded by her dependency—her addiction to him. For Alicia this situation created self-blame. She believed she was stupid or naive or crazy. Alicia couldn't accept how desperately she had chased this man if he really didn't care. To avoid this reality, she would regress, reach out, call him, and see if she could put everything back the way it was. But she couldn't. She had become too aware to go back.

But she was too afraid to go forward. Somehow, taking control of her life meant to her that she'd be alone forever—and she couldn't accept that.

Alicia did everything in her power to fight change. She tried to ignore and avoid the reality that her married lover would never make a commitment to her. She used her friends to hold onto the fantasy. They behaved codependently, listening intently when she complained about his abuse and her hope that it would change. She lied to herself and to him about what she wanted from the relationship. If she had put half as much time and energy into moving forward and taking charge of her life as she does into fooling herself about this man and their relationship, her life would have been straightened out months ago!

Alicia is not alone. Many women fight change as hard as they can. Displaced homemakers refuse to believe that their husbands would actually abandon them after all those years. Parents dealing with an empty nest refuse to believe that the children they sacrificed their lives for not only aren't appreciative, but have no respect for them. Workaholics refuse to believe that after spending years moving up in business, bringing in big accounts, and dedicating their lives to a company, the company could still fire them. Cancer patients refuse to give up the belief that "justice will prevail" when their self-sacrificing didn't protect them from a life-threatening illness.

Alicia's awareness caused her to panic. She couldn't accept her old behavior, yet she was afraid to move forward. Since her judgment had been so flawed in the situation with her lover, she was afraid to trust herself. When she could no longer depend on a man, she reached out to her friends, her mom, old boyfriends, her support group, and me—her therapist, trying to switch her dependency onto one of us. She called all of us every day, repeating over and over how frightened she was, expecting and hoping that we could make her feel better without her having to do anything for herself. I confronted her on her desire to be dependent on me—and her friends. She had trouble understanding that leaning on us wasn't much better than leaning on her married lover. The problem was not that the people around her were letting her down, the problem was her need to lean on someone outside herself.

She told me that she felt incredibly alone when she didn't talk to all of us. I told her I was glad she felt alone, that she must learn to face her problems alone in order to become self-reliant.

She said she thought friends were supposed to help. I explained to her that there was a difference between being supportive and being codependent. Allowing her to keep whining about her fear would be codependent, whereas my confronting her to move forward was being supportive.

She complained that no one was really there for her. I said that was true—she was driving us all crazy by constantly talking about her feelings but never taking action. I asked her when was she going to stop complaining and start putting her life back in order. She said she didn't think she could. I asked her what other options she had.

She became extremely depressed. She still didn't really *want* to take charge of her life. She still had really never finished Step One: Recognize, Understand, and Admit Your Emotional Dependency and Commit to Change. Before she could commit to change, she had to completely let go of the fantasy of being rescued by her married lover. Once she did, it threw her into crisis. Often it's not until we reach a crisis level or become so depressed that we can no longer stand to be where we are, that we change.

Being in a crisis situation is often frightening because others see it as failure, when it's simply a lesson in life—one of many that we all must learn. No one makes it through life without crisis. Each crisis that we face up to and resolve makes us stronger and makes it easier for us to face the next one. If we refuse to move forward when we're in crisis, we not only lose what we used to have—because we are beyond the point of going back—but we also lose the future. We die a little bit inside and become less able to connect to others. We return to denial because it's the only way we can survive when we don't grow. In order to grow, we must use the new information we've gained about the world and create change in our lives.

There are only a few options at this point—to grow and change and take control of your life *or* do everything in your power to withdraw back into denial, creating an emotional death—which Alicia was too far along to do—*or* panic and consider suicide as an option. Alicia was at this stage.

At her most desperate point, she dialed the phone number of everyone she knew. However, since they had all heard it before, her friends and her married lover all told her they were sick of her whining and refused to talk to her. She had called ten to twenty people to no avail. She hit bottom at that point, finally knowing that no one was willing to, or able to, handle the problem for her. She finally had to make a decision either to take charge of her life or end it. With my help and over a period of a day or two, she finally made a decision not to check out of life like her father had (he had died of cancer at a young age and Alicia always felt it was because he had been afraid to face his problems).

At my urging, Alicia called each of her friends back and told them that she was okay, but in the future they were not to let her whine ever again. If she tried to complain, she wanted them to say, "I care about you, but I can't fix it for you." This was her first real step toward breaking her dependency and making the decision to rely on herself. At the same time, she realized she still wasn't ready to take the steps necessary to take charge of her life that she had written down in her goals chart. Though she had worked through most of the program, she hadn't really completed Step Two: Withdraw, Separate, and Develop Your Own Identity—which she was now doing by telling her friends not to let her whine and by finally totally breaking it off with her married lover. She also hadn't completed Step Seven: Complete Your Adolescence Through Risk-taking and Experimenting. Her suicidal crisis had caused problems at work and they were pressing her for a resignation. Since she hated her job anyway, she decided to resign, took her money out of an IRA, packed up her car, and took off to see parts of the country she'd never seen before—and to find Alicia. The decision to experiment was her way of immediately and temporarily taking charge of her life and a step in front of taking control of her life long term.

Like Alicia, Vicki had started the steps many times but never completed them. She would refuse to take charge of her life and drop out of therapy. Before her mother's suicide, she had a good job and many boyfriends. The suicide threw her into such deep guilt and depression that she wallowed in it for three years. The more she wallowed, the more insecure she became. The more insecure she became, the more she isolated herself from men, gained weight, and felt inadequate at work. Like Alicia's, Vicki's life was spiraling downward. Although she had written letters to her father and thought she was comfortable alone (she was usually eating and reading escape novels), she realized she was following in her mother's footsteps by choosing not to deal with life. She had to go back and concentrate on her relationship to her mom. She finally began to get angry with her mother and her own stagnant behavior. That, along with beginning to take risks with men (which the support group pushed her to do) helped her start to gain control. She began to ask herself what she was feeling before she ate something and realized that she was using food as a tranquilizer. Starting on a diet and confronting her deceased mother were the two keys that finally helped Vicki take control of her life and move forward on the upward spiral.

She was never able to get back the old life that she mourned for, but she created a new one that was better. When she looked back she realized she was really faking happiness and control. The clues were there, but at the time she avoided them. Her lack of awareness had kept her semi-content until her mother's death, at which time all of her insecurities had come pouring out. She had patched her armor for several years, but now she was finally learning to deal with the realities of life.

When my sister was diagnosed with breast cancer she became paralyzed with fear. She asked me why I seem to be able to handle crisis and she can't. In fact, to her it looks like I *seek out* stressful events—from radio and TV shows to seminars and parental confrontations in my office. I told her that I've handled crisis and confrontation since the age of ten. I was therapist to mom and dad, while my sister panicked, withdrew, and cried over fear of abandonment. At forty, she still had no experience handling crisis and was totally unprepared for what she had to deal with. I, on the other hand, continued to make changes every time I felt unhappy—from divorce to quitting jobs to two major moves to facing an IRS crisis. Each time I faced a crisis, I learned more skills to use when facing the next one. Now I try to process each crisis as quickly as I can, having faith that there's a positive change on the other side. I see each crisis as a challenge, I no longer avoid it or give into the fear.

Handle Your Own Crisis

Follow these steps when handling your own crisis:

1. *Withdraw* and *feel the pain.*
2. *Allow the hurt to turn to anger.* Don't take self-pity too far.

There comes a time when you have to say, "So what am I going to do about it?"

3. *Ask yourself* again and again *what you really want,* instead of what you "should" do. What would make you feel better—both immediately and long-term? A trip to the beach? Moving to a different city? A friend saying, "I'm sorry?"

4. *Take a risk.* Ask yourself what you can do that might result in your getting what you want.

5. *Draw on your own strengths.* Don't allow negativity to run in your head. Replace any negative tapes with positive ones (e.g., "I'm smart, capable, attractive")—even if you don't believe it, yet.

6. *Don't try to escape, ignore, or avoid the problem or the feelings* with alcohol, drugs, food, etc. You'll just prolong dealing with the problem and these substances won't make it go away.

7. *Write out your anger* at those who've helped cause this problem (especially if you must wait to express it because of a divorce or a trial). Be careful not to dwell on anger at yourself or you'll become more depressed.

8. *Use friends for support,* but don't use them to ruminate over your past mistakes. If you do, they'll enable you to stay where you are. Instead, make a plan to deal with the problem with those who are causing it.

9. *Let the anger motivate you to positive action* using the Four Steps of Healthy Communication.

10. *Decide what lesson you've learned* from the crisis and how this information can help you in the future.

For an example of learning from crisis, Jackie's mother was brutally murdered by her mother's boyfriend. Jackie is beginning to find a lesson in the catastrophe. Her brother calls her a cream puff because she's too soft inside. She now sees that she learned this passive behavior of denial from her mother. Jackie will say, "I'm not angry about anything." And I'll say, "What about _____?" "Oh, yes, I forgot," she replies. Jackie has always pretended things were better than they were—like her mother's denial that her boyfriend ever abused her. The violent death of Jackie's mother is motivating Jackie to change and become stronger and more assertive.

Rewrite Your Script

Answer the following questions:

· What part of the fantasy you discovered in the last chapter do
you want the most?
· Why haven't you gone after it already?
· Are you getting something out of staying the same?
· Does your present situation arouse pity in friends and family?
· Do you feel like you're getting away with something when you
don't change?
· Do you really want to make the changes?
· Are you really sure you want your fantasy life?

So many people say, for example, "Yes, well, I'm forty years
old, I can't become a famous ballet dancer now. It's too late."
In the traditional sense, that's true. But you can still take related
actions: run a ballet school for children. Even if you have to hire
a dance teacher, you could be involved. Or you could develop a
ballet aerobics program and teach it in athletic clubs, or make
your own video dance tape. Be creative. Most people set their
goals too low. Set your goals high, take steps to get there, and
then you at least have a chance of getting close. This kind of
planning is taking responsibility for your life.

Combine Values and Decide What You Want

Early in my life, I accepted my parents' values and tried to adhere
to them perfectly. Then I rebelled and tried the opposite of my
parents' values. By the time I was thirty-five, I decided it was
time for me to come to the middle and decide who *I* wanted to
be. I decided I wanted my earlier, more attractive look back. I
lost fifteen to twenty pounds, began to wear make-up, and curled
my hair again. I spent time with people who were more involved
in the community than the transients I had bar-hopped with before. I stopped having one-night-stands. I quit drinking as much
and stopped experimenting with drugs.

I reevaluated my job as a therapist. I decided it wasn't so bad. It
was working within the school system that I didn't like. Since I al-

ready had my degree, I started teaching assertiveness classes at the local college and finally decided to start my own private practice working with women, instead of children. I started slowly, in a friend's law office, until I could afford an office of my own.

My strained financial situation kept me constantly coming up with new ideas to increase my business. I continually pulled myself out of the next financial bind. When my car broke down or I had a medical crisis, I came up with one more idea to make enough money to cover the expense. Sometimes I took a second or third job. Other times I came up with a workshop idea or a new way to get clients. Through this I developed financial security—not money in the bank, but security that within myself I had the skills to make it, no matter what.

Take Control

Build Financial Security

I've always admired people (usually men) who've made a lot of money, lost it all, then made a lot again—who after a bankruptcy can pick up the pieces and make another million. These people are financially secure. I don't mean they have money in the bank. What I mean by financial security is they are secure in their *ability to make money*.

Most women learned that financial security is access to money, not the ability to make it. Few women believe that financial security is an ability they can and need to develop within themselves.

Investors found out how financially insecure they were when the stock market crashed in 1987. Older women who haven't worked and who are widowed or divorced find out the same thing. As businesses across the nation close their doors, employees learn that pension plans are not financial security.

Security comes from within. The most clear-cut examples of people with money who are financially insecure seems to be adults living on income from trust funds. Clients of mine whose income comes from trust funds are often very nervous about money. They fear that if they lose their money, they could never make it back. They've never really had to put themselves on the line financially. They don't know how to start with nothing and make something. Though they have financial security in the traditional sense, female trust funders are literally the most financially insecure group I've worked with.

To develop financial security within yourself, you must face whatever you are most afraid of. For most women the fear is that with only themselves to rely on, they could never make enough money to live the life-style they want.

Peggy finally faced her fear of financial deprivation when she and Tom divorced because she had to give up the fantasy that Tom was going to take care of her. She had never researched possible careers, but was now forced to make a decision and earn a living. She now makes enough money as a real estate broker to buy herself the three-hundred dollar sweaters she and Tom always fought about.

Valerie was able to face her financial fears within her marriage. She felt controlled by Ken's money. If they took a trip to Hawaii on his money she felt like he expected sexual favors in return. When she felt pressured by him, she lost interest because she felt like a prostitute.

She couldn't really enjoy spending Ken's money because she felt obligated to "earn" it when she did. Guilt motivated her to focus on her career. She was able to save enough money so if Ken left her she would be OK.

Lana and Alicia, on the other hand, knew how to earn money. It was managing money that was their problem. Like them, I overspent in the past—secretly hoping that one day someone or something would bail me out. It took an IRS crisis to force me to take control of this area of my life. You may need to seek out financial counseling—from consumer credit counseling to a good accountant to a good stockbroker, depending on your own personal needs.

There are books that can help—*Money-Love* by Jerry Gillies,[1] and *Think and Grow Rich Action Pack!,* by Napoleon Hill.[2] Both books can help you change false beliefs you may have about money, spending, and deserving to be rich. They also have steps to help you make a financial plan for the future.

Find Happiness in Your Career

We all need a purpose in life. We need to feel needed. A woman often tries to make a man and/or family her purpose in life. If she does this, her neediness usually ends up pushing the man away, leaving her without anything. However, you can end up feeling empty if you make your job your sole purpose for living. On the other hand, if you know your "real" purpose or passion in life, you then have an internal direction that can lead you. You will never lose your "self" when you lose a job because your internal guide will lead you to another job or perhaps another career. For example, early on I wanted to save other children from going through the frustrations I felt as a child so I became a school counselor. After working with children for a while, I realized that I needed to be working with parents because children didn't have enough power to make the necessary changes to avoid the turmoil in their homes. That decision led to my desire to help couples develop relationships before they even had children, and finally to helping singles find healthy mates.

Many women today work, but few have careers and even fewer have a purpose. Women may have made hasty job choices in order to meet financial needs. They program computers, and are financial planners, sell real estate, or return to teaching. Some had their husbands set them up in pseudo-careers that they later learned would never really make money. I am not saying that these jobs are not challenging and fulfilling but they often do not involve a passionate desire.

If you're looking for a career that you love instead of a job, you need to begin by looking inside yourself.

1. Go through old memorabilia, scrap books, report cards. Remember what you were good at, remember what you enjoyed.
2. Listen to people when they say, "You always amaze me when you _____." "I can't believe how you _____." Write down the things people praise you for. Then think about how you could use these strengths to make money.
3. Pick a book like *Wishcraft* by Barbara Sher with Annie Gottlieb[3] and digest it slowly. What positive things have come from your past and your interactions with your family? Maybe you were the caretaker or the clown. What can you do with those skills today? Accentuate the positive, minimize the negative.

4. Accept your strengths and weaknesses and use them accordingly.
5. Let go of false beliefs about success, such as:

   • Men won't be attracted to me if I'm too successful.
   • You must be ruthless to really make it.
   • You have to know everything in some field to be an expert.

6. Give up excuses you may use to hold yourself back such as:

   • "I need more education."
   This excuse often covers up insecurity and a desire to avoid action. If you do need more education, get it while you work.
   • "I need money to get started."
   Borrow or start small.
   • "It's too late now."
   If it really is, like becoming a singer or doctor at age sixty (which probably still isn't too late), pick it up as a hobby or go into a related field.
   • "If only I wasn't so in debt."
   Use debt to make you more creative about earning and managing money, don't let it overwhelm you.
   • "If only I was appreciated."
   We all want to be appreciated more by others. You may feel more appreciated if you do something you enjoy because you'll appreciate yourself. You'll never be as appreciated as you want until it no longer matters to you.
   • "If only I were younger."
   People live a very long time these days. You've got plenty of time, but you must start now. It's never, never too late. Women over sixty are going back to college and starting businesses.
   • "If only I knew what I wanted to do."
   There's no better way to find out than by starting somewhere, anywhere! And only you know where to start. The answers are inside you.

Have the Social Life You Want

Many of my single female clients say, "I hate bars. You never meet anyone wonderful in a bar, so I never go." This is their excuse to avoid taking charge of the social area of their lives. I ask them where do they go to meet men, and the answer is often, "Nowhere." They don't want to learn how to flirt, discourage men they don't like, or dress and act in ways that attract men. Social situations like bars frighten them and they don't want to be ashamed or embarrassed by doing what it takes to overcome their fears. A woman who feels comfortable by herself in all types of bars can probably handle most other social situations, so why not use the most intimidating place to practice? Improving social skills will increase a woman's chances of meeting the kind of man *she wants* in her life because she can do more of the choosing. A woman certainly doesn't have to frequent bars to take charge of her social life, but she must have a plan of some sort. I met the man I married, the man I lived with, and my present partner in a bar.

My own plan to take charge of my social life included a variety of places to go and things to do, not only to meet men, but to develop a sense of belongingness. I had recently moved to Denver and did not yet have a network of friends. I took adult education classes, joined a singing group, looked for events each weekend in the paper, *and* I frequented the bars. I even moved my temporary office to a more permanent plush location where I thought I would not only attract the type of clients I wanted, but also the type of men *I* found most interesting. After a short time, several of my clients named certain bars nearby that they frequented and thought I might enjoy. I began to go there after work. I developed a sense of belongingness. I became good friends with a female bartender who made sure I met every eligible man and gave me the scoop on all the rest so I would know who to avoid. It was indirectly through her that I met the man I'm with today.

Women who are married can still take charge of their social lives—either with their husbands or without them. You can ask your husband to join you in planning a social life. Perhaps you can agree that you will take charge of making social arrangements every other weekend. If he doesn't go along, make plans without him and he might later change his mind.

Create an Image to Reflect the New You

Most women are not completely satisfied with the way they look. Many of us are still trying to live up to external standards of perfection. When this happens, we become tough on ourselves. We try to lose weight through rigid diets and exercise programs that may cause more harm than good. We begin to think we should be perfect—the way our family and society taught us, instead of accepting ourselves just as we are. Striving to have a perfect body or lose weight perfectly can discourage us. We'll bounce back and forth between trying to take charge and giving up.

Often when our self-esteem starts to improve, the extra weight drops off naturally and other self-destructive health patterns like smoking and drinking also begin to change.

Sheri, the airline stewardess, was only ten or fifteen pounds overweight when she came to see me. After she worked through the program and began to feel better about herself, the excess weight dropped off with no effort at all.

As our self-esteem improves, our image needs to reflect our new self-confidence. It may be time for a new hairstyle. Experiment with your appearance. Your make-up may be outdated. You may want to attract "classy" men, but still have a "hippie" image. Who do you wish you looked like? Try to come as close to that image as possible, keeping in mind your own physical strengths and weaknesses. Seek out an image consultant. Fantasize about the look you want. Pose in front of the mirror in different outfits. Cut out pictures and put them on the wall as role models. Look through magazines and cut out "looks" that appeal to you. Start a file of the pictures. Be creative in defining your new positive image. Be sure it reflects the new, more positive and self-assured you!

Maintain Emotional Strength

As I've said before, we've often misinterpreted controlling or holding in our emotions as emotional strength. Repression of feelings not only catches up to us at a later date, but also keeps us from growing up emotionally so that when we are faced with a major crisis we find we are not able to handle it maturely.

We discussed communication of feelings in Chapter Seven. It's necessary to be emotionally honest and express anger, love, hurt, fear, etc., in order to get close to others and develop and maintain intimacy. To be able to maintain emotional strength you need to take the following steps:

When faced with an emotional situation, ask yourself:

- What am I feeling?
- Why am I acting this way?
- Why am I so irritable?
- What do I need to deal with that I am avoiding?
- Who, or what, upset me?

Trust Yourself: Don't let anyone talk you out of your feelings or tell you that you are overly emotional or overreacting. Trust your intuition, your gut-level feelings are usually correct.

Nurture Yourself: We all crave more nurturing and most of us look for it outside ourselves. This is one way we hand over our power. We must learn to take care of ourselves first in order to make that craving go away. Talk to the little girl inside and tell her she'll be OK. Tell her she's a good person. Tell her she deserves the best in life. Ask her what she wants and try to give it to her. Take good care of her. Be the good mother she didn't have.

Act Soft Yet Strong: It's important to be able to recognize your full range of emotions. It's healthy to tell others that you feel hurt when, and if, they hurt you. But if someone still continues to attack, it's time to express your anger. The difference between being a victim and taking control is setting limits when someone continues to attack by saying, "I will not allow you to treat me this way." You need to be able to express *all* your feelings including love, warmth, compassion as well as anger, hurt, and frustration. This is being soft, yet strong.

Demand Respect from the Men in Your Life: Although insecure men often choose weak women, strong men don't respect women who don't take charge of their lives. In a crisis, women more often cry rather than fight, believing someone else (preferably a man) will step in and resolve the situation. Women often look for the easy way out rather than face the conflict head on. Until women learn to fight back in the game of life—instead of thinking it's not feminine—we won't have men's respect.

Men have learned a different language than women—a language of competition, aggressiveness, and success that we were never taught. In high school, we admired the girls who were prettiest and/or who could attract the most men. Boys, however, admired other boys who were able to win—at sports, at breaking rules, at doing whatever was necessary to be successful. What they didn't learn in school, they learned in the service, or gambling, or on the job. When they fight, they "kick ass." They use gambling analogies and talk about knowing when to "hold 'em" or "fold up" or "walk away" or "run." When they call someone a "bad ass," it's a compliment. To describe other men, they use terms like "He's a Top Hand" or "He can run with the Big Dogs."

To gain entry emotionally into the "old boys' club," you must become a "Top Hand." "Top Hands" run their own lives. They don't wait for others to do it. They stand up to other "Big Dogs" and hold their own. They don't take abuse from anyone. Becoming a Top Dog doesn't mean you become a bitch. You can be warm and feminine, until and unless you're attacked. But when attacked, the softness must go out the door and the more appropriate reaction of aggression must replace it.

I gained entry into the "old boys' club" the night I confronted my boyfriend's boss, Donald, who is a rich, phony womanizer. Donald was bragging to me about his "perfect" relationship with his wife and I knew that he had made a pass at my girlfriend. I confronted him. I told him that I knew that he had tried to cheat on his wife and that I didn't buy what he was saying. He stuttered and tried to talk his way out of the confrontation, but eventually backed down. Afterwards, each time he saw me, he made some degrading comment or sarcastic remark. I confronted him again and again. He finally gave up and tried winning my approval instead. Alan was proud of me for not being intimidated. He told the story to his friends and they all started calling me "Pit Bull."

Most of Alan's friends tested my strength at various times and in various ways—coming on to me, suggesting to me that Alan might be seeing other women, etc. I never retreated and I never suggested that Alan stay away from his friends. I worked each issue through with Alan and stood up to each man until I earned their respect or they stayed away from me.

You may think, "They sound like jerks. Who wants their respect anyway?" But we're fooling ourselves when we say that.

We retreat because we're afraid of these men and then we continue to let men intimidate us. If you want the respect of a certain man or men, you have to take the risks necessary to earn it.

You'll know when you've earned it. The men will say, "She's a keeper." In other words, "this woman is OK, she carries her weight." They won't say this when you cower to them or they see you desperately trying to please them.

Behavior Modification

We need to modify our behavior whenever possible. Start to break the habit of repressing your feelings. When someone upsets you, force yourself to call them and tell them right away. It's embarrassing to have to bring it up six months later or to yell at one person when you are angry at another. Use the embarrassment to motivate yourself to deal with your feelings at the appropriate time so you won't have to suffer the consequences of inappropriate behavior.

Staying in Control of Your Life

Setting Limits With Yourself

Alicia found that getting started was the most difficult step in changing her life. She felt so overwhelmed by all the areas she needed to work on. She wanted to clean her house, plan a budget, confront her friends, lose weight, and begin to meet men. Because of her perfectionistic attitude, if she was not immediately successful, she usually quit right after she started. As a child Alicia was over-controlled by her parents and never learned inner control. Someone else had always set the rules so she had difficulty being inner-directed. In order to become self-reliant, she had to stop waiting for someone to control her. Alicia had to learn to set her own internal limits. For example, she made some of the following agreements with herself: "I won't call any of my friends until I've cleaned the kitchen," "I won't watch TV until I've written one confrontation letter," or "I won't buy a new outfit until I've paid my bills."

Another one of my clients can't set limits with herself in sexual situations because of the sexual abuse she suffered as a child.

This is common with victims of sexual abuse. Since she was unable to stop her babysitter from sexually molesting her, she learned she couldn't say "No." Today she really enjoys sex, and even though she knows that she becomes addicted to men when she sleeps with them too soon, she has had difficulty stopping herself. So she promised herself to start setting sexual limits with men. She started by scheduling her first date with a new man in the daytime or during lunch or with some other event to follow an evening date. By eliminating the possibility of ending up in bed with the man, she keeps her promise to herself.

To be in control of your own life, you must be in touch with who you are and who you are becoming at all times. You must create a way of continually checking in with yourself. Some women choose to keep a journal. Some of my clients come back in for a three-month or six-month check up. My own personal method is to regularly schedule time alone. During this time, I do everything possible to allow any feelings I am unaware of to come to the surface. Only then can I deal with them in a healthy way and maintain control over my life.

Part III
Learning to Love Again

Now that you've completed the program and become more self-reliant, you no longer need to fear losing yourself in a relationship with a man. You can risk being soft and vulnerable, knowing that if a man tries to take advantage of you, that you can express your anger and set limits with him. You will no longer stay in a relationship, trying to prove to a man that you're good enough. Instead, you will realize when the problems are *his* and know when to get out.

Trust yourself—trust that you have the power to love without losing yourself.

11

Intimacy Without Addiction

Finding My Mirror Image

I had given up. I told myself, "Who needs a man anyway? They only cause me pain." After all, I've been with quite a few, and it didn't work with any of them. I married a man like my father, who wanted to control me. I tried living with a free-spirited hippie. All the men I had met were either wimps who wanted me to take care of them or macho types in three-piece suits.

I was nearing forty, and it was time I accepted the fact that I would probably be alone for the rest of my life. I visualized myself in a beautiful house in the mountains, with cats and flowers, sitting in the sun alone, writing. Instead of an "old maid" picture like I'd feared in the past, I was able to see a happy, vital woman who was in charge of her life. I decided to make it come true. By age thirty-seven, I had bought that house, filled it with plants, bought a new sports car, thrown myself into my work, become self-sufficient and independent, and shared all this with no one but my two cats.

I laughed when I heard about classes on finding your soul mate. Instead, I taught seminars on how to give up looking for Mr. Right.

I continued to date and enjoy men. But I made a clear decision that there would never be a man living in my house. As soon as I became completely happy as a single, I met *him*.

One night at a bar a man I knew vaguely was drunk and harassing me. Then a tall, dark, handsome forty-one-year-old stockbroker walked up and said to him, "It looks like it's time for me

to get you out of here." He introduced himself, apologized for
his friend's behavior, took his friend, and left. I sat there in
amazement, thinking, That's just the kind of man I've always
wanted. . . . Where did he go? Who was that masked man?

It was months before I ever saw him again.

In the meantime I was dating several men—a Washington,
D.C., lawyer with whom I had just spent time in Cancun; another
man, with a cabin in Wyoming, where we took fabulous weekends riding his dirt bike through mountain meadows past elk and
wildflowers; and a boyfriend in Vail, with whom I skied on winter
weekends.

What I didn't have was what I wanted—a sensitive yet strong
man I loved and respected and who felt the same about me. I
wanted a man who could be warm and loving—yet could handle
his own life. A man who could have fun with me, yet give and
receive emotional support. A man who could be my best friend.

I had never really known a man like that. The men I knew that
were responsible were workaholics or bores—or both. The playful
men I knew usually turned out to be flakes.

I wondered about this man I had just met. He seemed different
than the rest. A few months later, my sister asked me what kind
of man I wanted. I said, "A man like this Alan that I met." Then
I described to her what I thought he was like. "I want an attractive, classy, strong man who can also be warm and emotional. I
want a man with integrity, a man I can respect. I want a man who
is just like me, but male."

The next time I saw him was at a private party at a local bar.
I had just finished giving a lecture to the local Business and Professional Women group. This time I went over and asked him to
dance. We had drinks. We talked. Then he asked me to drive him
to his car. All of a sudden I noticed that he had on a wedding
ring!

It stopped me cold. I'd been through this before. I knew I liked
this man, and I knew that if I got involved with him under these
circumstances, it would cause me a lot of pain. I agreed to drive
him to his car, but all the way there I let him have it! "You
married men are all alike! You want to have your cake and eat
it too! How dare you spend the whole evening with me and be
married? I'll drive you to your car, but that's it, buddy!"

He tried to tell me that he wasn't like most married men, but

I told him I didn't buy it. "They all say that! There's no way to talk your way out of being married, so don't even try." As we approached his car, he opened his door, looked me straight in the eyes, and said, "Unlike most married men, I'm not going to try to kiss you goodnight." We parted, mutually rejecting each other, which would later lead to mutually respecting each other.

It was months before I saw him again.

What I didn't know about this man was that for the last couple of years, he and his wife had been in marriage counseling. Their problems were close to coming to a head. When his wife quit counseling, he continued. He had learned about himself, evaluated his life, his fears, and his fantasies. He had told his therapist that he wanted a "vital" woman in his life, a woman who could be a partner, someone strong enough to hold her own. His stay-at-home wife accused him of looking for a business woman in a silk suit, briefcase, and high heels. He didn't deny it.

As I saw him from time to time, we were polite and friendly, but nothing more. He would often buy me a drink, making it clear that there were no strings attached.

Not once in the eight months we knew each other before his separation did we ever schedule a meeting to see each other. But we were both excited whenever we ran into each other. We discussed business issues, problems with secretaries, I told him about my clients, the men I dated, and the trips I took. We never discussed his relationship with his wife or any possible relationship between the two of us. We truly became friends.

One night, again at the bar where we first met, we saw each other, and as I started to leave, he said, "Let me buy you a drink. My buddies and I are celebrating because my wife and I decided to get a divorce. Now you have no excuse not to go out with me." My reply? "I never wanted one."

We made arrangements to get together in two days. He came to my house in the mountains for a picnic in the afternoon. I was excited, yet confused. I asked myself a number of questions before he arrived: Was he telling the truth? What if he changes his mind? What should I do? I'm attracted, but is he safe yet? Should we meet somewhere else? What might happen? What did I want to happen?

When he drove up and got out of his car, I couldn't believe how great he looked in his shorts. I'd always seen him in his business clothes, and he in mine. We couldn't take our eyes off each other.

We sat in the sun and talked about life and relationships and what we've always wanted in a mate. We talked about support and equality. We seemed to think alike and be looking for the same things.

We kissed. We held each other. I felt turned on. We discussed how we felt. We discussed that it was too soon to make love. We decided to wait until he was moved out of his house to have sex, which would be in thirty days.

In the next month we had one date a week. We had dinner and drinks and made out in his car, listening to fifties music. It was as if we were sixteen again.

When the thirty days were up, much to my surprise he kept his word and moved out.

The first time we made love was in front of my fireplace listening to "Songbird." We talked and laughed and explored each other for hours.

It seemed too good to be true. The next morning I woke up in a panic, riddled with questions. Should I have slept with him? Will this ruin it now? Will he disappear? Do I know him well enough?

I told him of my fears. He asked what I needed. I told him, "To know you better." He really opened up and we talked all afternoon. I felt better. We were closer now.

I told him that most men are never that open. He said he was already invested in me. He wanted to be close to me. He said he respected me from the beginning, when I wouldn't see him while he was still married. He had been intrigued for some time as he watched me in my red silk dress and red high heels, frequenting the bar with other men. He had enjoyed becoming friends. He had learned to trust me like one of the guys when we discussed mutual business problems. He had decided I was different from other women he knew. Why should he be afraid of opening up to me?

It's now three years later, and the relationship is better than either of us could have imagined. Our love has grown deeper, our sex life gets more and more exciting and passionate as our trust grows, and our respect for each other is greater than ever.

The funny thing is that it's been relatively easy. Both of us did a lot of work on ourselves before we ever met. We've both made numerous mistakes. We've broken the old patterns we learned about relationships from our parents. By the time we met, we were pretty clear about our identities, values, goals, and what we wanted from a relationship with the opposite sex.

We've had issues to deal with in our relationship, like any other couple. But we've talked and worked them out.

I did it right this time. I didn't rush in. I didn't sleep with him too soon. I didn't accept playing second fiddle to another woman. I didn't pressure him. I went on with my life. I wasn't desperate. I was willing and able to live a happy life without him or any man.

He did it right too. He didn't pressure me. He didn't start something new until his old relationship was resolved. He didn't make promises he couldn't keep.

He's the best combination of a businessman in a three-piece suit and a sixteen-year-old playmate a woman could ever dream of. He's responsible and yet playful; he's classy, yet down-to-earth; he's gorgeous, yet not stuck on himself; he's strong, yet warm and sensitive. And he's exactly what I asked for: a reflection of myself—only male.

Fear of Intimacy

But if I had met Alan years before, our relationship would never have worked. I wasn't ready for a healthy relationship before (and neither was he). I had to make myself happy alone first. Back then I was still afraid of being engulfed by a man. I was only attracted to men who were as afraid of intimacy as I was.

Only a few years before, I had walked into a therapist's office and told her that I was unhappy with my relationships with men, and that I thought I *might* have a fear of intimacy. After all, I was dating three men—one was married, one was gay, and one was living in Australia.

I had my problem analyzed—not that it took a therapist to figure it out—but I didn't know what to do about it. Back then I hadn't resolved any of my parental issues or even acknowledged my intense anger or emotional dependency issues. I was in therapy early in my Aspen days, when I was in my rebellious, experimental phase, but didn't have these issues identified. In those days I was a hard core feminist and had learned to reject men before they had a chance to reject me. I rationalized that all men either wanted to control me or were afraid of intimacy, and that my only defense was to sleep with them, send them on their way, and pretend it didn't matter to me.

That's also what Anne from Chapter Eight did, but not quite in the same fashion. She was thirty-four and had been divorced a couple of years when she joined my support group. She was thin and attractive, had no children, and was moving up in her position at a bank. It was hard to believe that she never had a date. She joined the support group complaining, "I want to find out what's wrong with me. Why doesn't anyone ever ask me out? I look in the mirror and I know I'm not ugly. When I do start dating someone, it lasts only a few months. Once I show him I care, he says I'm getting too serious and disappears. It was so easy when I was eighteen. They chased me. What's wrong? Am I just not as attractive? Are there really not enough men?"

The men in the support group assured Anne that her problem was not her looks but her attitude. They said she seemed cool, distant, and unapproachable. They asked her if wearing a ring on her left ring finger was in fact, an intentional way to distance men. She was shocked. She had no idea that her fear of intimacy was showing. Anne's jaded attitude came through more as disinterest or conceit than as the true fear it was, and it kept men at a distance. With no men approaching her, her self-esteem stayed low, making her even more desperate when she did meet someone she liked.

Anne didn't realize that her fear was making her act different than she felt. She wanted to be close to a man, but feared both the possible rejection and the closeness. So she set herself up to fail. When she dated a man, she was careful not to let him know how much she cared or that she wanted to be married, for fear he would run away. Because of this, she attracted men who were looking for the strong, career-oriented type of woman. When after a few months into the relationship, Anne let her vulnerable, needy side come out and began to push for a commitment—these men ran. Thus, proving Anne's theory that men will reject you if you let them know you care, and also continuing her belief that something was wrong with her because she did want a commitment from a man. This kept her hiding behind a facade—for fear of showing her true, imperfect self—and keeping her destructive pattern going.

Anne was somewhat comfortable in her pattern because she could continue to believe that all men were jerks and that it was hopeless anyway—thus justifying her fear of intimacy. Why was Anne so afraid of intimacy? She was raised in a traditional family where her father ruled the roost and showed no emotions and her mother had no identity at all. Anne, on the one hand, wanted a relationship with a man, but on the other, she didn't want to pay the price she thought necessary to have one. This kept her in a push/pull, love/hate conflict with men, similar to the one many other women experience today.

Anne's fear of intimacy came more from not being able to trust herself than anything else. She seemed unable to keep a man from hurting her. Anne had to learn that confrontation and expressing anger are a healthy part of relating to a man—and using those skills helped her learn to trust herself.

Once Anne took the risks necessary to express her feelings and wants, she was able to set limits with men and overcome her fear.

Anne worked through the program. Earlier in the book, I discussed how she confronted her father about his treatment of her as she grew up, his lack of sensitivity and emotionality in their present relationship, and his treatment of her mother. Anne also confronted her mother for never holding her father accountable and trying to keep Anne from doing so. She confronted them both on why neither of them protected her from the uncle who came on to her when she was a child, which still makes her believe that men only want one thing.

Once Anne confronted her father and found out that he really loved her and that he had no idea he was hurting her, she lost much of her fear of being close. This helped her start trusting men. As she continued to date, using her new communication and confrontation skills, she learned much more about men.

Anne experimented with standing up to her dates and saying no to sex. She also stopped pretending she didn't want to get married. She took charge of her social life and joined a singles dating club, met a man she really liked, and they're now living together. Surprisingly, it's her idea not to marry yet. She wants to be sure they can work out the issues of living together that her parents had problems with before making that kind of commitment.

When I first started dating Alan, I was still very distrustful of men. I was enjoying him, but at the same time waiting for, and expecting, him to screw up. I held back emotionally, planning to have to someday walk away, like I had with all the other men once they showed their true colors.

We had been dating for about two months and had just left a bar when I told him I was going home. He asked that we talk a few minutes. We did. He said I seemed so afraid. What was I afraid of? I told him that I wasn't afraid of anything; it was just that he was in the middle of a divorce, and it wasn't safe for me to get too involved with him. After all, he still had a lot of "stuff" to work out from his marriage. He looked me straight in the eye and said, "I have a question. Since you've been divorced for fifteen years, and I've been in the middle of a divorce for two months, why is it that I constantly hear about your ex-husband? I think you're the one who still has issues to deal with! I feel like I'm always being punished for what your ex-husband and father did to you. I'm not them and I won't treat you that way."

Our relationship took an immediate turn for the better. I knew he was right and I admitted it. Not that he didn't have any intimacy or divorce issues to deal with himself, but I was the pot calling the kettle black. I was accusing him of something I hadn't worked through myself. I had usually gotten away with it. Most men had been intimidated enough by me to never call me on my own fear of intimacy. My "therapeutic" comments about them usually worked to back them off. If I didn't push men away with this type of accusation, I often put them off by acting extremely professional and superimportant or by talking incessantly about other men in my life. These were my defenses. But Alan broke right through them. I knew I'd met my match! Because of this, I gained respect for him and we became much more intimate. He had broken down my walls, not maliciously or to hurt me, but to be closer to me. I trusted that this man would be emotionally strong enough for me to lean on at times, and that I wouldn't always have to be the strong one. Maybe, just maybe, things could be different with this man.

My "wall of fear" didn't automatically disappear with Alan, but as he says, "Together we took down one brick at a time." He said he knew I wasn't like his ex-wife, but he had to continually remind me that he wasn't like my ex-husband, my father, or the men I dated in Aspen. He proved to me that he wasn't.

Ten Keys to Finding and Developing a Healthy Relationship With a Man

1. Become Approachable. For many women, it's difficult to drop the facade they've worked for so many years to develop. Karen, the attorney who stood up to her married boyfriend on money issues, works daily in a male-dominated world and has had much difficulty learning to be vulnerable. Her only experience with being vulnerable was when she became totally weak and needy in her relationship with her married lover, and she certainly doesn't want to be like that again. But she realizes that one reason she doesn't meet many men is because she usually looks and acts too intimidating.

I told her that to become approachable again, she needs to combine the softness and vulnerability she felt when she was young and naive with the knowledge and savvy she's gained over the years.

When she experiments with trying to be more approachable, she often goes too far. She'll wear a sexy dress and laugh inappropriately one day, then feeling embarrassed, she'll get nervous and close off completely the next. It's as if there are two people inside of her—a serious lawyer and a playful little girl. Because she's afraid of showing the wrong part of her personality at the wrong time, she tries too hard. There are certainly appropriate times for each, but she needs to be more natural. On a day-to-day basis, she needs to feel a sense of integration of the two parts of her self.

The key is to learn to be soft yet strong. When you do this, you start out warm and friendly with a man. Then, if he hurts you or is abusive, you use your strength and tell him to stop. If he doesn't stop, you become as aggressive as necessary to stop him. When you know you can do this, you will no longer need to be afraid of men and will be able to let down your defensive facade.

2. Know Who You Are and What You Want. Just as in sports, with men it also helps to visualize and talk about the kind of man you want. Alan and I both had an image of what we wanted and we got it. We were also clear about our own self-images.

In the past, when my client, Barbara, found a man she liked, his life became her life. His friends became her friends. Because of this, the man usually became bored with her and ended the relationship. Like Anne, she always hid the fact that she was looking for a long-term relationship.

In her most recent relationship with Vic, a twenty-seven-year-old male psychologist, she isn't letting this happen. Even though she's presently unemployed, she has saved money and decided to go back to school and is not letting Vic run the relationship. Vic insinuated that her decision to go back to school was a bad one, and she made it clear to him that she didn't need another nonsupportive male in her life (she's the one who recently set her father straight about raining on her parade). He backed down immediately. She now knows that a man and a woman don't have to agree on everything to care about each other, they just have to respect each other's opinions. And she knows it's her responsibility to let a man know if she isn't getting the respect she wants from him.

Vic knows she's looking for a long-term relationship. At first, just like the men in her past, he pulled away from her when she told him this. She let it go for a few days and then called him, the way she would a female friend, and asked him what was going on. He told her he thought the relationship was getting too heavy. She said she wanted him to discuss that with her, not pull away. They did, and he says he's not ready for a commitment. She said that was fine, but that whenever he gets scared, she wants and expects him to talk about it—not pull away. He agreed. In the meantime, she says she intends to continue dating other men.

Often, relationships never get past this point because it's difficult for two people to have developed their identities enough to know who they are and what they want. Because few men or women have completed the separation process enough to have developed their own identities, most relationships end up built on need or power struggles. But don't let this depress you, by relating in a healthy way with a man, he will either become healthier or he will leave. (Note how this is different than trying to *fix* him.)

3. Have Realistic Expectations. Having realistic expectations doesn't mean that you can't want the best. My expectations of the kind of man I wanted were high. I wanted an attractive, loving, emotional, successful man. That was realistic as long as I was that kind of woman myself. If I'm overweight, it's unrealistic to expect a thin man to be attracted to me. That's also true with money. If I'm poor, I can't expect a rich man to be attracted to me—unless he's looking for an unequal relationship where he can have all the control. Alan also had realistic expectations. He had let go of the fantasy of having a woman "take care of him and make him happy."

Many women say they want a relationship but are afraid of intimacy. They tell themselves that every man is either too good for them or not good enough. What they are doing is rationalizing the fear. They search for a reason not to connect. Being realistic means not expecting others to be perfect, accepting a man as he is, but setting limits so you don't allow his imperfections to harm you.

4. *Understand Men and Their Imperfections.* Men are people too. They desire healthy relationships with women, but, like us, don't know how to have them. They are as insecure as women but in different ways. They fear failure in their personal relationships more than their careers, because they know they lack skills in this area. They fear not living up to the expectations of women, because they never seem to be able to make them happy. They fear being controlled by women, because their mothers controlled them. When in a relationship, men are as dependent or more dependent than women are, but instead of wanting to play out their dependencies, they fear dependency.

Men don't share their emotions because they don't know how. No one ever taught them. Now, as adults, they're afraid to show just how inadequate they are at emotional expression, so they avoid emotional interaction.

Just as we were taught to give too much, as our mothers did, men learned from their fathers to take the controlling, responsible, rescuing role. It's the only role they know, but most resent it and really want a partnership with a woman. But most men don't have a clue as to how to make that happen. Show them by setting boundaries.

5. *Strategically Plan for What You Want.* What do you want to accomplish? Marriage, or dating several men? Who is your target

market? A twenty-five-year-old athlete? A fifty-year-old busi-nessman? A thirty-five-year-old lawyer? A sensitive man? A rich man? Where will you find him? Health clubs? Dances? Legal conventions?

We must do more than look pretty to get the kind of man we want. Extremely beautiful women know that attractiveness doesn't necessarily get them dates. In fact, it often keeps men at a distance. Having a good product doesn't necessarily mean it will sell.

Use your business skills to help you find the man you want. Who do you want to expose this product—yourself—to? One of my female clients says she wants a man in a three-piece suit, but hangs out in country and western bars. She'll never find him there. Who is your target audience? What is your consumer's demo-graphics? How can you get high visibility? Make a plan based on your answers to these questions. I moved my office to the part of the city where the kind of man I wanted hung out. Don't be afraid to strategize.

6. Openly Communicate Feelings and Require the Same From Him. We have discussed in previous chapters the importance of being emotionally open and honest. But it's often difficult for most women to get a man to do the same.

Most of us have been taught, and believe, that the best way to get a man to open up and be intimate with us is to open up first. This is often true in our relationships with women because they tend to share more the more we share. But it often backfires in relationships with men.

When a woman opens up to a man who has been socialized to take care of women, instead of opening up to her, he more often will use the information to try and rescue her or control her. It's not usually intentional, it's just what men have been taught. So if a woman says she's worried about losing her job, a man is more likely to say, "Don't worry, I can help you find another one," than to say, "Mine's a little shaky too." Because of this, women must keep track of how much they open up to a man if they want to create an equal intimate relationship.

On the other hand, emotionally avoidant women who, like many men, are masking their insecurities with a tough facade, must be careful that they don't fall into the rescuing role. Especially today, there are just as many men as women who want to find someone to take care of them. The best way to keep this from happening is this: when a man complains about his job, income, living situation, or anything else, present a complaint of your own, and/or ask him what he plans to do about his problems. Be vulnerable. Tell him, "I understand. I often feel that way too." If he's simply looking for a momma, he'll run away. If he wants a healthy relationship, you'll be doing your part in creating one.

Most of us get confused about what a man "being there" for us means. My sister says that her husband is "there" for her. I say he's not. He provides well for her. He will "let" her do anything she wants to do. She can lean on him when she's upset, and he stays strong for her. That's a daddy role. Truly "being there" for someone means sharing emotionally—listening to and comforting, but also being vulnerable and allowing the other person to listen to and comfort you.

If a man is advising too much or leaning on you too much, you need to let him know that and ask him to either be stronger or more vulnerable so that the relationship can be equalized.

My relationship with Alan began with confrontation—probably more confrontation than was called for. As I told him what I thought about married men, he heard my negative feelings from the beginning. I never pretended I was someone I wasn't. As time went on, however, Alan behaved emotionally like most men do and didn't share his feelings as much as I did mine. He gave summaries about his day and held back his frustrations and vulnerabilities from me. He also had difficulty talking about issues from his past.

One day I was sharing a problem with him that had to do with my father. I asked him to share issues with me about his father. He said he didn't have any. I told him I didn't believe him. We argued. I told him that I felt that the relationship was getting out of balance. I had been more open with him than he had been with me, I decided to close up until, and unless, he started sharing, because I wanted an equal relationship with him. A few days later, when I hadn't shared much and had been spending more time away from him, he called and said he didn't like this, so what was it I wanted to know?

Be sure you don't wear blinders when you meet a man. We

often see only what we want to see, ignoring a man's flaws and magnifying his strengths. We often fantasize, and in our imaginations turn a man into what we want him to be, rather than seeing what he really is.

Don't think, "He'll be different with me," or, "His wife doesn't understand him," or, "He'll change because he loves me." Women fool themselves when they're desperate for a man.

Look for his flaws. Are they problems that can be worked through? Ask, "What does he have to offer me?" "What does he really want?" Not, "What do I think I can change him into?" Before you invest in a man, find out the following:

- Why did his last relationship end?
- Does he recognize the part he played in his last breakup?
- What was his childhood like?
- How does he get along with his family?
- Does he control his relationships or allow himself to be controlled?
- What anger does he have about women?
- What are his long-term goals?
- Has he ever been in therapy? If needed, would he consider it?
- Who are his idols? Who were his role models?
- How does he handle money?
- Does he want children? If he already has them, what is his relationship with them like?
- Does he like or have pets? Why or why not?
- What are his values about money, religion, etc.?
- Is he an alcoholic, drug addict, workaholic, etc.?
- Who or what controls his life?
- Is he looking to rescue or be rescued by you?

By interviewing him, learn what his patterns are in relationships. Figure out what he might do to you and prepare for it. With this information you can work out your differences before they become issues that can kill the relationship.

7. Resolve Your Differences. Don't you wish relationships could stay as good as new without so much work? The reason relationships don't usually keep their spark is because couples fight over the same issues again and again without solving the problem.

Without resolution, resentment builds and the relationship dies.

With Alan, I tried to handle our potential differences in advance. One night over dinner, I suggested we discuss our political differences. He replied, "What are you—a solution looking for a problem? Are you trying to create problems in our relationship or what?" I told him that I was trying to resolve issues before they became serious problems. We had our discussion. We got closer that night and each and every time we had our "talks." He gradually began to realize that these talks work to prevent fights. Now, he often approaches me with, "Let's talk about anything that could go wrong before we leave on this trip, so we can prevent it." He's become a believer.

The first real fight Alan and I had was while we were just friends and accidently ran into each other in a bar. A mutual acquaintance insulted me, and I had confronted the guy, but he wouldn't leave, so I asked Alan to tell him to leave. He quickly retorted with, "You're a strong woman, handle it yourself!" For a while I would hardly speak to him. Then one night we finally talked it out. He said he was tired of rescuing women and asked, "Why can't women handle their lives themselves?" I told him I wasn't looking for him to take care of me, I just wanted the *support* of a friend. I told him I would have supported him in the same situation. We discussed the difference between rescuing and supporting and decided we *could* be supportive of each other. We came to a resolution about how we would handle the situation if it ever happened again. Now when we talk about the fight, we laugh, because nothing like that has ever been a problem again.

Women are often afraid to bring up differences to men for fear they'll be so far apart in their beliefs that they'll lose the relationship. Usually the opposite is true—the differences become greater when they go undiscussed. They turn into power struggles, with each person insisting that *his* or *her* way is the "right" way.

Fights are simply "corrections" in a relationship. Alan, who is a stockbroker, now relates our problem-solving to the stock market. He says, "The stock market continues to go up until all of a sudden something's going wrong and a correction is needed. Each correction usually causes a greater upsurge in the market, just as our confrontations do in our relationship."

No two people can always get along. Alan and I had several differences. One of them was that he was a very patient person and I was a very impatient person. At times we argued over which was the right way to be. After much discussion, we agreed that in some cases, patience is best, and in others, impatience is more appropriate. Interestingly, we've both changed and grown from the difference.

When you start dating someone new, find out what your differences are and discuss them again and again until you understand and come to resolution on them. Don't think that love will take care of it. If you can't come to resolution, then agree to disagree, promising not to attack each other and to respect each other's opinion. In bringing differences to resolution, each party must desire to solve the problem instead of taking an accusatory stance, or it will become a war. Each partner must think, "He's made mistakes and so have I, but where do we go from here?" To work it through, both partners must let go of "how it's supposed to be" and decide how they feel and how they "want" it to be. To come to resolution, both must discuss how each could have handled the situation better and make a commitment to do it that way next time. Here's how to fight fair.

1. Don't brush anger away with, "I shouldn't feel that way."
2. Handle anger when you feel it so grudges don't build up.
3. Anger should be conveyed to the person who hurt you before you tell anyone else about the situation.
4. Don't agree to do things you don't want to do, so that the "you owe me" attitude does not build up.
5. Never attack or criticize anyone. There is no such thing as "constructive criticism." Don't put your value judgments on others. Instead of saying, "That's stupid," own it by saying, "I feel angry when you say things like that."
6. Don't write anyone off until you've given them a chance to fix the problem. Tell the person how you feel and what you want and give him or her a chance to give it to you.
7. Don't rigidly fight for your way. Don't let your ego be at stake over every issue so that winning becomes more important than resolution.
8. If you make a sarcastic remark, ask yourself, "What am I really upset about?"
9. Don't seek revenge. Verbally express your anger instead.
10. Don't build cases against anyone.

8. *Equalize the Power.* It's difficult to keep power in a relationship equal. You must be aware of the possibility of it getting out of balance. Lana, of course, learned that the hard way with her doctor friend in Los Angeles. For months the relationship was great, and he was treating her like a queen. He began to criticize her so slowly and gradually that she didn't see what was happening until it was too late. Because of his own insecurities, he had to put her down to build himself up. I helped her see that this was what he was doing, and taught her how to search for his flaws. I told her that any man who is really secure in himself doesn't need to treat a woman abusively. To equalize the relationship, she prepared a "counter presentation" listing his problem areas. This helped her take him off the pedestal. Then she told him how she felt about what he'd done to her, said she wanted him to stop it, and then went through her list of his problems, aggressively confronting him. He backed down completely, agreed that she was right, and said he would make it up to her. He begged her to stay in the relationship. She actually flipped the balance of power totally in her favor. He has now turned into a wimp, showing no strength, and she's pulling out of the relationship. The longer the power stays out of balance, the more likely it is to totally flip to the other side after a major confrontation. This happened to my parents. Dad ruled the first twenty years, and mom ruled the last twenty. And none of those forty years were happy.

Power can be equalized even if you're the one with all of it. If you're in the power position, let him know you're tired of carrying most of the responsibility and are losing respect for him. To equalize power, you must not be afraid to confront, and express anger and/or lack of respect. And you must be willing to let the relationship go if it doesn't improve.

The power in a relationship usually gets set in the first few months. Marriage seldom improves the power structure, because once a deal is done, you have less power than before.

Alan and I did not have a power struggle at the beginning. Since we had become friends, mutual respect was already there. However, at times the power would shift a little. For instance, during his divorce, I felt that he was leaning on me too much for his happiness, and I told him I wanted him to be happy even when I wasn't around. I said I was losing respect for him when

I felt he couldn't be happy without me. He backed off and did more things on his own, and the relationship became balanced again.

If your identity is well-formed, you may not have to fight for power. At this point, Lana would not fall into the same trap that she did with the doctor.

9. Make Clear Agreements. On our first date, Alan and I sat in the sun and discussed what we wanted from a partner in a love relationship. Although our lists were not intentionally directed toward each other at that time, we were starting to make our first agreement.

Agreements need to be made early on, dealing with each issue as it comes up: who pays for what, how clean he keeps his apartment when you're there, his attitude when he talks to you, who prepares meals, and a host of other possible issues that could become serious problems in the future.

Alan and I have discussed every issue and come to agreements on each one. We agreed we didn't want children, especially since he already has one grown daughter. He's a smoker and I'm not. He promised to be considerate, and I promised to stay off his case. I also said I wouldn't pressure him to ski, if I didn't have to learn to play golf.

We decided to keep both of our houses—his in the city, mine in the mountains. We agreed to never mix our money and to share all mutual expenses and chores. We spoke of our goals and fantasies—a beach home, a trip to Sweden, money and investments we can live on in later years.

We also discussed the issue of monogamy early in a relationship and decided initially that we would both date others. We both knew what the rules were in our relationship from day one. As time went on we made a decision to change that agreement, but again we discussed it together before we made the decision. We worked out any and all issues that we felt could become problems in the future.

It's especially important to get an agreement regarding equality in the relationship. We must make it very clear to a man from the very beginning that we want an equal relationship—or no relationship at all. We're often so eager for love that we overlook the signs that the man we're dating doesn't really want an equal relationship. There may be clues that he expects us to take on the "wife" or "superwoman" role. Watch for these clues, bring them to his attention, and get them resolved before you go any further in the relationship.

Andrea thought she had a clear agreement with her husband, Terry. He worked as a lawyer in a downtown office, and she ran a dress-design business from their home. He made the house payments, and she paid for groceries and the children's clothing. She felt they had an equal relationship.

Before Terry married Andrea, he made it clear that he never wanted to support a woman. He wanted a woman who had her own career and could carry her weight in a relationship. In fact, before they married, he asked for a prenuptial agreement, though her assets were as great as his. What Andrea forgot to do was make sure he was going to carry *his* weight. She not only helped provide for the family but carried all the housework and child-care duties as well. Because she and Terry both had their own incomes, somehow she thought that made her relationship with him equal.

When I asked Andrea why Terry didn't help around the house, she defended him with, "But he helps when I ask. And besides, he just doesn't have time."

Later on, exhausted from trying to be a superwoman, Andrea decided it was time to change their agreement since she was obviously getting the short end of the stick. She decided to hold Terry accountable for carrying his share of the workload at home. First she prepared a list of all the household chores and the expenses paid by each. The inequity became obvious. Then she told Terry how exhausted and burned-out she was feeling and why, and asked for his cooperation.

She gave him two choices. She wanted him to take on half of the household chores, or, because she wants to be closer to her two young children, he could take a more traditional role and pay most of the bills. Either would take the pressure off of her.

Terry agreed to pay more of the expenses, and Andrea decided to temporarily cut back on her work. This solution would not be acceptable for a woman whose priorities were work, but it was a satisfactory compromise for Andrea. She gained free time and respect from Terry.

It might have been more difficult for Andrea to get Terry to help with half of the housework, especially since he already spent too much time at the office, and she'd let him get away with it for years. But it wouldn't have been impossible.

To negotiate the contract, both parties must state what they want, what they're willing to give as a trade-off, what will happen if certain variables change, and what happens when someone doesn't keep his end of the bargain.

10. Commit to the Relationship and Require the Same From Him.
Women usually make the mistake of committing to a relationship before the man does. Always continue to date other men until, and unless, he is committed to you—or you will give away your power and probably never get a commitment from him. Using the Four Steps of Healthy Communication, let him know how you feel, what you want, and that if he doesn't come around, you will continue to keep looking. Then back off, spend less time with him, and begin to increase your options. Often, this will make him change his mind, but don't count on it and don't do it just for that purpose.

Commitment to intimacy is the most important commitment you can receive. Many women settle for a commitment to marriage without a commitment to emotional intimacy—sharing and talking about their relationships. That's because it's often easier to get. I once spent time with a man I'd known who actually flew in from Austria to ask me to marry him, yet he wouldn't talk to me about anything emotional when we were together. He thought commitment to marriage was enough—that he shouldn't have to share of himself.

In all relationships, including friendships, you need to ask for a commitment from others to share honest, open feelings with you—both good and bad—and to let you know when they aren't happy with the relationship. Otherwise the relationship won't be able to grow, guilt and resentment will develop, and it will die. Here are some guidelines for building an intimate, nonaddictive relationship with a man.

HOW TO DO IT RIGHT

· Become friends first.
· Control yourself, not him.

- Keep separate friends and interests.
- Take alone time.
- Make romance a priority.
- Spend quality time talking.
- Develop a united front—"It's you and me against the world."
- Accept each other's differences.
- Don't overstep boundaries.
- Continually profess your love.

12

Maintaining an Equal, Healthy Relationship

Rex was forty and Leah was twenty-six. They met when he was taking a scuba-diving class that she was teaching. She also taught CPR, ran a consulting business, and looked great. He'd never met such a strong, beautiful woman and was immediately smitten. She was impressed not only by his lucrative computer business but by his urbanity, charm, and sensitivity. They dated and a year later were married.

They were incredibly happy and felt sure they had made the right decision. That is, until she started allowing him to take control of the relationship.

She had planned to enter medical school, but he convinced her it would be too hard on their relationship. She settled for nursing school instead. While she was in school he advised her on classes, helped her stand up to her supervisor, and edited her research papers.

As he helped her, she became more insecure about her academic abilities and convinced herself she would never have made it through medical school anyway. They moved to a house in the mountains, far from her scuba diving and her friends. She began to wait—for her nursing degree, for his sexual overtures, for his attention—for her *life* to improve. She felt unloved. She tried to make him love her by cooking for him and bringing him little presents. When that didn't work, she started to nag him about spending more time with her. In response, he began to watch TV and undertook more household projects. She nagged him even more.

They began to dread weekends, when they had the leisure time to talk. One Sunday morning the conversation took a nasty turn.

SHE: "You give more affection to your dog than to me."

HE: "Maybe if you weren't always nagging me about something, I'd feel more like being with you."

SHE: "You don't love me anymore."

HE: "I feel like I'm raising a child. You're not the vibrant, independent woman I fell in love with."

SHE: "You're never there for me. I didn't get married so I could be alone all the time."

HE: "You want to take away all my freedom. I'm tired of it. If you hassle me this way one more time, I'm leaving for good."

She felt frightened and feared being abandoned. Faced with the Big Ultimatum, she was torn between suppressing her feelings or losing her man. He felt frustrated and guilty. He didn't want to hurt her like this, but he couldn't live with a woman who constantly complained. He mourned for the strong woman he had married; she, for the supportive man she had married.

They came into my office, asking, "What happened? What went wrong? Is it salvageable? What can we do to fix it?"

Leah and Rex made the common mistakes that many couples make in relationships. Though Leah appeared strong and competent, she didn't really feel that way inside. When she met Rex, she put him on a pedestal. Though she did want to go to medical school, she was somewhat relieved when she didn't have to go through all that work; after all, Rex had been working for some time in his profession and was doing quite well financially. She believed his strengths could make up for her insecurities.

Ten Mistakes Women Make in Relationships

1. Trying to Control Him Instead of Ourselves. Leah had tried to get Rex to stay home, give her attention, and make her happy. Leah had to give up the idea that Rex had the power to make her happy and decide to make herself happy. It took awhile to let go of this fantasy, especially since she was living with him. She had difficulty separating from him enough to start the program. Living with a man while you break dependency on him is sort of like working in a bar while you break an alcohol addiction. I didn't ask her to actually move out, just to pull away emotionally and spend time alone to complete the steps in the program. She struggled and struggled, until one day, I told her that I had a fantasy of starting a clinic for women obsessed with men just for this reason. I described it as a combination of an alcohol/drug clinic and Club Med, referring to the Club Med in Cancun where I often went to spend alone time in a social environment. The next week, she came in grinning, saying she was ready to make me an offer I couldn't refuse. She said, "What if we go to Club Med together for a week? I pay, you give me two hours of therapy every day, and we work through this program and get it over with." We left two weeks later.

Away from her husband, she was a different person. At Club Med, she was able to experience herself again and explore new and old interests. She was able to take control of her life. She got back into scuba diving—which helped her remember she was good at some things. She wrote confrontation letters to both parents. And most important, she was able to go back to her husband with a plan and the determination to equalize their relationship.

She told him she would either figure out how to be happy within the marriage, or she would be forced to leave. She told him that she realized she had sacrificed too much in the relationship, and that it was his turn to do the sacrificing. Then she told him that she was going to try to get into medical school next fall, even if it meant moving away from him temporarily. He was upset because he wanted a child, and he felt that waiting until she finished medical school would be too long.

She said she did want children and would consider having a child first, if he would agree that when the child was two, he'd take full responsibility for it while she went back to school. He agreed, and she said, "By the way, would you mind putting that in writing?"

2. Meshing Our Identities With His. Because Leah wasn't clear about her own identity, she eagerly meshed it with her husband's. And certainly, it wasn't all her fault. Rex welcomed and even expected it.

We're taught that when we're in love, "we two shall be one." We believe that if we're really in love, we will naturally merge our identities with his. We think that being in love means having the same beliefs, values, and goals. We often feel insulted and unloved when our mates don't agree with us. We start practicing *we think*, whereby we assume that if we love our spouses, we should think the same way they do, and vice versa. We also think we should spend our time together sharing the same activities— he should come to the opera whether he enjoys it or not, and we should go to baseball games, whether we enjoy them or not. When romantic partners attempt to merge identities, most often the woman gives hers up, although men are often guilty too. But sacrificing on either or both parts doesn't make the relationship better. They not only lose the differences that attracted them to each other in the first place, but they also begin to take responsibility for their mate's faults and ultimately, their mate's happiness.

Certainly, the "we" that Leah and Rex had become had no sparkle. Neither of them were as exciting as they were before they married. She stopped scuba diving. She didn't mingle with her friends at the hospital because Rex put them down by saying they had the "social worker" mentality. He no longer went hunting because Leah didn't approve. He stopped mountain climbing because Leah gets altitude sickness. Each tried to make the other happy. Their lives had evolved around holding the other back from being themselves.

3. *Looking for a Father Figure.* My grandmother always said, "It's just as easy to marry a rich man as a poor man." And it's probably true. But if you marry a man who has more money than you do, you are almost guaranteed to have an unequal relationship. The person with the money has the power. Besides, men who bring money into the relationship often think they don't have to give anything else. That's certainly what Rex believed. Besides, he had expectations of his own. He believed that if he provided money, it was Leah's responsibility to mother him and take care of his personal needs. Many women who look for a rich man don't realize that this is usually the expected trade-off.

My female clients continually get angry at me over this issue. They still want a man with money and use the excuse that "because of the inequities that continue in the job market,'' they deserve to find a man who has or makes more money than they do. And they want to believe that if a man *does* have more money, it doesn't necessarily mean the relationship can't be equal, does it? Surely I shouldn't expect them to date men on the same income level as theirs.

The truth is that the greater the difference in income, the more unequal the power usually is. However, Valerie was able to equalize her relationship with Ken even though he made much more than she did. She made enough money herself that she had the capacity to leave, which gave her ''enough'' power. She also no longer allowed Ken to use his money to control her. When he tried, she made it clear that she'd be glad to move to a smaller house where she could afford to make half of the house payment.

Relationships in which the man becomes the father and the woman becomes the mother, or vice versa, are relationships set up to fail. Both parties develop resentments similar to those they felt toward their parents. Leah enjoyed Rex's support—both financially and his help with school work—but she also resented his control. Rex enjoyed Leah's cooking and pleasing attempts but also felt more and more obligated by them. The resentments certainly put a damper on their sex life. After all, who wants to have sex with their parent? Parental roles in relationships kill the spark more quickly than anything else.

4. Spending Too Much Time Together. When people are constantly together, they get on each other's nerves. I used to tell my mother, when she'd beg me to lengthen my visits with her, ''Don't take it personally, mom. I love you. It's just that I can't be around anyone constantly without getting irritable, and I don't want to let that happen.'' No matter how strong we are or how clear our identities are, when we are in the continual presence of another person, we begin to *react instead of act.* We begin to be swayed by that person and his beliefs. We lose touch with ourselves. We begin to believe what *we think* rather than what *I think,* whether we want to or not.

In fact, when two people live together on a daily basis, it's much harder to keep the spark alive, particularly for women. Women are so used to giving to others that they usually feel guilty when they don't think of others' needs first. It's much easier for a woman to fall back into her old patterns than try to be herself, particularly if a man puts pressure on her—and especially if he calls her selfish when she doesn't cater to him.

That's what happened to Jackie's mother, Marjorie, who was murdered by her boyfriend. Jackie was working with me on her assertiveness issues and realized that she learned her passivity from her mother. Her mother's boyfriend, Carl, constantly criticized Marjorie, and Marjorie allowed his criticism. A few times, Jackie mentioned to her mother that she didn't like what he did, but her mother defended him.

Carl had always been controlling and he especially had a problem with the fact that Marjorie had started making more money than he did. His insecurities about that, and a very rough childhood that left him feeling unloved, kept him constantly pressuring her to show him more and more love. Each time Marjorie did something for herself or her children, he took it personally and called her selfish. Part of her believed his accusations—since her mother used to call her that. She couldn't see just how sick this man was and that she would never be able to do enough to make him feel loved. It was *his* problem, not *hers*.

Carl ended up shooting Marjorie and then put a gun to his own head. Jackie had no idea that the abuse was so serious. She came to find out that, ever since her mother had moved in with him a few months before, he had been beating her, but few people knew it.

Though this story is much more drastic than our everyday experiences, it makes its point. Living together and/or marriage never make a relationship better. Any problem left unresolved in a relationship will be intensified when you constantly spend time with someone. As long as a woman has the power to walk away, she has the capacity to change the way a man treats her. As Jackie says, "When my mother and her boyfriend fought before they moved in together, mom was at least able to go home before the tension escalated to this point."

Many people today are choosing different life-styles than the day-to-day living together of traditional marriages. Some couples have bicoastal residences, others are building houses next door to each other. Some are even deciding not to marry because they've tried it before and see how living together can often destroy love.

Because Alan and I learned this in our past marriages, we've chosen not to marry and to keep separate residences. All the time we spend together is by choice. We feel this is a major reason that the spark in our relationship has not only *not* diminished but has increased. We've discovered the importance of allowing the other person time to miss us.

Besides, couples who spend all their time together are not as likely to plan quality time together. Years ago, I stopped planning quality time with my best friend, once we became roommates. We assumed we'd see each other a lot, which we did, but we rarely discussed anything more than bills, housework, and other day-to-day topics. The friendship died. This is what happens in many marriages, and it is certainly what happened to Leah and Rex's relationship, as well as Peggy and Tom's.

5. Not Keeping Romance a Priority. Couples get wrapped up in their work, children, and the daily maintenance of the household and put romance on a back burner. The spark in a relationship must be tended in order to keep it going—special quality time must be set aside each day or at least once each week. Women must insist that dating continue. But it's not just a woman's responsibility.

After marriage, many women try to hold onto the romance, but men seldom do. Women, like Leah, often tend to think that they must carry *all* the responsibility for romance and emotional closeness in the relationship. They believe that if they don't carry it, there won't be any. Since women usually carry that burden, men don't have to do it themselves. Though women complain about this responsibility, they seldom insist that a man handle it. Just like the laundry, he'll never take the initiative if it's already done.

Andrea, who we discussed earlier, used to beg Terry to plan quality intimate time with her. He always promised he would but never followed through. When she asked for leisurely Sunday mornings in bed, he always had a golf game or work to catch up on. He even became too busy and too tired to have sex.

Andrea used to leave love notes around the house, believing that if she did, he might reciprocate. She used to call him several times a day at the office and prepare his favorite meals, only to be disappointed when her special considerations were not only not returned or appreciated, but they often simply irritated him.

Surprisingly, as she became more available, he became more scarce.

She had told him again and again how she felt, but admitted to me that nothing was working. I asked her to stop being the romance giver and begin taking charge of her own happiness instead.* She did. She began to ask friends to go to dinner and to plays. She decided to take her children on a long-awaited trip to Africa, instead of waiting for Terry to find the time to go with them. She's making sure that she has the emotional closeness she wants from her friends. She often invites Terry to join her when she has plans but goes without him now when he's too busy. As a result, Terry has become curious about Andrea's evenings and has recently been asking if he can join her.

Don't continually handle the romance if he doesn't return it. On the other hand, if he does, then have fun surprising your partner with special cards or other romantic gestures that he especially enjoys. Here are a few suggestions.

- Invite your husband out to lunch or dinner, and then surprise him by taking him to a hotel room, where the champagne is already on ice.
- Make a photo collage of your relationship from its beginning to present.
- Buy ten cards and send him one each day.
- Rent a limo for the evening. Be driven around while the two of you sip champagne and do whatever else your hearts desire.
- Have a professional photographer photograph his favorite part of your body. Enlarge it, crop it, and frame it.
- Listen and pay attention to any fantasy he mentions, such as, "I'd love to be passive and have a woman seduce me." Dress the part and play the role.
- Write a relationship history, remembering all the good times you've had together. Give it to him.

Each mate needs to remind the other on a regular basis what it is they love about each other. Never say, "You know I love you." Tell him you love him and why, and ask him to do the same.

*The earlier in a relationship this is done the more likely it is to work. Also, it will not work if he doesn't really love you.

Take time to nurture the relationship. Constantly look for new ways to bond. Spend long periods of unstructured time together, having fun and doing things spontaneously. Discuss feelings about movies, current events, values, life's little frustrations. Remind each other of your love. Become a mutual-admiration society.

6. Avoiding Issues. Many couples have learned how to avoid each other. The man often makes work his life, and the woman makes the children hers. In dual-career relationships, they both often use work and children to avoid each other. Then they avoid household issues by hiring a maid. On weekends, they run errands or become couch potatoes. They become experts at putting off emotional problems, hoping they'll go away. Rex and Leah tried to communicate, but each time they did, it never went anywhere. Leah would hold in her feelings until she exploded and verbally attacked Rex. Rex would walk away because he felt he should protect her from his bad feelings. Both were at fault. Both needed to learn to express their feelings as they felt them, rather than holding them in and/or walking away. When couples hold in their anger, a wall of resentment begins to cover all loving feelings.

Leah never let Rex know how much it hurt her to move away from her scuba diving, her friends, and a city where she could pursue medical school. On the one hand, she wanted him to know how she felt about it. On the other hand, now that she had *him,* she thought she shouldn't feel upset about losing those things. So instead of telling him how she felt, she nagged him to make up for her losses and pressured him to make her happy.

Her resentments and his frustration with the nagging were building a thicker and thicker wall. Neither were taking the emotional risks necessary to bring the issues into the open and resolve them. The thicker the wall became, the less they talked about anything—for fear of blowing up the entire thing. The ironic twist to this is, the whole relationship *will* blow up if you don't discuss and resolve the issues.

7. Going Outside the Marriage to Meet Our Needs. The old coffee klatsch of the past, in which the neighborhood housewives got together and talked about their children, has changed to career women gathering in the office lounge to discuss the most recent scenario in their marital indiscretions.

This is what Bonnie and her friends do. A few years ago, a *People* magazine survey reported that women were finally having affairs almost as often as men were.[1] Is this movement toward equality? I don't think so.

The movie *Fatal Attraction* was very popular in 1988. Many people who were having affairs were frightened, though some just decided that they should be more secretive. I believe that if Dan Gallagher, the movie's main character, had talked to his wife as soon as he realized that his lover was obsessed with him, he could have prevented much of the disaster. And if he *had* talked to his wife *before* the affair about their sexual problem (their daughter interfered with their sexual activity), the whole situation might have been prevented.

They needed to come up with solutions together. Maybe they needed to get away for a long weekend—just the two of them. Maybe bedtime for the child needed to be earlier—and shared by both—with a nightcap for them afterwards.

When a woman or man goes outside their relationship for intimacy—whether sexual or emotional—the relationship is in trouble. Often both emotional intimacy and excitement are missing, but can be repaired if both partners will work at it. However, some men only feel safe being emotionally intimate with women they're not married to, because these women have no control over the men's lives.

Often, an affair will help keep a bad relationship together when it needs to end. The "other woman" becomes the enabler for the man to relate to so he is able to stay distant from his primary relationship. For instance, Karen's affair initially kept her and her lover more content in their marriages because their emotional and sexual needs were being met by each other. But, in the long run, that's not what Karen really wanted. She finally left her marriage but then realized that she wasn't Brian's first and only affair, and that he would probably never leave his wife. It hurt her to discover that Brian would probably find someone else to fill the role of mistress if she broke up with him. That's how he had kept his marriage bearable for years. And if she were able to win him someday, what made her think he wouldn't cheat on her?

Karen wishes now that instead of jumping into her affair, she would have tried to work out the issues with her husband before divorcing him. Not that she feels she could necessarily have saved the marriage, but she would feel better about herself if she had handled it that way.

8. Creating a Power Struggle. Everyone knows that the key to a good relationship is communication, but it depends on what you communicate. Some couples constantly communicate "It's your fault." "No, it's yours." They constantly blame each other. They often communicate "shoulds," i.e., "This is the way you *should* act if you're a good husband, lover, father, etc." That kind of communication kills love and puts the same perfectionistic ideals on us that our parents did.

These couples spend the rest of their marriages fighting that *their way* is the "right" way: "I told you that was the way to do it." "Why don't you ever listen to me?" And in the age-old fight between men and women, the man usually believes that logic is the way to solve a problem, so he accuses his partner of "over-reacting" and being overemotional and irrational. She believes that an emotional response is the "right" way and accuses him of being cold and insensitive. The truth is that there is no right and wrong where feelings and perceptions are concerned. But each partner puts his or her ego at stake. Each rebels against the other as they did with their parents.

When a man hurts us, we tend to believe that he did it on purpose and doesn't really care about us. Often he doesn't even know he hurt us, so the first thing we need to do is tell him we're hurt and discover if the hurt was intentional. When we don't do this, we immediately want to hurt him back. We feel we have to fight back to preserve ourselves—this is how the war begins. Also, the feeling that someone doesn't love us brings out all the old insecurities we felt as a child when our parents scolded us, our peers laughed at us, or we lost someone we loved. This insecurity makes the power struggle more intense and makes us feel we have to prove we are right to prove that we're okay.

Take Paul and Joyce for instance. He's always been a wild cowboy. When he met Joyce, who seemed to be as wild and crazy as he was, they were sure it was meant to be. They had a ball—until they got married and had a child. Now she's upset when

Paul isn't home at 6 P.M. Why does he have to party so much? Feeling alienated, she reached out to the church for support. The church helps her feel right when she verbally beats him up with, "You *should* do this and you *shouldn't* do that." The resentment is growing and he seldom comes home anymore. He says, "She knew what I was like when she married me, and I'm not going to change for her." He stays out later than he wants to—just to prove she can't control him. She changes the locks and once nailed his burned steak to the door when he missed one too many dinners. They go round and round and neither will end the war or leave the marriage.

My mom and dad were in a power struggle like this for almost forty years. And each one screamed regularly, "You're killing me!" But the desire to win the war was greater than the desire to be happy.

9. *Not Setting Limits.* Leah let Rex overstep his boundaries when she let him help her with her homework and the confrontation with her boss. There is a difference between "supporting" her and "handling it" for her. Support would have been letting her know he believed she could do it, while "handling it" for her made her feel more insecure. Leah's increasingly insecure feelings were her clue that Rex was going too far, and she needed to tell him.

When she felt insulted by Rex, she thought, "I'm sure he didn't mean it. He was just trying to help." She probably also thought, "That's just the way men are. They're used to taking charge."

Once I asked Alan to read a letter I had written to my father. He told me that he thought it was too strong, then let me know he'd hate to get a letter like that from his daughter. He thought I should wait to mail it and take time to think it over. I was terribly hurt. I had worked on the letter for weeks and was so proud that I had it ready to send. I didn't want Alan's criticism or approval, I just wanted to share it with him. I told him that he had overstepped his boundary and that I didn't want him to evaluate my letter, only read it and support my attempt to resolve an issue with my father. Now when I give him something like that to read, he asks if I want his feedback or not, and I tell him if I do. I give him the same respect. Just because two people love each other does not give them the right to analyze, evaluate, and criticize everything the other does.

We often want to believe that if a man cares about us, he will be fair, and we won't have to tell him what we want and don't want. We won't have to keep score. But it's not true. It's our responsibility to let him know our needs. It sounds so cold and calculating to say, "I cooked last time," or, "It's your turn to clean the bathroom," but if we don't we'll end up resenting him. Don't keep score and then hold it in, however. It's very important to share the scoreboard as you go along.

10. *Not Knowing When to Give Up.* There could come a time when you've worked and worked on the relationship and decide that the resentments are too great to be resolved. Peggy and Tom tried to resolve their issues, but the resentments ran too deep. They had talked about their feelings, gone away on vacations without the children, and even temporarily separated and worked on themselves. But no matter what they did, they could not recreate the spark, so they divorced.

What do you do if he won't cooperate? Women often complain that they're willing to work on the relationship, but their husbands aren't. It's impossible to build or have a healthy relationship without both parties cooperating. *You alone* cannot fix the relationship. You must insist that he join you in marriage counseling and/or the two of you create your own plan for putting the relationship back together, such as: "We'll discuss the problems and work on them every Wednesday night; we'll spend every Saturday involved in quality romantic time; we'll get some books on recreating the sexual spark;" etc.

If he will not cooperate, you must accept the fact that your relationship with him is over. Often the reason he won't cooperate is that he knows he doesn't have to—because he believes you'll never leave, no matter what. Until you accept the possibility of the relationship being over, you will not be strong enough to clean it up.

If you really want to keep the relationship, don't leave until you've gone through the four steps of healthy communication, with your ultimatum being your threat of leaving.

But, before you walk out, put your ducks in a row. Have all the variables covered—where you'll live, how you'll support yourself, who your emotional support system will be, what you'll say to friends, how you will spend your weekends and holidays, and so on.

Prepare your case in advance. Make it convincing and know which "wants" are negotiable and which are not. Before making your presentation, prepare for the worst. Visualize yourself losing, leaving, and being okay. Then, go in with that attitude.

If the relationship ends, expect to feel sad that it didn't work—no matter who ended it. Feel the pain. Feel the rejection and the embarrassment. Even cry.

Don't accept all the blame. It's important not to think that you were the problem. It's important not to feel like a failure. Don't get stuck feeling sorry for yourself or putting yourself down. Sure, if you had tried harder to be the person he wanted you to be, it might have lasted longer. But you would have lost something greater—yourself.

If this person gave you no chance to fix the problem, it may feel unfair. Let him know how angry this makes you. Hold him accountable. Ask questions and demand that the person explain what happened—until you understand it. Then get angry at what he did to you, and let him know in a letter or in person. Use the anger to empower you, but don't become caught up in getting even. Try and figure out what went wrong. Become introspective. Maybe you were too naive. Maybe you should have asked more questions or confronted the situation sooner. There's always something you could have done differently. But don't beat yourself up. Instead, decide how you will do it differently next time and make a commitment to that. Take the knowledge you gained from your mistakes and use it in your next relationship.

Women often stay in bad relationships because the relationship feels normal—just like home did. They also stay because they'd rather be with *any* man than no man at all. They fear loneliness more than they fear abuse. They also fear having to run their lives on their own. They don't want to support themselves or have to make decisions. Pressure from family or guilt about hurting their partners also keeps women in bad relationships. Don't let these issues hold you back when you know in your gut that it's over.

Signs of a Marriage in Trouble

1. You hold in your feelings because you fear hurting him or being abandoned by him.
2. You feel held back by him because he controls you or you constantly feel the need to sacrifice for him.
3. You feel that you're working against each other instead of together, probably because your values and goals are different.
4. You feel like nothing you ever do pleases him, because he's probably overly critical and/or has the impossible expectation that you should make him happy.
5. You have no common goals that you know of because you basically live separate lives.
6. He gives nothing to you emotionally, though he may give you "things."
7. You are attracted to other men or at least are fantasizing about them.
8. You look for reasons not to come home or stay at home.
9. Obligations, not desire, rule your behavior, because you try to be a good wife even though you're really not into it anymore.
10. You resent having all or none of the responsibility and control in the relationship.

Making It Work

If you want to make your relationship work, you have to give up the myths you've been taught about how marriage is supposed to be. It is not his job to make you happy and never will be. Until, and unless, you can give up this myth and complete your own identity and take charge of your life, you cannot have a healthy relationship with him. You will be stuck in the patterns of your parents. You will believe that you must sacrifice for those you love, that husbands and wives have certain roles they should follow, that obsession is love, that a man should automatically know how you feel and what you want without your having to tell him, and that denying problems will make them go away. You must let go of these ideas to have a healthy relationship. But what if you've already made these mistakes? Is it too late to clean up?

Ten Steps to Put the Spark Back in Your Relationship

1. Recognize, admit, and work through any destructive patterns in your own life by completing the Eight Steps to Emotional Intimacy Without Addictions.

2. Using the Four Steps of Healthy Communication, resolve old resentments and past issues with your partner, coming to an agreement as to how each problem will be handled in the future. (You may need a therapist to help you with this if there are many resentments.)

3. Recreate your "Life Before Mate" identity. Stop sacrificing, and enjoy your own interests, friends, and other pursuits in life. Live by your own value system.

4. Create and maintain your own personal power. Don't blame your mate for your life. Be a whole person and do whatever you need to do to stay in charge of your life in all areas: financially, socially, emotionally, physically, and in your career. Ask your mate to do the same.

5. Accept your mate's humanness. He isn't perfect, but neither are you. Don't judge. Instead, set limits about how you will and won't be treated and ask him to do the same.

6. Be emotionally honest from now on and get a commitment from him to do the same. Tell him how you feel, what you want, and what you'll do if you don't get it. Make and get a commitment to be continually intimate with each other.

7. Let go of the old expectations of marriage and make a list of new, healthier guidelines for your relationship, which you both agree on, such as: Tell the truth no matter how much you think it will hurt, because it will hurt worse if you lie; no criticizing or living by the "shoulds" of others; no "sacrificing for" or feeling "obligated to" each other; listen to each other and be sure each has heard what the other said before responding.

8. Tell your mate what your expectations and desires are in the relationship. Let him know what you want.

9. Discuss common goals and differences in values, and plan your future together so that both of your needs get met.

10. Constantly look for new ways to bond. Spend long periods of unstructured time together having fun and doing things

spontaneously. Discuss everything. Do unexpected romantic things for each other. Continually remind each other of your love.

Can You Change an "Old-style" Man?

One reason many single women fear marriage is because we haven't known many wives who've been able to maintain a position of power. There are bitchy wives who scream and yell, and mothering types who rule through guilt. But seldom do we see true partnerships. In marriage, men often become liabilities—more trouble than they're worth. But it *is* possible to turn them into assets.

It's often difficult to get men to become team players when they've been raised to be the coach. No matter how much power you have going into the relationship, you will have to work very hard to maintain it once the vows are made and the negotiation is over.

Valerie's husband, Ken, was certainly an "old-style" man, but Valerie was able to change him. When Valerie got involved in her career and began to feel stronger, Ken tried to intimidate her by saying, "You're not the woman I married. You've changed, you've become money hungry. You've got screwed-up values. You're ruining our relationship!" He usually ended his sermon with an ultimatum: "If you're not willing to be there for me, I'll just find someone who is."

Valerie's *first step was to seek out support from others*—friends, family, and a therapist. She came to me and I helped her with the *second step—to work through the program in this book and build up her self-esteem* so she could stop fearing Ken's threat of abandonment. Her *third step was to secure her own financial future.* She reviewed her personal finances—the income from her job, her savings, and her spending. Her *fourth step was to figure out her back-up plan*—how she would handle an apartment and other expenses and what else she would do if she and Ken split up. Her *fifth step was to call his bluff.* In fact, Valerie counter-intimidated him with, "If what you want is a nursemaid or femme fatale in the bedroom, feel free to go find a young, brainless woman who will feed your ego like I used to do, because I will never be that person again."

Women are usually afraid to take a risk like this for fear of being left. Or they confront but don't follow through. However, it becomes easier when you realize that men are usually more afraid of being alone than women are. They just don't admit it as readily.

To Valerie's surprise, Ken backed off. So she didn't stop there. She took the *sixth step—she made it clear that she would no longer accept the relationship like it was before.* And she was not bluffing. She told Ken,

> "I'm tired of being a shadow of you. My career feeds my ego just as yours feeds you, and I'm not willing to give it up. I'm sorry I got started in my career late in our marriage, but it's your turn to understand. I supported you while you climbed the ladder, and I expect you to do the same for me. I want an equal relationship with equal decision-making. Will you try to work this out with me or not? If not, I'm willing to give up the relationship, but I'm *not* willing to give up my career or my identity."

Ken agreed to work on it, although Valerie had prepared for the worst. Her *seventh and last step was to start communicating what she wanted from the relationship and from Ken.* She had held her tongue in the past about who she was and how that was different from who Ken wanted her to be. She let him know that she wanted vacations together without his family joining them. She made it clear that she would no longer pick up the slack around the house. She told him that he would have to be at home more when his children came to visit because she resented the responsibility. She made him understand that instead of his advice, she wanted his support and understanding from now on.

Valerie's relationship with Ken changed. And when Ken stopped controlling the relationship, she was able to give him much more of what *he* wanted—love and affection. She didn't feel constantly angry as she used to. She even began to feel more sexual toward him.

Interestingly enough, with Valerie's new attitude and way of behaving, it's not only Ken that's treating Valerie differently these days. Her boss and her father have made some real changes too.

Valerie had to let Ken know that times have changed and so have the rules for relationships.

New Rules for Relationships

1. Be determined to be selfish enough to make yourself happy. Don't let him or anyone else talk you out of it. Don't try to keep him from making himself happy, either.

2. Encourage each other to have separate friends and interests. You can't always like the same things. Enjoy the parts of your life that you don't share.

3. Resolve financial issues. Make clear agreements about who pays for what and what that means. If you have expectations, talk about what they are.

4. Schedule regular time apart, not only with friends, but also time alone to stay in touch with who you are and how you feel. Travel separately at times, spending weekends alone. Don't forget to allow yourselves time to miss each other.

5. Express feelings when they arise instead of keeping a secret scorecard.

6. If you already have a scorecard, empty it right now by cleaning up the resentments. Make a list and ask him to do the same. Tell him your grievances, from big issues like, "I've never forgiven you for making me get that abortion," to those that seem trivial like, "It drives me crazy that you never put the cap back on the toothpaste." Discuss how each issue can be resolved. Then let go of them. Before you can care about him again, you need to understand why he hurt you and be guaranteed that it won't happen again.

7. Don't take on new relationships to make up for problems in this one without trying to fix the problem first. When there are problems, tell your husband that he's not meeting your needs and let him know that if these issues don't get worked out, you will either leave him or get your needs met elsewhere.

8. Don't participate in power struggles. You can say, "I know that's how you see it, but it's not how I see it, or how I feel. I would like you to listen to my position and try to understand it and then I'll do the same with you, okay?" If you still can't reach a resolution, agree to disagree and not to fight about it again.

9. Set limits about what you will and won't accept by using the four steps of healthy communication. If his behavior doesn't

change, let him know that three strikes and he's out. For instance, if he doesn't come home to meet you for dinner when he says he will, after three times of waiting, you will stop planning dinner with him.

10. Compromise, but don't sacrifice. If he doesn't compromise, get out. It won't get better, it will only get worse.

Living Happily Ever After

Alan and I don't have a dependent relationship or a totally independent one. We have an equal, supportive relationship. I don't need him and he doesn't need me. But we want to always have each other in our lives.

We're not jealous or possessive with each other, because we feel sure of each other's love. Not that there are never doubts, but when there are, we talk about them.

We encourage each other in business, and if I call him, or he calls me, and says, "I have to work late," or, "I'm going to stay later with my friends," we usually encourage and support each other. If we are upset, we say so and compromise.

We don't tell each other how to run each other's lives. If we do want advice, we ask for it by saying, "Tell me what you would do." We're careful not to cross over each other's personal boundaries.

We keep our money separate and take turns paying for dinner or buying groceries. If either of us has a particularly good week or month financially, we'll treat. But it's never expected.

We admire each other's ethics and morals. Our values are similar. We feel equally attractive, and we therefore don't play on each other's insecurities.

We seldom fight, because we resolve each difference as it comes up. When we face a new crisis, we make resolving it an immediate priority—even if it takes staying up all night. We continually profess our love for each other, both in words and actions. The spark continues to grow.

We know there will be future issues to resolve, and we're willing to work at the relationship. However, we do hope, and expect, to live happily ever after. And most of all, we plan to keep having fun together and enjoying each other forever.

Part IV
The Self-Reliant Woman

You should now understand why your life hasn't been the way you wanted it to be, why you have either let men control you or you've controlled them—and how to change it.

If you have completed the program, you're now ready to love again—this time while remaining self-reliant.

However, after completing the program, you may say, "I'm still not happy," or, "I still don't feel as good about my life as I want to." Becoming self-reliant is a process you will continually work on throughout your life and will never fully perfect.

If you still feel uncomfortable with yourself, it may be because you haven't given up the fantasy of being rescued by someone. You can't get the benefit from this program until you do that.

If you are holding onto that fantasy as Alicia was, you may not yet be ready to change. You may need to experience more of life or go through a few more bad relationships or have a major crisis before you're ready to take charge of your life. You must be motivated to give up your love addictions and become emotionally self-reliant before this program can work.

Sometimes we must go over something again and again before we get it. Sometimes we haven't really identified who has hurt us the most and resolved it. Maybe you will need to go back and see if there is some part of the program that you haven't finished. For instance, you may have confronted your parents, but, like Andrea, it may have been your sister who affected you the most. Or in Alicia's case, her brother had as much impact on her as her parents did, and it took confrontation of him before she could let go of her married lover. Maybe you've confronted all of your family but didn't do it with gusto because you still don't really believe it's their fault—you're still holding onto the blame and beating yourself up. If so, you need to spend time alone again trying to get in touch with your anger. If that doesn't work, you may need to seek the help of a therapist.

Maybe you still haven't taken control of all areas of your life because it can take months or even years to do so. But if you can start improving just one area you will begin to feel better. Vicki's weight loss gave her the strength and confidence to take charge of the other areas of her life.

Some of the women who come to see me seem unable to feel better because they're so used to feeling depressed that depression has become a big part of their identity. They don't want to, or don't know how to, give it up.

To become self-reliant you must be willing to give up the old, unhappy you. You must be willing to give up old beliefs and values that haven't worked. You must be willing to trust yourself more than anyone else.

Once you trust *you*, you will no longer need to lean on others. You will be ready to become the authority over your own life and ready to become your own therapist.

13

Becoming Your Own Therapist

It's important that in the end you learn to rely on no one—including a therapist—except yourself. That doesn't mean that you can't have supportive friends or a therapist you see from time to time, of course. However, you need to know how to handle a crisis of your own, know when you're making a decision that's right for you, and know how to get what you want without asking others to handle it for you.

However, you may need to seek out therapy or a support group to help you through the program. It's usually easier to handle confrontations that come from a professional or someone who is not involved in our lives. If you decide to choose a support group to help you, be sure it's small enough to allow intimacy and feedback. Also, in my experience, groups with both men and women work better than all women's groups. Men provide valuable feedback. Also, it's easier to work out father issues and boyfriend/husband issues if you can role-play a situation with a male.

Therapy or Not?

You may want to try the program alone first and see if you can do it on your own. If you have trouble with it, you may need to seek outside support. As far as I know, however, there are very few therapists that can, and will, take you through all the steps in this program—because they've never heard of the program and, more importantly, never completed the program themselves. Most of them who have not confronted their parents would be just as afraid as you are to do it, and therefore might even try to talk you out of it.

If you do turn to therapy, be careful that you don't set up another emotionally dependent relationship. Be sure that your therapist helps you take charge of your life rather than holding you back. Ultimately, the goal is to become your own therapist and process and work through issues on a regular basis before they become major problems.

If you are in therapy and something about your situation begins to feel too familiar—the therapist treats you the way one of your parents, siblings, or last boyfriend did—look at the situation carefully. Get in touch with how you feel. Tell your therapist how you feel and what you think is happening. Use the therapeutic situation to work it through. Stand up to him or her the way you couldn't stand up to your parents as a child. Don't repeat the victim role you felt before. Tell him or her how you feel, what you want, and that if he or she doesn't treat you differently, you'll find a new therapist.

When Alicia came to see me, she was very angry at her last therapist. As far as she was concerned, he was one more weak man who judged her but didn't have control of his own life. He made her feel bad about her affair with the married man. She didn't tell him that, she simply quit, leaving a large unpaid bill. She felt like she "got" him, because she knew he was such a wimp that he'd have trouble confronting her with it. With my help, she was able to confront him on the phone. She also paid off the bill.

The therapist's office should be a place where you can be the "real" you that you've had to hide from others before—a safe place to express the full range of your emotions, including anger. If you don't feel safe doing this with your present therapist, you're with the wrong one.

However, don't always assume the worst about your therapist, either; after all, a therapist is a human being with problems and imperfections like your own. It's when he or she takes those problems out on you that you have to take a stand. Don't go in with blind trust. Make him or her earn your trust. Don't accept that your therapist knows more about you than you do yourself. Be sure he or she respects your feelings and values. Therapists often advise you according to the latest theory. It's your responsibility to ask if this theory has been tested and whether it's worked in your therapist's own life.

Remember that this is one more relationship that needs to be healthy. You'll have a tendency to relate to your therapist in an unhealthy way since that's how you've related to friends and lovers all your life. Be sure and let the therapist know what your patterns are, and give him or her the power to confront you on them when necessary.

Be sure you're with a therapist you like and "click with," someone who is impartial (not just a feminist or religious counselor—unless those are your particular values), and someone who is not personally involved in your life. Don't try to be friends with your therapist, or you could damage the therapeutic relationship, because then he or she will no longer be able to be impartial.

This program is a confrontational one and, therefore, a passive therapist probably cannot help you through it. You need someone who can be direct, someone who has the strength to "call you on it" when you use your typical defenses or behave in an unhealthy way. Your therapist needs to be able to point out when your actions don't match your words or when you are being abusive to him or her.

Alicia's previous therapist needed to, first of all, collect his fees from her as he went along, as he knew money management was one of her problems. And second, he needed to ask her why she was resistant about paying him, and if she had some unresolved anger toward him. After all, he's the therapist, and it was his responsibility to run his business appropriately. Alicia's behavior was unhealthy, but that's why she was there to see him.

Therapy should allow you to:

- reveal your true self without fear of being criticized.
- communicate your full range of emotions.
- feel safe sharing your innermost fears and concerns.
- feel supported.
- learn how to exert greater control over your life.
- see and understand the way you relate to others.

Don't Play Therapist With Others

It is important to feel proud of the "new" you, but don't get cocky and overzealous and decide that the whole world now needs to become like you or to follow in your footsteps.

In EST and some of the other programs like it, you are encouraged to drag more people into the program so that they too can be saved. This encourages dependent behavior. Don't do this with my program. If you do, you will be doing to others what society did to you—trying to force one point of view across as the "right" or "only" way. This promotes dependency on the program—not independent thought. It promotes resentment, not openness, to new ideas. I was, and still am, resistant to those who pressure me to believe that their way is the way I should do it. Let's not turn our own insights into a responsibility to save the rest of the world from what we perceive as their stupidity.

Instead, just be a good role model for others. And if friends ask for information on why you're progressing so well, give it to them, but don't cram it down their throats. If you tell them that the key to your self-reliance was confronting your parents, and they say they would never do it, let it go. You may want to say, "You're fighting me on this, so I'm going to stop telling you about the program. If and when you really want the information, let me know and I'll give it to you then."

The most important reason not to play therapist with your friends and family, however, is because it's not good for you. It's codependent, "rescuing" behavior. It will drain you and put you right back into your old mode of taking care of others' needs rather than taking care of yourself. The altruistic act of "helping" others is the most common and widely accepted way of avoiding one's self. It's a trap.

Alicia tried to do this. She told me that she was taking her therapy back to all her friends. Because of this, she was staying with friends who needed something from her, not making new friends who could have an equal, healthy relationship with her. She needed to tell them to get their own therapy, and she needed to leave them behind if they didn't grow. Alicia had trouble understanding why her friends didn't seem to "get it." She had a hard time realizing that people aren't always ready to grow when you want them to be, and most of her friends weren't ready.

Friends often have ulterior motives. They want us to be like them so they will feel secure. If they're miserable, they want us to be miserable—not because they're malicious, but because they're being self-protective. You can "invite" your friends to grow and change along with you, but you cannot take on the burden of trying to get them there. Your investment in their growth cannot be greater than their own. You have to accept the fact that they may not be as motivated as you or may be getting something out of being miserable.

Make an attempt to turn certain codependent friends from the past into supportive ones by using the Four Steps of Healthy Communication. For instance, you may have a friend who continually whines to you about her life, and you've been allowing her to do so. Try to change the way she relates to you by using these four steps. But, first, you must decide that if her behavior doesn't change, you are willing to end the relationship. This allows you to take the risk. Next, call her and tell her that her whining upsets you and drags you down. You do care about her, but her problems don't seem to be getting any better, and it's upsetting to you. By listening to her whine, you feel you may be encouraging her to wallow in her problems. You *want* the relationship to change. You're going to set a limit with her and listen only to those problems that she's doing something about. If she has no plan of action, don't allow her to talk about the issue. This encourages her to find her own answers instead of leaning on you. Tell her you want your relationship to be more of a two-way street, whereby you also share *your* problems. Ask her if she will do this. If not, the relationship must end or go to a more superficial level (acquaintance) in which you just do fun things together now and then.

Surround Yourself With Healthy People

Relationships cannot always be expected to be permanent. People must choose to grow with us or we must leave them behind. Even my mother, who wanted me to stay married, now says, "Think what your life would be like if you were still married to Andy!" If you allow your friendships to become more important than your personal growth, you'll stagnate. You will be sad and feel a loss as you move on, but it is necessary to let go.

One part of becoming your own therapist is surrounding yourself with people who are healthy and do for you what a good therapist, who is not codependent with you, would do. That means a friend or lover or family member who, without caring more about your growth than you do, can give you honest feedback, whom you can be your "real" self with, whom you can communicate your full range of emotions with (and they can do the same), and who can take and give confrontation and support.

The New You

Once you begin to take the risks necessary to change your life, you will feel more in control and should be able to see the light at the end of the tunnel. Usually, one success builds on the next, and you feel like you are on an upward spiral toward happiness.

But your journey is not over. In fact, it never will be. You will begin to see life as constant change, and hopefully, you will begin to look forward to the next challenge it brings. That's what keeps life exciting.

There will always be something to deal with, but as you learn to handle problems and crises, instead of avoiding and denying that they exist or alternatively collapsing in depression, it will get easier.

You will learn that things happen for a reason, and that if something painful or strange occurs, there may be some lesson you still haven't quite learned about life, and you can use this situation to make your life better in the future. Most problems and crises can be turned into something positive. I know it's hard to believe that it could be for the best when someone you love dies or you get fired from your job. But maybe you were too dependent on that loved one or that job, or maybe you would have never looked for something better if you weren't forced to.

When life throws us a curve, initially we are upset. But if we work through the painful emotions and then let go of them, we can begin to see the good that can come from the situation.

Staying on Track

The key to staying on track is staying in touch with yourself. In being your own therapist, continually ask yourself:

- Am I being myself?
- Am I being good to myself and giving myself a break when I make mistakes?
- Am I trusting myself more than others?
- Am I staying in touch with my feelings?
- Am I facing issues head-on?
- Am I emotionally honest with myself and others?
- Am I using the Four Steps of Healthy Communication to express myself?
- Do I let others know how I feel about life? About them?
- Am I setting boundaries with others?
- Do I let people know when they hurt me, and what I'll do if they keep doing it?
- How do I feel about my parents and other authority figures?
- Have I worked through my anger enough to begin to see some good in my parents and to relate to them as equals? If not, what else must I do?
- Is my life basically under control and in balance? What areas do I need to work on?
- Am I reaching my goals and moving forward?
- Is my life changing?
- Am I able to be vulnerable and confrontational?
- Am I happy?

If you ignore any part of your life, you become vulnerable to others' attacks and control over you. Weak areas are ''hot buttons'' that others can use to intimidate, manipulate, and control you.

Because others will believe differently than you do, and because there are more of them living ''normal'' codependent lives rather than ''healthy'' functional lives, you will need something to hold onto. Go back over your journal, look at your notes, and finish this program by creating a new set of guidelines by which to live your life. Create your own Bible with your own commandments to give you the strength you may need in times of crisis or loneliness. Below are my personal guidelines. Create your own according to your beliefs and values.

MY BIBLE

On love: Obsession, possession, and needing someone is not love. Love involves respect and sharing intimate emotions, including anger.

On marriage: Create your own guidelines. The rules of traditional marriage traps can destroy your relationship.

On children: Set limits with children, but treat them with respect. Teach them to enjoy life, not to be afraid of it. Don't pass on your destructive patterns.

On giving: Stop giving when you get nothing back. Giving too much is a sign of addiction to approval.

On eating and drinking: Enjoy everything in moderation. Don't obsess.

On work: Take your passion in life and make it happen, but don't make it your entire life.

On joy and sorrow: Expressing a full range of emotions is normal and keeps you feeling alive.

On material things: Accumulate and enjoy your wealth, but don't make it more important than people.

On abusive behavior: It's your responsibility to tell others when they hurt you and to tell them to stop it! Allowing others to victimize you will cause you to victimize others.

On authorities: Don't be intimidated by anyone in the role of authority or give anyone power over you.

On freedom: Vow to stay on your own track. Enjoy being yourself instead of who others want you to be. Do what you want instead of what you "should" do.

On emotions: Be able to feel and express the full range of emotions, from anger to hurt, sadness to excitement.

On pain: Pain can't be avoided. It can make you stronger if you emotionally experience it and follow that with action.

On self-knowledge: Self-knowledge equals confidence. Do whatever is necessary to understand why you are the way you are so you can love yourself.

On teaching: Share the knowledge you've gained, but only with those who request the information.

On friendship: Friends who've become a liability hold you back in your life. If you can't turn them into an asset, let them go.

On time: Your time should be valued and never given away—except to yourself. Don't waste it by waiting for things to happen.

On good and evil: The possibility of both exists in all human beings.

On pleasure and fun: The enjoyment of life is what makes it worth living.

On beauty: Beauty is important on both the outside and inside. Expressing anger doesn't make you ugly; repressing it does.

On values: What's right for you may be different from what's right for someone else. Don't blindly accept others' values or place yours on them.

On power: Confront issues and people to gain and maintain power over your own life instead of trying to control others.

On behavior: Make sure your actions match what you say you believe. Maintain your integrity by not becoming a hypocrite.

On communication: Be emotionally honest with everyone. Be vulnerable with those you trust and aggressively angry with those who try to hurt you.

On future: Make your fantasies come true. Decide what you want and take the risks to get there. Let no one stand in your way.

On intimacy: Create intimacy anytime you want it through self-disclosure and requesting it back. You'll never have to feel lonely again.

On balance: Balance your life with: work/play, responsibility/silliness, alone time/social time, activity/quiet, interactive/contemplative, confrontational/vulnerable.

On death: Death cannot be avoided, but the fear of it should not keep you from living.

MY TEN COMMANDMENTS FOR LIFE

1. Don't continue giving to someone who doesn't give back. Stop somewhere between the first and third time.
2. Spend plenty of time self-nurturing, or you'll start to need and crave nurturing from others. If you don't make yourself happy, you'll look for someone to do it for you. Self-nurturing energizes and gives you confidence and control.
3. Think of your own needs first. Don't intentionally hurt others,

but don't spend your time worrying about their feelings. Their feelings are their responsibility.

4. Don't restrict yourself regarding what you should and shouldn't be like because you're a woman. Allow yourself the full range of feelings and behaviors.

5. When someone hurts you, it's your responsibility to tell them you're hurt. If you don't, they won't know to stop it and may continue hurting you.

6. Dare to be different.

7. Never lose the relationship with yourself.

8. Never trust anyone else more than yourself.

9. When crises happen, pull back and regroup. Then come out fighting.

10. Always do whatever is necessary to remain a healthy, happy, vital person.

Have You Arrived?

None of us reach the point where we'll never again feel needy or insecure, or we'll never slip up, and/or we'll never let someone intimidate us. We all get frightened and feel overly vulnerable at times. So forgive yourself when you're not perfect. Once you've broken your addiction to love and become self-reliant, you are in a small select group of women who are truly confident most of the time.

You will no longer be treated like a child, because you won't allow it. You will trust your own decisions. You will give yourself more leeway when you make mistakes because you'll have more confidence and will know that mistakes mean growth. Others will seek you out because, with a clear identity, you will be a more interesting person. You will learn to take as well as give. You will stop whining, because you will change the things in your life that you don't like. You won't be lonely, because you'll be able to make healthier connections with people and create intimacy whenever and wherever you choose. You won't be intimidated by people in positions of authority. Basically, you will be in control of your own life and your own happiness. And you will always be able to be the real you.

Thirty Characteristics of an Emotionally Self-Reliant Woman

1. She knows that it takes more than one thing—money, a man, an education, or a family—to make her happy. She wants balance in her life.
2. She has close friends who are supportive, with whom she can celebrate successes, but none who are codependent.
3. She has a sense of belonging, because she's created a social life by seeking out others like herself.
4. She loves her alone time because she enjoys her relationship with herself.
5. She has a home she's proud of, one that reflects her true personality and makes her feel safe.
6. She makes her own justice because she knows justice doesn't automatically prevail.
7. She doesn't blindly trust others; her trust has to be earned.
8. She communicates with power. She lets others know immediately how she feels, what she wants, and what she'll do if she doesn't get it.
9. She's in charge of her own finances.
10. She controls her destiny—she knows what she wants in life, has goals, and is taking steps to reach them.
11. She feels a sense of passion for her work but doesn't try to make it her entire life.
12. She nurtures herself because she knows she can't give to others if she doesn't take care of herself first.
13. She lives in the reality of what is, rather than how she wishes things were.
14. She consults with experts—from doctors to stockbrokers—but none of them control her life.
15. She values herself and her time and only spends it with those who treat her with respect.
16. She takes charge of her life instead of blaming others.
17. She is her true self with others, rather than being what she thinks they want her to be.
18. She is not afraid of conflict and sees it as an opportunity to get a problem solved.
19. She follows her own values instead of the ''shoulds'' of oth-

ers, and she defends her values, but doesn't try to put them on others.

20. She treats herself with the same consideration and respect she wants from others.
21. She looks as good as she feels. Her image reflects her self-worth.
22. She has a full range of emotions and behaviors that she acts from.
23. She has an equal relationship with her parents, or if they won't cooperate, has no relationship at all.
24. She compromises but doesn't sacrifice. She sets limits with others, but after giving them a chance to come through for her, discontinues the relationship if they don't.
25. She's a risk-taker.

WITH MEN

26. She doesn't send the double message: "I'm strong but please take care of me."
27. When a man tries to intimidate her, she counter-intimidates because she knows from his behavior that he's more afraid than she is.
28. When a man pulls away, she checks out why by asking him what the problem is, telling him to be honest with her, and accepts the truth when he tells her.
29. She tells a man what she wants in time for him to give it to her, not on her way out the door.
30. She knows men are no stronger than women, so she treats them, and expects from them, the same that she expects from her female friends.

Remember, Love is *not* fear, jealousy, guilt, or resentment. Love is *not* sex, control, being taken care of, or sacrificing. Healthy Love embraces:

—attraction,
—mutual respect,
—emotional honesty,
—sharing of values and goals, and
—commitment to the good of each other.

That's the difference between love and addiction.

Vow to break the patterns of your parents. Vow to have a "functional" happy life. Lana, by the way, is still single, but recently met a man who fits none of her past glitzy stereotypes about men and she may be falling in love with him. Peggy is working and supporting herself selling real estate; she has now found a man who *does* want to make love to her. Andrea's marriage is happier than ever, and her two sons are becoming happy and confident—she is thrilled that she is not passing destructive patterns down to her children. Alicia is losing weight, changing her career, dating several men, and taking risks in every area of her life. She's even exploring her off-the-wall fantasy of being a biker mama. Valerie is still married and has become her own therapist. She decided to complete the rest of the program on her own, in her own way—and in doing so, has taken control of her life. And Sheri just called to say she's met the man of her dreams—a gorgeous, twenty-seven-year-old cowboy from Montana who is on the rodeo circuit. They're getting married in October.

You can turn your life around too. You can even meet the man of your dreams and live happily ever after. But not until you become the woman of *your* dreams will you become the woman of his!

TWO-YEAR UPDATE

Lana married the man of her dreams only recently, moved to Texas, and is reportedly incredibly happy. Peggy is divorced, self-reliant, and living in Vail. I lost contact with Sheri, but Anne is still living with her boyfriend and is happy.

Valerie realized she had more work to do with her parents and came back in for further guidance. She finally had the major confrontation with her parents she needed and they didn't speak to her for a year. It wasn't until she had major surgery that they came around.

Alicia totally ended her relationship with the married man by sending his wife the love letters and taped phone conversations she'd kept. She never heard another word from either of them. She then moved to Washington, D.C., and got on with her life.

And Diane, whose minister had sexually abused her, took the

minister to court and won a large settlement—without a gag order. Of course, the Presbyterian minister just went on to another church—but that's a different story.

And once Andrea's children left home, she decided she wanted a different life and a man who could be more intimate. Since she wasn't afraid to take risks, she left her husband and went back to an old boyfriend from years ago who had become a deeper, warmer person since his terrible ski accident in Aspen years ago. I was invited to her wedding, where upon she gave me flowers and a card saying, "I'm so happy, it could never have happened without you." I cried the entire time.

And Alan and I have had to face more issues, especially some concerning his male friends and the male value system. But facing these issues and resolving them has helped me formulate ideas for my next book, *Holding Men Accountable.** Alan and I worked our issues through and are still incredibly happy and incredibly in love—after five years.

*Title may change.

Appendix I

Diagnostic and Statistical Manual of Mental Disorders (Third Edition—Revised), American Psychiatric Association, Washington, D.C., 1987, pp. 222–223.

Diagnostic Criteria for Major Depressive Episode

A. At least five of the following symptoms have been present during the same two-week period and represent a change from previous functioning; at least one of the symptoms is either (1) depressed mood, or (2) loss of interest or pleasure. (Do not include symptoms that are clearly due to a physical condition, mood-incongruent delusions or hallucinations, incoherence, or marked loosening of associations.)

   (1) depressed mood (or can be irritable mood in children and adolescents) most of the day, nearly every day, as indicated either by subjective account or observation by others.

   (2) markedly diminished interest or pleasure in all, or most all, activities most of the day, nearly every day (as indicated either by subjective account or observation by others of apathy, most of the time)

   (3) significant weight loss or weight gain when not dieting (e.g., more than 5% of body weight in a month), or decrease or increase in appetite nearly every day (in children, consider failure to make expected weight gains)

   (4) insomnia or hypersomnia nearly every day

   (5) psychomotor agitation or retardation nearly every day (observable by others, not merely subjective feelings of restlessness or being slowed down)

   (6) fatigue or loss of energy nearly every day

   (7) feelings of worthlessness or excessive or inappropriate guilt (which may be delusional) nearly every day (not merely self-reproach or guilt about being sick)

   (8) diminished ability to think or concentrate, or indecisiveness, nearly every day (either by subjective account or as observed by others)

   (9) recurrent thoughts of death (not just fear of dying), recurrent suicidal ideation without a specific plan, or a suicide attempt, or a specific plan for committing suicide

B. (1) It cannot be established that an organic factor initiated and maintained the disturbance

   (2) The disturbance is not a normal reaction to the death of a loved one (Uncomplicated Bereavement)

Appendix II

Choosing A Therapist

(From ''Choosing The Right Therapist,'' Carolyn Bushong, *New Woman Magazine,* June, 1988, pp. 55–58.)

Studies have shown that having a therapist you like is the most important factor in ensuring the success of your therapy. If you're on a tight budget, call a mental-health clinic in your area, as they usually operate on a sliding scale. If you can afford the $50 to $120 that a session usually costs, you can call your local professional association for social workers, marriage and family counselors, psychiatrists, and psychologists. Some cities may also have a Psychotherapy Referral Service listed in the Yellow Pages. But the best way to find a good therapist is by personal referral. Ask for recommendations from friends who have similar values and goals. Get as much information about the therapist as you can from them.

Then call several recommended therapists to inquire about their theoretical orientation, policies for scheduling and payment, length of time the therapy will take, and other questions that are important to you. Set up a face-to-face interview with one or more of them. Use your intuition when you evaluate the therapists, as well as the factual information they give you. Did you feel the therapist understood you? Was he or she clear about policies? Was the therapist someone you could admire and respect? Did he or she seem sincere? Did the two of you click? Research shows that this ''click'' is essential for getting good therapy.

You should:

- choose someone you like, admire, and feel comfortable with.
- get enough information from your therapist to satisfy yourself that he or she is qualified to counsel you.
- let your therapist know when you're not getting what you want.
- monitor your progress.
- make sure you don't become too dependent on your therapist.
- trust your gut feelings more than your therapist's authority.
- terminate therapy when you feel you're ready.
- be open to change. Realize that growth means change in both behavior and beliefs. Don't be afraid to let go of old habits that aren't working for you, and find new ways of relating to others and living your life.
- set goals with your therapist.
- get a second opinion if and when you feel uncomfortable with your therapist.
- realize that when therapy doesn't work, it's often because therapist and client are mismatched.
- report any therapist who abuses you sexually or otherwise. Unethical behavior should be reported to the local government agency in your state that regulates the profession, such as your state board of the American Psychological Association.

Notes

Introduction

1. Bushong, Carolyn, with Kathryn Kanda, "Single, Secure, and Satisfied," *New Woman,* September 1986, 84.

Chapter 2: Why We Lose Ourselves in Love Relationships

1. Subby, Robert, *Codependency, An Emerging Issue* (Hollywood, FL: Health Communications, 1984) p. 26.

2. Peele, Stanton, *Diseasing of America* (Lexington, MA: Lexington Books, 1989), n.p.

Chapter 3: Step One

1. Bushong, Carolyn, "How to Succeed at Love Without Really Trying," *New Woman,* September 1989, 57.

Chapter 4: Step Two

1. Moddi, S. R., *Personality Theories: A Comparative Analysis* (Homewood, IL: Dorsey Press, 1972), p. 296.

2. Schultz, Terri, *Bittersweet: Surviving and Growing From Loneliness* (New York: Penguin Books, 1976), p. 93.

3. Lindbergh, Anne Morrow, *Gift From the Sea* (New York: Pantheon, 1975), p. 24.

4. Keen, Sam, and Anne Valley Fox, *Telling Your Story: A Guide to Who You Are and Who You Can Be* (New York: New American Library, 1973), p. 14.

5. Ibid., p. 18.

6. Ibid., p. 22.

7. Prather, Hugh, *I Touch the Earth, the Earth Touches Me* (Garden City, NY: Doubleday & Co., 1972), n.p.

8. Keen, *Telling Your Story,* p. 28.

Chapter 5: Step Three

1. Prather, Hugh, *Notes to Myself* (Moab, UT: Real People Press, 1970), n.p.

2. O'Neill, Nana and George O'Neill, *Shifting Gears* (New York: Avon Books, 1975), p. 41.

Chapter 6: Step Four

1. Bradshaw, John, "Our Families, Ourselves: The Paralyzing Grip of Perfectionism," *Lears,* March 1990, 86.

2. From interview with Kevin Leman, Ph.D., in *Bottom Line/Personal,* March 15, 1990, 11.

3. Ibid.

Chapter 7: Step Five

1. This questionnaire was copied directly from a booklet put together by the Counseling Department at Southern Illinois University, Edwardsville, IL, in 1971.

2. Jourard, Sidney, *The Transparent Self* (New York: D. Van Nostrand Co., 1971), p. 32.

Chapter 8: Step Six

1. Forward, Susan, *Toxic Parents* (New York: Bantam, 1989), p. 23.

2. Ibid., p. 252.

Chapter 9: Step Seven

1. Goble, Frank, *The Third Force: The Psychology of Abraham Maslow* (New York: Pocket Books, 1971), p. 52.

2. Plummer, Joseph T., "Changing Values: The New Emphasis on Self-Actualization," *The Futurist,* Vol. XXIII, No. 1, 11.

Chapter 10: Step Eight

1. Gillies, Jerry, *Money-Love* (New York: Warner Books, 1978), n.p.

2. Hill, Napoleon, *Think and Grow Rich Action Pack!* (New York: Hawthorne Books, 1972), n.p.

3. Sher, Barbara, with Annie Gottlieb, *Wishcraft* (New York: Ballantine Books, 1979), n.p.

Chapter 12: Maintaining an Equal, Healthy Relationship

1. "Unfaithfully Yours: Adultery in America," *People,* August 18, 1986, 85.

About the Author

Carolyn Bushong is a psychotherapist in private practice specializing in relationships, and a love advice columnist for *Complete Woman* magazine. She has an M.S. in counseling and a B.S. in education with more than twenty years' experience in the field. She is a former columnist for the *Rocky Mountain News* and regularly writes feature articles for national magazines such as *New Woman*, *Cosmopolitan*, and *Complete Woman*. Her articles have been syndicated in newspapers around the country since 1984, and she is presently syndicated internationally. A frequent guest on television and radio talk shows, Bushong has appeared on *Oprah*, *Donahue*, *Maury Povich*, and *Sally Jessy Raphael*.

Bushong lives in Evergreen, outside Denver, Colorado. She maintains her psychotherapy practice in the Cherry Creek/Denver area. She also conducts psychotherapy by phone for those who are interested in her techniques but do not live near Denver. For further information, call 1-800-548-1888.